T0305042

Water Management in Arid and Semi-Arid Regions

To Professor David Pearce, who unexpectedly left us, when this book was completed.

David, you will always be an inspiration for us, the younger generation of environmental and resource economists. Your loss will be deeply felt but your legacy will endure long into the future and all over the world.

Water Management in Arid and Semi-Arid Regions

Interdisciplinary Perspectives

Edited by

Phoebe Koundouri

Department of Economics, University of Reading; Department of Economics/CSERGE, University College London, UK; The World Bank Groundwater Advisory Team (GW_MATE); Coordinator of ARID Cluster of Projects, European Commission 5th Framework Programme

Katia Karousakis

Department of Economics/CSERGE, University College London, UK

Dionysis Assimacopoulos

National Technical University of Athens, Greece

Paul Jeffrey

School of Water Sciences, Cranfield University, UK

Manfred A. Lange

Geophysical Institute, University of Muenster, Germany

Edward Elgar

Cheltenham, UK • Northampton, MA, USA

Published by
Edward Elgar Publishing Limited
Glensanda House
Montpellier Parade
Cheltenham
Glos GL50 1UA
UK

Edward Elgar Publishing, Inc.
136 West Street
Suite 202
Northampton
Massachusetts 01060
USA

A catalogue record for this book
is available from the British Library

ISBN-13: 978 1 84542 423 7
ISBN-10: 1 84542 423 9

Printed and bound in Great Britain by MPG Books Ltd, Bodmin, Cornwall

Contents

Contributors

Dionysis Assimacopoulos, Professor, School of Chemical Engineering, National Technical University of Athens, Greece

Juan Bellot, University of Alicante, Spain

Maria Bertaki, Research Fellow, NAGREF-Institute for Olive Tree and Subtropical Plants, 73100 Chania, Crete, Greece

Andreu Bonet, Departamento de Ecologia, Universidad de Alicante, Spain

Kostas Chartzoulakis, Senior Researcher, NAGREF-Institute for Olive Tree and Subtropical Plants, 73100 Chania, Crete, Greece

Antonia Alkistis Donta, Senior Research Fellow, Centre for Environmental Research, University of Muenster, Germany, Lecturer at the Network for Interdisciplinary Causal Research, Hannover, Germany, in Co-operation with the University of Hannover and the University of Applied Sciences, Hannover, Germany

Denise Eisenhuth Research Assistant, Depto de Ecología, Universidad de Alicante, Alicante

Mary Gearey, School of Water Sciences, Cranfield University, UK,

Paul Jeffrey, Principal Research Fellow, School of Water Sciences, Cranfield University, UK

Katia Karousakis, Research Fellow, Department of Economics/CSERGE, University College London, UK

Phoebe Koundouri, Senior Lecturer in Economics (B), Department of Economics, University of Reading, UK; Senior Research Fellow, Department of Economics/CSERGE, Department of Economics, University College London, UK, and Member of the World Bank Groundwater Management Advisory Team (GW_MATE), the World Bank, US

Manfred A. Lange, Director, Institute for Geophysics and Director, Center for Environmental Research Coordinator, Westfälische Wilhelms-Universität Münster, Germany

Marita Laukkanen, Senior Researcher, MTT Agrifood Research Finland

Sébastien Loubier, BRGM, France

Rodrigo Maia, Associate Professor, Faculty of Engineering of Porto University (FEUP) Portugal

Guadalupe Ortiz Noguera, PhD student, Department of Sociology I, University of Alicante, Spain

Juan Peña, PhD researcher, Departamento de Ecología, Universidad de Alicante Spain

Natasa Ravbar, ZRC-SAZU, Slovenia

Jean Daniel Rinaudo, BRGM, France

Juan Rafael Sánchez, Departamento de Ecología, Universidad de Alicante, Spain

Andreas Schumann, Professor for Hydrology and Water Management, Faculty for Civil Engineering, Ruhr- University Bochum, Germany

Julio César Tejada, Ecología Terrestre, Universidad EARTH, Costa Rica

Ezio Todini, Department of Earth and Geo-Environmental Sciences, University of Bologna

Antonio Aledo Tur, University of Alicante, Spain

Tatjana Veljanovski, ZRC-SAZU, Slovenia

Acknowledgements

My overwhelming debt is to the European Commission, Fifth Framework Programme, for financially supporting the ARID Cluster of projects and to the responsible scientific officer of the Commission, Dr Panagiotis Balabanis, for his enthusiasm, support and encouragement throughout the years of the interdisciplinary research effort that was conducted within the ARID Cluster.

I am also indebted to my co-editors (the coordinators of the individual projects of the ARID Cluster) and all the contributing authors of this book, for their devotion to the completion of this book in a relative short time. I am also grateful to every single one of the 80 researchers working for the ARID Cluster, as well as the external scientific panel of the cluster, Professor Evan Vlachos, Professor Bernard Barraqué and Iacovos Iacovides, for providing us with feedback from many scientific disciplines, as well as filed experiences, that enriched our way of thinking about integrated and sustainable water resources management and broadened our understanding of the scientific and policy issues involved in the implementation of the EU Water Framework Directive.

I also wish to thank my publisher, Edward Elgar Publishing, whose staff was enthusiastic about this project from the beginning. I owe special thanks to Catherine Elgar, my commissioning editor.

Finally a special debt is owed to my partner, family and friends, who understand my enthusiasm (and time devoted) to working towards a better management of the European waters.

Phoebe Koundouri

PART I

Introduction

1. Water management in arid and semi-arid regions: interdisciplinary perspectives – an introduction

Katia Karousakis and Phoebe Koundouri

Water deficiency in many arid and semi-arid regions in Southern Europe is becoming a major constraint for economic welfare and sustainable regional development. These water-deficient regions are characterized by high spatial and temporal imbalances of water demand and supply, seasonal water uses, inadequate water resources and poor institutional water management. Appropriate strategies and guidelines for water management are necessary for the formulation and implementation of integrated sustainable management of water resources.

The recently adopted Water Framework Directive (WFD) clearly demonstrates the EU's intention to respond to this challenge through an integrated multi-objective approach for water management. There is a clear need to develop and evaluate strategies for integrated water resources management (IWRM) in Southern European water-deficient regions through multi-perspective approaches that take into account economic, technical, social, institutional and environmental constraints. In particular, there is a pronounced need to learn to cope with rapid social changes, efforts for economic development and escalating water demands in a continuously changing environment.

The aim of this book is to present the culmination of results from the ARID Cluster of projects, which examine water scarcity and demand in arid and semi-arid regions, as well as participatory and adaptive approaches for appropriate management strategies. Experience and lessons learned are derived from various case studies, which examine competing water use patterns, comparing governance structures and how these have evolved in response to scarcity, and structural and non-structural instruments to address water deficiency.

The ARID Cluster is supported by the European Commission under the Fifth Framework Programme and is contributing to the implementation of the Key Action 'Sustainable Management and Quality of Water' within the Energy, Environment and Sustainable Development programme. The ARID Cluster project was initiated in 2001 and will be completed in 2006. The ARID Cluster brings together three distinct, yet related research projects dealing with water management in arid and semi-arid regions. In particular, its purpose and objectives amount to bringing together the results of three cross-disciplinary approaches to sustainable and integrated water management, so as to develop effective and efficient policy recommendations that can feed directly into the water management decision-making processes.

These are the Aquadapt project, focusing on a co-evolutionary approach to adaptive, integrated management under changing utilization conditions; the MEDIS project, addressing conflicting demands and varying hydrological conditions for the sustainable use of water on Mediterranean islands; and the WaterStrategyMan project, which seeks to develop strategies for regulating and managing water resources and demand in water-deficient regions. The nature of the work undertaken in the three projects has evolved primarily through the use of case studies, thus providing important insights into the issues of water scarcity under different socio-economic and environmental conditions. The purpose of the ARID project is to identify and evaluate common issues and challenges that exist across the three projects and to determine the means by which these can be addressed most efficiently. Finally, one of the underlying objectives of ARID is to examine what policy implications these results may have for the implementation of the Water Framework Directive.

Chapters 2 and 3 compose Part II of the book, which focuses on strategies for regulating and managing water resources and presents some of the main results of the WaterStrategyMan project of the ARID Cluster.

In Chapter 2, Professor Ezio Todini, Professor Andreas Schumann and Professor Dionysis Assimacopoulos present the WaterStrategyMan Decision Support System, aiming to define an appropriate methodology for supporting decision-makers in the sustainable and integrated water resource planning in arid and semi-arid regions. In the context of the EU Water Framework Directive, the systematic evaluation of water management interventions should be performed for a long time horizon, simulating long-run accumulative effects and anticipating potential future changes and uncertainties. Selected methodologies and indicators should assist decision-makers in identifying the appropriate policy and management instruments in relation to regional economic growth and environmental sustainability. Multidisciplinary information is needed for the analysis of water management strategies and plans, and the evaluation of their effects, taking into account economic, hydrologic and environmental interrelationships. This objective was accomplished through the development of a procedure based on the simulation of alternative water availability and demand scenarios and the evaluation of the effect of alternative water management options and instruments. The procedure was formalized in a prototype decision support system (WSM DSS), designed to simulate the impacts of different water management options and strategies, integrating the economic principles of the Water Framework Directive 2000/60/EC. Since 2004, the WSM DSS is being applied to river basins and regions in Greece, Italy, Cyprus, Portugal, Israel and Spain, aiming to assist in the formulation of alternative water management strategies following the principles of integrated water resources management (IWRM). The chapter ends with some concluding remarks on potential further application and future developments and extensions of the system.

Chapter 3 by Professor Rodrigo Maia is intended to supplement Chapter 2 by demonstrating the development and evaluation of alternative water management scenarios through the application of the DSS on the Ribeiras do Algarve River Basin, which is located in the Algarve region, Portugal. This river basin is situated in the southern stretch of the country and covers a total area of 3837 km^2. The climate in the basin is Mediterranean, characterized by rainy winters and dry summers, as well as precipitation with varying spatial and temporal distributions. Currently this region is the most popular tourist destination in mainland Portugal, where there exists conflict between different uses of water resources, especially between the tourism sector and agriculture, as well as infrastructure deficiencies, poor groundwater quality, high losses in secondary water supply networks and inadequate irrigation methods. The application of the DSS tool takes place in two phases. In the first phase, stakeholders' opinions are analysed to formulate appropriate water management responses. These include: (1) structural opinions for supply enhancement including dam construction, network enhancements, desalination, new boreholes for groundwater abstraction and reduction of network losses; (2) demand management options comprising of water reuse and improvement in irrigation methods; and (3) socio-economic measures, addressing domestic and irrigation water price adjustments. The second phase involves the formulation of strategies using the available options. In particular, two different strategies were considered: (1) one reflecting the dominant water management paradigm in the region; and (2) another reflecting a new, shifting, paradigm. The main goal of both water management options and strategies is to achieve 95 per cent coverage for domestic use and a minimum of 80 per cent coverage of irrigation demand, while adhering to a maximum use of 80 per cent of aquifer recharge. The chapter concludes with a description of a strategy that could be able to achieve economic sustainability, as required by the cost recovery principle of the Water Framework Directive.

Part III of the book focuses on sustainable use of water on Mediterranean islands and addresses the conflicting water resources demands under varying hydrological and socio-economic conditions. The results presented in this part of the book derive from research efforts of the MEDIS project of the ARID Cluster, which uses a stakeholder participatory approach to integrated and sustainable water resources management.

Chapter 4, by Manfred Lange, Antonia Alkistis Donta and the MEDIS consortium, focuses on climate change and vulnerabilities to drought on Mediterranean islands. The vulnerability of a system depends on its sensitivity to external changes and on its adaptive capacity that will reduce the impacts of those changes on the system. Assuming that sensitivities to droughts of arid and semi-arid regions are relatively stable, the vulnerability of a given region to water scarcity results from the impact of changes in water availability not to be compensated by adaptation. Reducing vulnerability to droughts therefore requires effective adaptation strategies. In devising such strategies, a number of aspects or dimensions need to be considered: the physical and environmental dimension, the economic and regulatory dimension and the social, institutional and political dimension. These aspects will have to be considered holistically, which requires an interdisciplinary research design. In this chapter, the authors briefly review some of the concepts of integrated assessments of climate change. This provides the basis for looking at issues affecting present adaptability to water scarcity in arid and semi-arid regions related to the three aforementioned dimensions. Moreover they discuss briefly how global change might affect some of the adaptabilities and suggest various strategies to enhance adaptive capacity, with regards to islands in the Mediterranean.

In Chapter 5, Kostas Chartzoulakis and Maria Bertaki focus on water use in agriculture in Mediterranean islands. They argue that sustainable water resources management in the major Mediterranean islands (Cyprus, Crete, Sicily, Corsica and Mallorca) is closely related with water use in agriculture, which uses more than 50 per cent of available water resources. This percentage ranges from 55 in Corsica up to 82 per cent in Crete. It is also the sector least efficient in water use, since irrigation efficiency is less than 55 per cent. The demand for irrigation water is high in all islands even though only a small percentage of agricultural land is irrigated, ranging from 8.8 in Mallorca up to 33.4 per cent in Crete. In all islands, water for agriculture comes mainly from groundwater sources, while only in Corsica is surface water the sole source of irrigation water. Treated wastewater, although it is a valuable irrigation water resource, makes a very low contribution to irrigation (1 and 7 per cent in Cyprus and Mallorca respectively). Among the crops dominating in Mediterranean islands, citrus, fodder and open-field vegetables are the high water-demanding crops, while olives are the less water-demanding crop. Modern irrigation systems have been widely used the last few decades in all islands. Localized (drip or mini-sprayer) irrigation systems are mainly used for tree crops and vegetables, while sprinkler irrigation is dominant for fodder crops and some vegetables. The growing water demand in Mediterranean islands makes the rational use of irrigation water extremely important for agricultural development to be sustainable and for the environment to be conserved. To meet these goals, aspects related to water management in agriculture are discussed in this chapter, with emphasis on irrigation application, soil and plant management practices, water pricing, reuse of treated wastewater, farmers' participation in water management, and capacity building.

Part IV of the book is composed of Chapters 6 and 7 and focuses on a number of economic issues that emerge as vital for efficient water resources allocation and the optimal implementation of the Water Framework Directive. This section has a strong economic focus and derives from the research of a group of economists in the ARID Cluster.

In Chapter 6, Katia Karousakis and Phoebe Koundouri present a typology of economic instruments and methods for efficient water resources management in arid and semi-arid regions. In particular, this chapter provides the economic perspective to implementing integrated water resources management, and describes the valuation techniques and economic instruments that have been developed and are available to help price water efficiently, and allocate it to its highest-valued user as required by the EU Water Framework Directive.

Chapter 7 by Marita Laukkanen and Phoebe Koundouri presents an analytical attempt to approximate the behaviour of economic agents in groundwater extraction under two possible scenarios, namely coordination and no coordination between the agents. This is a formalized experiment to investigate the potential of organizing irrigated agricultural regions in irrigation divisions; that is, to investigate whether social welfare can increase from implementing irrigation divisions in a water basin. This is an economic policy that could prove efficient in the implementation of the WFD. In particular, the authors analyse a game with N farmers that extract groundwater from a common aquifer of small storage capacity. Their aim is to compare the socially optimal, myopic and feedback extraction strategies, the latter arising from competitive interaction between extracting agents. The main extension to existing literature is that the authors consider heterogeneous farmers, facing uncertainty deriving from stochastic rainfall. The farmers differ in terms of their choice of irrigation technology, which results in different farmer-specific impacts on the aquifer recharge rate. The implications of the different strategies on extraction rates, groundwater table levels and welfare attained, are illustrated via simulations based on data from the Kiti aquifer in Cyprus.

Part V of the book introduces the co-evolutionary approach to adaptive, integrated water management. Chapters 8 and 9 of the book present some of the main results from the research conducted by the Aquadapt project, which investigates the potential of such an evolutionary approach to integrated water management.

In particular, in Chapter 8 Tur et al. focus on socio-cultural determinants of water utilization and they have three specific objectives. The first objective is to understand the political, socio-cultural, economic and technological determinants of collective and individual water consumption. The second objective is to investigate the attitudes of consumers towards water as a communal resource, as a social right and as a commodity. The third objective is to understand the linkages and the differences between four case studies to determine the scope of local, regional and international integrated water management challenges. These objectives are investigated in four selected areas of study, namely, the Herault watershed in France (survey conducted by BRGM), the Kras plateau in Slovenia (survey conducted by ZRC-SAZU-School of Water Sciences), the Marina Baixa region in Spain (survey conducted by Alicante University), and the Nene catchment in the UK (survey conducted by Cranfield University). The chapter has been structured around the following points: firstly, the description of the socio-economic features of the four catchments that will allow us to contextualize the results obtained and to infer from the data to the social use of water; secondly, an explanation of the undertaken methodology; thirdly, the comparative analysis of the basic frequencies gathered in the survey; fourthly, to show the results from the profile analysis; and finally, to offer some general conclusions on a shared culture of water in Europe.

Chapter 9 by Andreu Bonet, Juan Bellot, Denise Eisenhuth, Juan Peña, Juan Rafael Sánchez and Julio César Tejada, investigates evidence of landscape change, water usage, management system and governance co-dynamics in South-Eastern Spain. The authors argue that the identification of the co-dynamic processes between landscape, water usage, management system and governance is crucial to determine the causes of structural change in a socio-natural system of semi-arid Spain. A clearer understanding of the co-dynamic processes that can occur in socio-natural systems could help to further illuminate the rapid and unforeseen changes that are inherent to the environmental, socio-economic and governance contexts within which water supply and demand patterns develop. The processional logic is that if co-dynamic processes cause structural change in socio-natural systems, then structural change could offer the key through which to identify the characteristics of both the type of resilience and the adaptive capacity that maintain the long-term sustainability of a socio-natural system. The literature pertaining to the concepts of resilience and adaptive capacity recognizes that resilience refers to the potential of a natural or social system to reorganize or restructure. The problem in this study is that there has been a history of both inter-basin and intra-basin water transfers (that is, engineering resilience) introduced to stabilize the hydrological system. While engineering resilience maintains the global stability of the hydrological system, it could have ultimately locked out the desired type of co-dynamic processes and structural change that can lead to the creation and testing of alternative water sourcing and usage practices. The result of continued and increasing engineering resilience to maintain stability of the hydrological system diminishes both the adaptive capacity of other ecological systems, and social adaptive capacity. In this chapter the characteristics of the type of resilience the authors are interested in locating provides a socio-natural system with the potential to adapt or reorganize in a desirable way following disturbance-driven change that is caused by significant and regular water transfers. Therefore the ultimate challenge is to locate the reciprocal co-dynamic processes that promote the type of structural change that increases the ecological as well as the social resilience and adaptive capacity of the water-using communities in the Marina Baja. The aim then is to analyse structural change in both the natural as well as the social system and the nature of the reciprocal co-dynamic processes that promote either ecological and social adaptive capacity.

In Part VI the final chapter of the book brings together the common themes, issues and problems that have been identified throughout the research conducted in the ARID Cluster in a manner which enables conclusions and policy recommendations to be drawn that can feed into the Water Framework Directive.

PART II

A strategy-developing approach for
regulating and managing water resources
and demand in water-deficient regions:
the WaterStrategyMan project

2. The WaterStrategyMan decision support system

Ezio Todini, Andreas Schumann and Dionysis Assimacopoulos

2.1 INTRODUCTION

In the context of the EU Water Framework Directive, the systematic evaluation of water management interventions should be performed for a long time horizon, simulating long-run accumulative effects and anticipating potential future changes and uncertainties. Selected methodologies and indicators should assist decision-makers in identifying the appropriate policy and management instruments in relation to regional economic growth and environmental sustainability. Multidisciplinary information is needed for the analysis of water management strategies and plans, and evaluation of their effects, taking into account economic, hydrologic and environmental interrelationships (McKinney et al., 1999; Bouwer, 2000; Albert et al., 2001). Complex integrated modelling, when based on comprehensive information systems, can meet those objectives. Under this context, a variety of models and decision support systems have already been developed for simulating and optimizing water allocation and quality in different water resource systems. However in most cases the systematic formulation and evaluation of alternative policies is lacking.

This chapter aims to summarize the work accomplished in this field through the EU-funded WaterStrategyMan project (Developing Strategies for Regulating and Managing Water Resources and Demand in Water-Deficient Regions, Contract No: EVK1-CT-2001-00098) for the definition of an appropriate methodology aiming to support decision-makers in sustainable and integrated water resource planning and management in arid and semi-arid regions. This objective was accomplished through the development of a procedure based on the simulation of alternative water availability and demand scenarios and the evaluation of the effect of alternative water management options and instruments. The procedure was formalized in a prototype decision support system (WSM DSS), designed to simulate the impacts of different water management options and strategies, integrating the economic principles of the Water Framework Directive 2000/60/EC. Since 2004 the WSM DSS is being applied to river basins and regions in Greece, Italy, Cyprus, Portugal, Israel and Spain, aiming to assist in the formulation of alternative water management strategies following the principles of integrated water resources management (IWRM).

This chapter is structured as follows: first, a summary of the review of existing decision support systems is given, in order to provide the background for the development of the WSM DSS; then sections 2.3 and 2.4 present the framework of the development, the modelling approach of the new DSS and some user interface aspects, while sections 2.5 to 2.10 give a brief overview of the different modules and principles incorporated in the DSS. Finally, the chapter ends with some concluding remarks on potential further application and future developments and extensions of the system.

2.2   EXISTING DECISION SUPPORT SYSTEMS

The first phase of the development of the WSM DSS concentrated on the extensive literature review of methodologies and decision support systems developed during the last few years by research groups and organizations. DSSs analysed were:

- MIKE BASIN, by the Danish Hydraulic Institute (DHI, 2003);
- DSS for Water Resources Planning Based on Environmental Balance, developed within a project funded by the Italian Cooperation with Egypt (ET&P, 2001);
- BASINS (US EPA, 2004);
- A Spatial Decision Support System for The Evaluation of Water Demand And Supply Management Schemes, by the Technical University of Athens (Manoli et al., 2002);
- IQQM, by the New South Wales Department of Land and Water Conservation, with collaborative assistance from the Queensland Department of Natural Resources (QDNR), (NSW, 1999);
- ENSIS, by the Norwegian Institute for Water Research (NIWA) and the Norwegian Institute for Air Research (NILU), (Bakken et al., 2001);
- REALM, by the Victoria University of Technology and the Department of Sustainability and Environment, in the State of Victoria, Australia;
- MULINO, of the EU-funded Mulino Project (Giupponi et al., 2004);
- RIBASIM, by Delft Hydraulics (WL Delft Hydraulics, 2005);

- WEAP, by the Stockholm Environment Institute and Tellus Institute (Stockholm Environment Institute, 2005);
- WATERWARE, of the European research programme Eureka-EU487 (Fedra and Jamieson, 1996; Jamieson and Fedra, 1996a, 1996b);
- AQUATOOL, by the Universidad Politecnica de Valencia, Spain (Andreu et al., 1996);
- IRAS, by the Civil and Environmental Engineering Department of Cornell University and Resources Planning Associates Inc of Ithaca, NY (Loucks, 1995; Loucks et al., 1996).

All the above DSSs have been analysed as potential tools for sustainable water resources planning, within the context of the Water Framework Directive, and for providing insight as to potential aspects that could be integrated in a more coherent and adaptive methodology. The main outcome of the analysis was that most commercially available packages include extremely sophisticated components, but are deficient in the integration of interrelations between the different social, environmental, economic and technological dimensions of water resource planning. Additionally, the assessment of demand and environmental feedbacks on alternative structural and non-structural management approaches is in most cases incoherent and missing.

2.3   THE FRAMEWORK OF THE WSM DSS

The WSM DSS was developed as a GIS-based package with the objective to emphasize on the conceptual links between the different components and aspects of water resource system management, instead of merely focusing on a detailed description of the physical systems and related phenomena. The DSS was formalized around a procedure aimed at assessing the impacts of current and future water resource planning and management on the basis of scenario simulations. The main procedural steps are described in Figure 2.1.

The assessment of current and future state and impacts implies the use of appropriate indicators, in order to provide the decision-maker with a broad analysis of the water system. These indicators describe not only quantitative aspects, but also water quality patterns, social constraints in water usage, environmental impacts of policy measures and the progress achieved for a more sustainable development of water resources. Economic analysis issues are also accounted for, through the estimation of direct, resource and environmental costs.

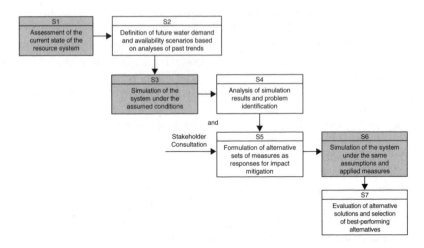

Figure 2.1   Procedure for assessing the impacts of alternative strategic options and formulating alternative solutions

The WaterStrategyMan (WSM) approach and the modules of the WSM DSS have been formalized under the 'Driving forces – Pressures – State – Impacts – Responses' structure of indicators (DPSIR), as proposed at European level by the European Environmental Agency (Smeets et al., 1999) (see Figure 2.2).

The two pre-processors of the DSS, the water availability and the water demand modules, are used for the analysis of driving forces and the estimation of the pressures exerted on the water resource system. Driving forces, defined as natural phenomena and activities not easily controlled (Walmsley, 2002), are here represented by climate change, demographic growth and land use pattern change. Pressures are quantified in terms of pollution loads generated by human activities, water resource availability and demand estimations. The kernel of the WSM package, the water allocation module, simulates water distribution in the resource system and calculates indicators that assess its state. Finally, the postprocessor of the DSS (evaluation module), assesses impacts of driving forces and pressures, and compares the effect of various alternative strategic measures (responses).

2.4   THE WSM DSS ARCHITECTURE

The decision support system has been implemented in Visual Basic.NET using the Arc Objects COM technology by ESRI, which is also the platform

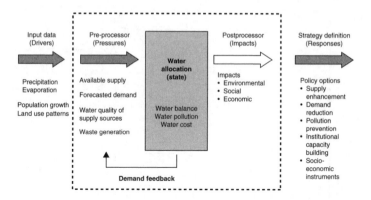

Figure 2.2   The DPSIR framework applied in the WSM DSS prototype

for the GIS Database. The tool was designed according to the four-step schema presented in Figure 2.3 that involves: (1) the database; (2) the object model linked to mathematical models for water allocation, quality and economic estimations; (3) a logical coordination unit, responsible for the communication with external models; and (4) the user interface which allows for the definition of parameters related to the simulation and the presentation of results through customizable charts, tables and maps. Water management strategies or single interventions can be simulated under different scenarios and compared, and the decision-maker or the analyst can formulate responses to mitigate water stress impacts with respect to their objectives.

The operational framework of the DSS is based on the concept of a water management scheme (WMS), defined as a set of scenarios for variables that cannot be directly influenced by the decision-maker (that is, rainfall patterns constituting a water availability scenario and population growth formulating a demand scenario) and the application of one or more water management interventions. A WMS is defined in terms of a database containing information on the water infrastructure at a certain region and reference year, at which the implementation of scenarios and strategies begins. A base case is always present, serving as input for the creation of new WMSs. User interaction with the DSS falls under three functional groups, accessed via a hierarchical navigation tree: (1) base case editing, allowing for the editing and introduction of new data for the reference year; (2) creation of WMSs, providing the capabilities for defining scenarios on water availability and demand, definition of strategies and visualization of results and for conducting a parametric economic analysis; and (3) evaluation,

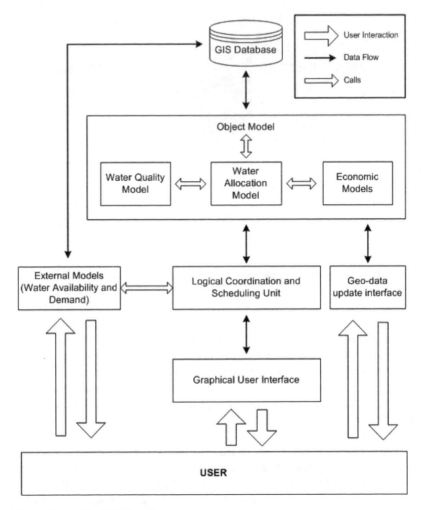

Figure 2.3   The DSS architecture

which permits the comparison of different WMSs according to a predefined set of indicators (Figure 2.4).

All specific regional data are stored in an ESRI GIS Database (geodatabase). Special attention has been given to the portability of the DSS. The developed object model, analysed in the following section, with the interlinked mathematical models can easily be transported to other GIS environments since most GIS functions are implemented outside the modelling procedures and algorithms.

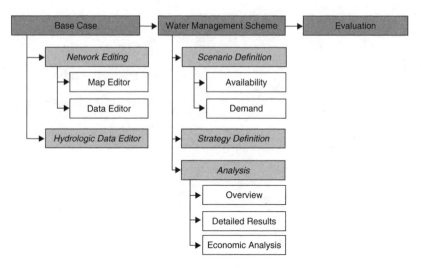

Figure 2.4   The DSS operational framework

In the WSM DSS, water resource systems are modelled on the basis of geometric networks. A geometric network is described as a set of junctions (points) and edges (polylines) that are topologically connected to each other (Figure 2.5). In the object model of the DSS, junction elements are conceptualized as water nodes while the connections between them are the water links. Network elements are drawn over the map of the area under consideration.

Water nodes are classified into three categories, (1) supply nodes standing for alternative water supply sources and characterized by the monthly available supply; (2) demand nodes modelling water uses and flow requirements; and (3) transshipment nodes standing for treatment plants and generic network junctions. Water link objects are classified in four categories according to the connectivity rules of the network and the particular modelling requirements of the DSS: supply links (pipelines and canals), conveying water from supply sources to demand nodes; groundwater interaction links (recharge and discharge), representing the natural interaction between surface and groundwater bodies; return flow links, conveying return flows from consumptive demand uses to receptor bodies (surface or groundwater) or wastewater treatment plants; and river links, representing the natural course of a river water body. An overview of the object model for water nodes is presented in Figure 2.6.

The object model of the water resource system implicitly specifies a number of connectivity rules, in order to ensure the proper modelling of a

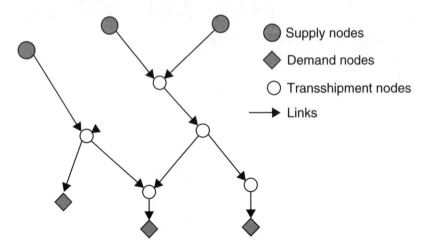

Figure 2.5   Network representation of a water resource system

water resource system and its correct simulation by the WSM Decision Support System. Modelling requires that some types of edges (water links) have a specific type of start or end junction, or both. For example, ground-water recharge links can only originate from surface water nodes (reservoirs and river reaches) and should end only at renewable groundwater nodes. Additionally, junctions modelling particular types of water sources such as non-renewable (fossil groundwater) or importing from neighbouring regions cannot have incoming edges of any type. To ensure therefore the integrity of network data within the database, network connectivity is modelled within the WSM Decision Support System, with a set of rules that specify which type of junction can be connected to other junction types, and with what types of edge.

2.5   USER INTERFACE ASPECTS

The general flow of the user interface follows the layout of Figure 2.4. An example of the implemented user interface (results visualization section) is presented in Figure 2.7.

The maps of the area and of the water network are visualized in the map editor panel of the DSS interface (Figure 2.8). The geographic layers of network elements are directly linked to the graphical user interface, allowing for network modifications, feature editing, additions and deletions (Figure

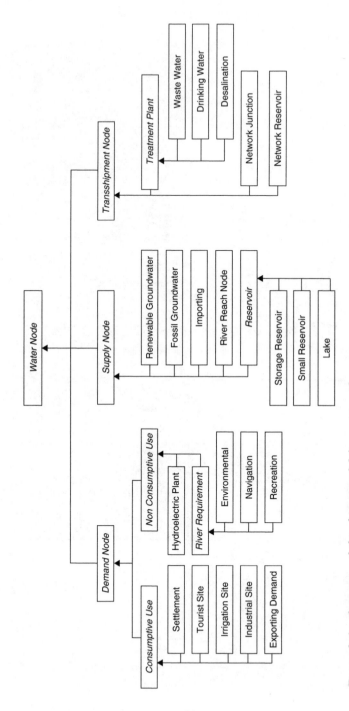

Figure 2.6   Overview of the object model for water nodes

21

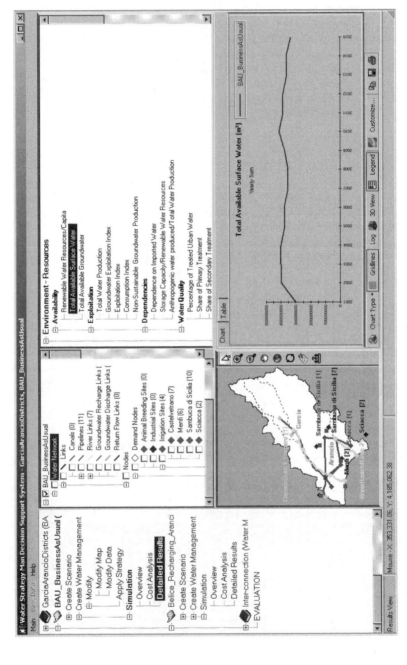

Figure 2.7   Presentation of results in the WSM DSS prototype

22

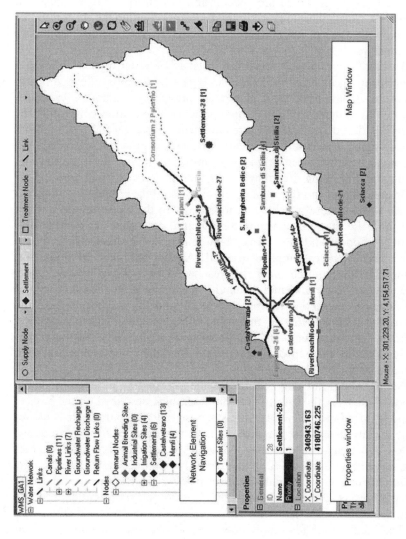

Figure 2.8   The map graphical user interface of the WSM DSS prototype

23

2.8). The analysis and visualization of the geographic features are supported by basic GIS functions such as zooming, panning, map refreshing, labelling and distance measuring.

The different demand or supply nodes are characterized by appropriate data, some of which are general and descriptive, that is, name and identifier, while others are used to model the node within the water resource simulation, that is, water quality parameters and various economics parameters.

Demand nodes are characterized in terms of water quality by average concentrations of predefined variables typical of the return flows, different according to the node type, each one representing a different water use. Furthermore demand nodes require specific information concerning the variables that drive their water requirements, based on the type of water use. Demand drivers for settlements are the residential and seasonal population, as well as the per capita daily consumption rate. For irrigation sites and animal breeding sites, they are respectively the cultivated area and the crop area shares, and the number of animals and the consumption rate per head. Units of total production, together with the consumption rate per unit and the share of consumptive demand, determine the demands for industry nodes, while the energy requirements of hydroelectricity plants drive their non-consumptive demand. Among the demand nodes, the minimum flow requirement of river reaches has been also considered under the name of 'environmental demand', which stands for the water volume necessary to preserve both the aquatic life and the geomorphologic and hydraulic characteristics of the rivers. Other demands affecting the river reaches symbolize requirements for navigation and for recreational purposes. Data for these three nodes concern the water volumes that have to be assured on a monthly basis.

Supply nodes not only require specific information in terms of operational data, as in the case of artificial reservoirs, described on the basis of capacity, dead volume, release rule, stage area and loss parameters, but they also require descriptive physical data such as distance from sources and catchment area for river reaches. As far as the aquifers are concerned, they are described and modelled in an extremely simplified way, and their data requirement is: capacity, initial storage, number of wells, rate of sustainable production, catchment area and specification of conceptual connections with rivers.

The quality data for supply nodes specify the initial conditions of the system before simulating the water allocation, while the economics data for demand nodes address pricing methods, water selling prices and the demand elasticity of water users. This latter defines the reaction of the users to the change of price, according to the rule that an increase of price corresponds to a decrease of demand. Costs for supply nodes include: depreciation period and construction cost of the infrastructure, which are used to calculate the annual equivalent cost, and costs for operation, maintenance and energy consumed per unit water volume abstracted, which form the running costs.

All the data charactering the nodes and links are stored in the geo-database and loaded in dedicated panels of the WSM DSS graphical user interface. From this interface, the values can be entered to define the case study or to update it. The navigation through the list of nodes, in order to access the data panel for the single geographic element or to highlight it on the map, is supported by the object manager panel of the graphical interface: the nodes and links of the water network are listed in a tree shaped view, similar to the folder tree view of Windows Explorer, and they are classified by type, according to their water function with respect to the allocation (for example demand nodes, supply nodes or treatment nodes) and according to their specific water use or resource type (for example industrial, domestic, aquifers, storage reservoirs and so on). Categories can be expanded by clicking on the plus sign or collapsed by clicking on the minus sign, according to the desired level of detail. Each type of node is marked with its own coloured symbol, such as circles, squares or rhombi. This symbol characterizes each node on the regional map that displays the water network and the physical features. Each network node or link has a user-defined name, and its unique identifier (ID) that appears next to the name in brackets.

The schematization of the water network within the WSM DSS and the data entry for all the geographic elements contribute to the first step of the water resource analysis procedure: assessment of the present status of the resource system. It is the basis for the development of step two, namely the selection of water scenarios.

2.6   FORMULATION OF WATER AVAILABILITY AND DEMAND SCENARIOS

The objective of the water availability module of the WSM package is to estimate the amount of water that is available in a water resource system, to be allocated to the existing demand users. Water sources considered comprise surface water, such as artificial reservoirs or natural lakes and the river network system, and groundwater, both renewable and fossil. The availability module generates monthly time series of forecasted available water for each modelled water source. These availability scenarios, along with the respective demand scenarios represent the basic information required to estimate the water allocation in the system. Results can be obtained in the following two ways:

1. by defining a set of customized years to be repeated in time, based upon the real observations at existing monitoring stations; and
2. by estimating run-off and natural recharge from a surface water balance performed on a monthly time step.

In the first case, 12 monthly values of run-off and recharge must be defined for each reservoir, river reach and renewable groundwater node in the network (Figure 2.9). These data should represent a normal (average) year, obtained from existing recorded data. Variations of the normal year can be created through the assignment of monthly positive or negative rates with respect to the normal year values. Customized years are then combined into the sequence that defines the scenario.

The alternative way for defining water availability scenarios is based on a lumped water balance at the watershed scale. Presently, it is in fact performed by a soil moisture balance module based on the hydrological modelling approach known as the ARNO Rainfall-Runoff Model (Todini, 1996). A set of maps are required in this case, among which are those of the definition of the hydro-geological catchments relevant to aquifers and lakes, the Digital Elevation Model (DEM) of the area, the saturated hydraulic conductivity of soils and soil moisture capacity as a function of soil types, land use map, monthly maps of precipitation, reference evapotranspiration and temperature, containing monthly data for the normal year. Given the DEM and the geographical position of the river reaches, maps of the corresponding upstream sub-basins are generated through the use of common GIS functions. Once these watershed maps are created for all water source elements, mean values of meteorological and pedologic information are calculated for each. Water balance is performed on a monthly time step over the entire simulation horizon. As a consequence, input data (rainfall, temperature and reference evapotranspiration) are required for the entire simulation horizon.

Scenarios for these variables are generated in three alternative ways:

1. by repeating the average year, or a user-customized year, for the entire duration of the scenario;
2. by defining an annual or monthly increment over the entire horizon, thus determining a yearly or monthly trend (Figure 2.10);
3. by building up a sequence of previously created years, similarly to the previously mentioned approach.

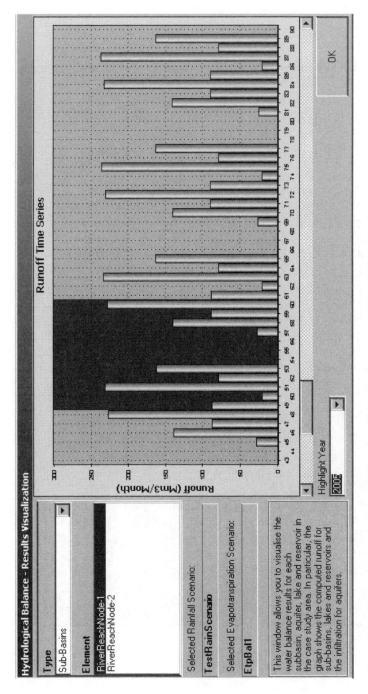

Figure 2.9 Generating a scenario from run-off time series in the WSM DSS prototype

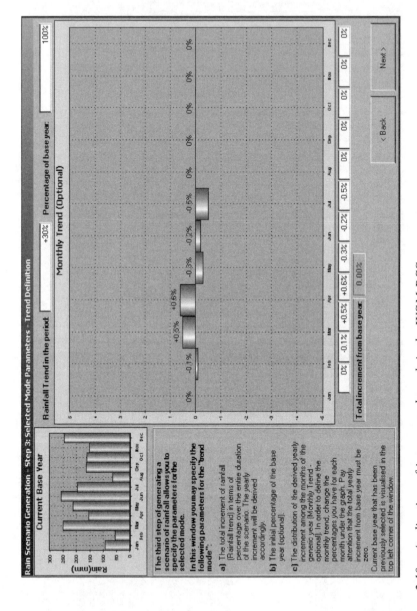

Figure 2.10   Application of inter-annual trends in the WSM DSS prototype

Generation of evapotranspiration scenarios can be performed on the basis of either potential evapotranspiration (ETP) or temperature maps, according to data availability. In the latter case, mean values of evapotranspiration for each altitude class of the DEM of the region are obtained through the corrected temperature values (in order to take into account the altitude distribution of the region) on the basis of the Thornthwaite formula. Time series of available run-off and infiltration, which correspond to the defined water availability scenario for the selected water sources, are then generated and used with the output of demand forecasts for estimating the water allocation in the system.

The water demand module produces forecasted time series of water demand for all water uses, generated by specifying appropriate growth rates to the key variables (drivers) that govern demand pressures, such as population for domestic use, cultivable area and livestock for agricultural practices, production growth for industries and minimum required energy production from hydropower plants.

In addition to the a priori evaluation of water demand trends, and for being able to assess the effects of non-structural measures, that is, pricing reforms, a Demand Feedback Loop functionality can also be activated. The concept is that water demand can vary reasonably either because of demand management measures and incentives, or due to socio-economic reactions (for example reduced water consumption under shortage conditions, or migration of population when quality of life drops below certain limits). Within the WSM DSS, the feedback option allows for modifying the demand scenarios along the simulated time horizon: variables that model specific trends, such as population or cultivable area, are influenced by water deficits that occur in a user-defined number of previous years. An example is presented in Figure 2.11.

2.7   WATER ALLOCATION

The kernel of the WSM DSS, that is, the water allocation model, performs the simulation of water allocation through the system. The model uses as input the pressures and drivers defined by the pre-processors of the DSS, and acts as an intermediate step in the assessment of state and impact indicators that allow for the evaluation of each water management option and strategy. In the WSM prototype, a simulation approach was preferred that aims to minimize water shortage under limited water supply (Manoli et al., 2001). Economic optimization models, aiming to maximize the social welfare surplus, require the monetary valuation of environmental impacts; this, in combination with the complex modelling of societal objectives,

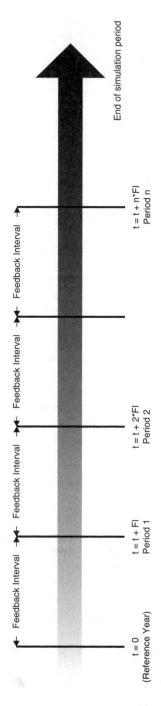

For each period n:

- Seasonal population$_{n,max}$ = Seasonal population that can be sustained according to water received during period n-1
- Irrigated area for each crop$_{n,max}$ = Area that can be sustained according to water received during period n-1
- Livestock number for each animal type$_{n,max}$ = Livestock number that can be sustained according to water received during period n-1

Figure 2.11   The feedback functionality for demand as integrated in the WSM DSS prototype

developmental priorities and property rights, which in most cases are subject to many constraints, limit the applicability of a DSS.

The implemented algorithm at each time step estimates the flow on the network (that is, a set of link flows) that minimizes the water shortage on all demand nodes under four types of constraints: supply, demand, flow conservation and link capacity. The model is solved by first constructing a reduction to a standard MaxFlow problem and then using the Ford-Fulkerson method (Lestor et al., 1962), also known as the augmenting-path maximum flow algorithm.

In situations of water shortage, distributing the water available from the various supply sources to the connected uses creates conflicts. The allocation model can solve this problem using two user-defined priority rules. First, competing demand sites are treated according to specified priorities. Those can express social preference or constraints, economic preference (prioritization to activities with highest economic values), or a system of water rights. Where a particular use can be supplied by more than one resource, supply priorities are used to rank the choices for obtaining water. Supply priorities in this case express: (1) cost preference; (2) quality preference of uses (for example domestic or industrial use) for supply sources with high water quality; (3) need for the protection of resources and the formation of strategic reserves.

2.8   WATER QUALITY AND ECONOMIC ANALYSIS MODELS

Water quality of water sources, effluents from demand nodes and treatment plants, and of water carried in each water link in the network in general, is described by the concentrations of the pollutants and variables considered, namely: salinity, chlorophyll, ammonia nitrogen, nitrate nitrogen, coliform bacteria, total phosphorus, heavy metals, biochemical oxygen demand and dissolved oxygen, suspended and inhibiting matters, and adsorbable organic halogens. The key concentrations simulated are those at the modelled water supply sources: groundwater, river reaches, artificial and natural lakes. These concentrations are distributed throughout the system together with the allocation of water to the nodes, according to the paths traced by the network links, and can be modified by the pollutant load production of demand nodes and by the treatment process of the plants. The concentrations at supply nodes are updated at each time step using two different algorithms, according to the quality parameter type.

For some, the continuity equation on the loads is applied: the variation of load in the volume stored in the supply equals the difference between the incoming and the outgoing loads. The total incoming load derives from the loads of the links carrying water to the supply node, while the outgoing load is computed from its current concentration. For heavy metals, total phosphorus, suspended and inhibiting matters, and adsorbable organic halogens a heuristic proportionality approach is used. Incoming loads are compared to the most recently measured (MRM) values, which are used as a reference, and water quality is assumed to improve proportionally if incoming loads are lower than the MRM, and to worsen otherwise.

One of the innovative aspects of the WSM DSS prototype is the tentative implementation of the cost-recovery principle, according to the requirements of the Water Framework Directive (2000/60/EC) and the relevant Guidance Document. The WSM DSS, according to the results of the water allocation algorithm, estimates financial (or direct), environmental and resource costs and associates these with the particular uses in accordance with the polluter-pays principle.

Estimation of direct costs associated with the provision of water supply and treatment is straightforward, depending on the amortization of capital investments, and energy, operation and maintenance costs associated with each part of the infrastructure. Their allocation to the respective uses is performed according to the annual volume of water supplied to each use that determines the share of infrastructure used by each user.

Two types of environmental costs have been incorporated, one for the abstraction and consumptive use of freshwater resources (both surface and groundwater) and one for the discharge of polluting effluents from demand activities. Estimations are based on a cost-based valuation method, where (external) environmental costs are approximated by the cost of mitigation measures. The sensitivity of the ecosystem is accounted for through the use of vulnerability coefficients, measuring the impact of abstractions of effluent discharges on the specific water body. In order to cope with data availability constraints, as well as different estimation techniques, various models have been incorporated for each type of environmental cost.

In the selected approach, resource costs are associated with the scarcity rent of freshwater resources, defined as a surplus, the difference between the opportunity cost of water and the per unit costs of turning that natural resource into products (for example agricultural crops for farmers, industrial production and so on). The estimation of opportunity costs is based on the computation of the water values for the different users. Values for irrigation are estimated according to the revenues from crop cultivation and the alternative value of land, whereas for animal breeding they are associated with net profit from livestock. Water values for industries are a function of the yearly production and the value of the product unit, while for domestic use, and in the absence of the urban demand curve, values are

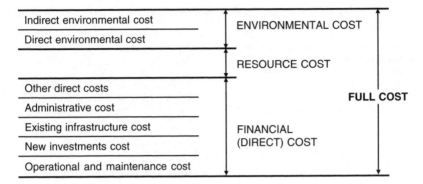

Figure 2.12   Cost elements considered in the economic analysis of the WSM DSS prototype

most regularly estimated as the marginal cost of the most expensive supply source under use.

In addition to the above, a series of economic indicators such as private and social welfare surplus have been introduced in order to assist in the ranking of alternative water management measures and strategies during the evaluation stage.

2.9   MODELLING OF WATER MANAGEMENT OPTIONS

A characteristic of the DSS is that it predefines a number of 'abstract' water management instruments (actions) and incorporates them as methods into the system. Those methods modify the properties of network elements accordingly or introduce new ones, related to water infrastructure development. An 'abstract' action becomes 'application specific' by the user-definition of its magnitude, time horizon and geographic area of application. An initial set of actions taken into consideration is presented in Table 2.1.

Incorporated actions are mainly focused on measures to deal with the frequent water shortages occurring in arid regions. The main aim is to either enhance supply, promoting the protection of vulnerable resources through structural interventions, or to regulate demand through the promotion of conservation measures, technological adjustments for increasing the efficiency of water use, and pricing incentives.

Instruments and measures not available in the DSS can also be modelled through changes to the network structure or function (for example the

Table 2.1   Summary table of policy options and actions incorporated in the WSM DSS prototype

Policy options	Actions
Supply enhancement	• Unconventional/untapped resources • Exploitation of surface waters and precipitation (direct abstraction, dams, reservoirs) • Groundwater exploitation • Desalination • Importing and inter-basin water transfer • Water reuse • Improved infrastructure to reduce losses (networks, storage facilities)
Demand management	• Quotas and regulated supply • Irrigation method improvements • Recycling in industry and domestic use • Raw material substitution and process changes in industry
Social-developmental policy	• Change in agricultural practices • Change of regional development policy
Institutional policies	• Economic policies (water pricing, cost recovery, incentives)

introduction of cisterns in a settlement is modelled as a small reservoir with total capacity equal to that of the sum of the individual cisterns, set just outside the settlement).

2.10   INDICATORS AND EVALUATION

In addition to the indicators and indices that are directly used for the evaluation of water management strategies, the DSS provides a number of additional time series of indicators and indices based on the primary data that are either modelled by the system or entered as initial data. Their purpose is to provide the user with additional information on the evaluation process and the behaviour of key parameters influencing the water system. Time series are visualized at a monthly base or aggregated yearly. Specific indicators characterize the various spatial entities of the water network, such as

Table 2.2   Additional time series of indicators in the WSM DSS – Water Management Scheme level

Category		Indicator
Environment resources	Exploitation	Total water production
		Groundwater exploitation index
		Consumption index
		Non-sustainable groundwater production
	Dependencies	Dependency ratio
		Anthropogenic water produced/total water production
	Water quality	Percentage of treated urban water
		Share of primary treatment
		Share of secondary treatment
		Share of tertiary treatment
Social indicators	Pressures	Agricultural demand per ha
		Tourist per inhabitant
		Water abstractions per capita
	Deficits	Domestic deficit as percentage of demand
		Industrial deficit as percentage of demand
		Environmental deficit as percentage of demand
		Hydropower deficit as percentage of demand
		Irrigation deficit as percentage of demand
Economics		Direct costs
		Environmental costs
		Resource costs
		Revenues from water billing
		Rate of cost recovery
		Benefit from water use

settlements, industries, storage reservoirs and river reaches, while aggregation is also performed on a water management scheme level (Table 2.2). According to the type of network element they refer to, different categories of indicators are estimated, such as: exploitation, dependencies, water quality, pressures, deficits, cost/revenues and water quantity. In the exploitation group, there are variables such as total water production and consumption index, groundwater exploitation index and non-sustainable groundwater production index. Dependencies relate to the needs for water imported from neighbouring areas and the recycled and desalinated water produced over the total water production.

Evaluation of alternative schemes is based on a multi-criteria approach that takes into account the entire simulation horizon. In a first step, time series of indicators are computed, describing the behaviour of the water system in terms of environmental, efficiency and economic objectives (Table 2.3), with the ultimate goal of assisting decision-makers in the selection of water management instruments that meet the goals of integrated water resources management.

Comparison is performed through a multi-criteria analysis based on the computation of statistical criteria for reliability, resilience and vulnerability (ASCE, 1998). The statistical criteria measure the behaviour of the monthly or yearly time series of each indicator with respect to the predefined range of satisfactory values that the indicator can assume. Reliability is defined as the probability that any particular indicator value will be within the range of values considered satisfactory. Resilience describes the speed of recovery from an unsatisfactory condition. Vulnerability statistical criteria measure the extent and the duration of unsatisfactory values. Performance for each indicator is computed as the product of the above criteria, and the relative sustainability index of each WMS is estimated as the weighted sum of the performance of the selected

Table 2.3   Initial set of indicators used in the evaluation procedure of the WSM DSS prototype

Category	Indicator
Environment/resources	Dependence on inter-basin water transfer Desalination and reuse percentage Groundwater exploitation index Non-sustainable water production index Share of treated urban water
Efficiency	Coverage of animal breeding, domestic, environmental, hydropower, industrial and irrigation demands
Economics	Direct costs Benefits Environmental cost Rate of cost recovery

indicators. An example of the evaluation results provided by the module is given in Figure 2.13.

In practice, the implementation of a measure introduces a response at a certain point of the simulation horizon, in order to overcome unacceptable and/or inadequate conditions estimated on the basis of the applied demand and availability scenarios. Alternative strategic options can be simulated as freestanding, under the same scenarios or diverse extreme climatic and demographic conditions. In the WSM approach (WaterStrategyMan Project, 2002–2005) the ensemble of scenarios plus a particular option is referred to as a 'Comprehensive scenario'. The main objective of the undertaken analysis is to determine the options that could be effective in meeting the targets set for each case study region, and estimate their potential extent, cost and environmental impact. The construction of alternative sets of strategic measures as responses or solutions to unsustainable conditions characterizes the fifth step (S5 in Figure 2.1) of the water resource analysis procedure presented in the introduction. After simulating the new strategies (step S6) using the DSS, the evaluation of the outcomes and effects of the application of the alternative strategies is performed (step S7). Thus the final output permits the ranking of alternatives, and the selection of those most appropriate for dealing with the water management issues encountered in the region under study.

2.11   CONCLUDING REMARKS

The WSM DSS prototype is a GIS-based software package that allows for water resource assessment, identification of boundary social and economic conditions, climatic drivers and demographic pressures, simulation and investigation of future forecasts and comparison of alternative policy measures. Special attention was given to ensure the portability and simplicity of its application. The simulation-based approach adopted for its development aims to simplify the level of data required in modelling complex physical systems. The package can work at different aggregation levels, depending on data availability and modelling scopes. As the system is simulation driven, the WSM DSS is not expected to provide an optimal answer to emerging water management issues; instead the approach is meant to provide insight to a series of possible solutions and options that could be effective in dealing with these issues, while at the same time addressing the principles of integrated water resources management.

The structure of the software is modular and open to expansion and improvements of the modelling core. Further improvements of the WSM DSS prototype will be oriented towards the description of the

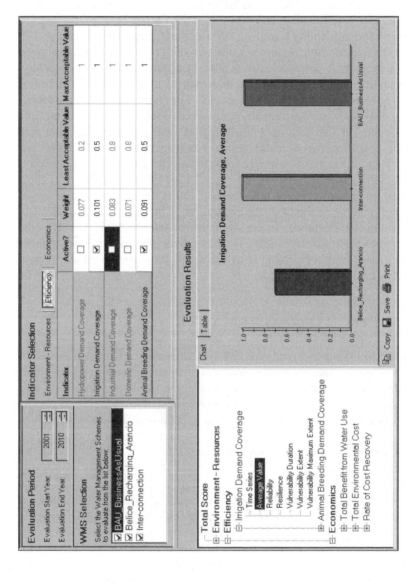

Figure 2.13 The evaluation module of the WSM DSS prototype

socio-economic reactions through the aggregation of indicators, for example describing the 'quality of life', or consumer willingness to pay. In addition, improved hydrological balance descriptions (Todini, 1995; Liu and Todini, 2002; Ciarapica and Todini, 2002) and their link to General Circulation Model (GCM) outputs could allow for the analysis of possible future trends under climatic change conditions, and the analysis of the effects of future uncertainty over current management practices.

REFERENCES

Albert, X., O. Mark, M.S. Babel, A.D. Gupta and J. Fugl (2001), 'Integrating resource management in South East Asia', conference presentation, Water 21 October 2001, 25–30.

Andreu, J., J. Capilla and E. Sanchis (1996), 'Aquatool: a generalized decision support system for water-resources planning and operational management', *Journal of Hydrology*, **177**, 269–91.

Bakken, T.H., K. Dagestad and B.M. Wathne (2001), *ENSIS – An environmental surveillance and information system*, proceedings from the IWA conference Berlin.

Bouwer, H. (2000), 'Integrated water management: emerging issues and challenges', *Agricultural Water Management*, **45**, 217–28.

Ciarapica, L. and E. Todini (2002), 'TOPKAPI: a model for the representation of the rainfall-runoff process at different scales', *Hydrological Processes*, **16** (2), 207–29.

DHI (2003), *Mike Basin, Manuals and Documentation*, http://www.dhisoftware.com/mikebasin/index.htm

Environmental Systems Research Institute – ESRI (2001), *ArcGIS 8 Users' Manual*, Redlands, CA, USA.

ET&P (2001), *A DSS for Water Resources Planning Based on Environmental Balance*, Final report, Bologna, Italy.

Fedra, K. and D.G. Jamieson (1996), 'The WaterWare decision-support system for river basin planning: II. Planning Capability', *Journal of Hydrology*, **177**, 177–98.

Giupponi C., J. Mysiak, A. Fassio and V. Cogan (2004), 'MULINO-DSS: a computer tool for sustainable use of water resources at the catchment scale', *Mathematics and Computers in Simulation*, **64**, 13–24.

Jamieson, D.G. and K. Fedra (1996a), 'The WaterWare decision-support system for river basin planning: I. Conceptual Design', *Journal of Hydrology*, **177**, 163–75.

Jamieson, D.G. and K. Fedra (1996b), 'The WaterWare decision-support system for river basin planning: III. Example Applications', *Journal of Hydrology*, **177**, 199–211.

Lestor, R., Jr. Ford and D.R. Fulkerson (1962), *Flows in Networks*, Princeton, NJ: Princeton University Press.

Liu, Z. and E. Todini (2002), 'Towards a comprehensive physically-based rainfall-runoff model', *Hydrology and Earth System Sciences*, **6**, 859–81.

Loucks, D.P. (1995), 'Developing and implementing decision support systems', *Water Resources Bulletin*, **31**, 571–82.

Loucks, D.P., M.R. Taylor (and) P.N. French (1996), *IRAS-Interactive River-Aquifer Simulation Model, Program Description and Operating Manual*, Ithaca, NY: Department of Civil and Environmental Engineering, Cornell University.

Manoli, E., G. Arampatzis, E. Pissias and D. Assimacopoulos (2002), 'A spatial decision support system for the evaluation of water demand and supply management schemes', *Hydrorama 2002, 'Integrated Water Management: The key to Sustainable Water Resources'*, 182–8.

McKinney, D.C., X. Cai, M.W. Rosegrant, C. Ringler and C.A. Scott (1999), *Modeling Water Resources Management at the Basin Level: Review and Future Directions*, International Water Management Institute, SWIM Paper 6.

NSW Department of Land and Water Conservation, Centre for Natural Resources (1999), *Integrated Quantity and Quality Model (IQQM)*, http://www.dlwc.nsw.gov.au/care/water/iqqm/.

Smeets, E., R. Weterings, P. Bosch, M. Bchele and D. Gee (1999), *Technical report No 25 – Environmental Indicators: Typology and Overview*, European Environment Agency – Academic Press.

Stockholm Environment Institute (2005), 'Water evaluation and planning system', *User Guide for Weap2*, http://www.weap21.org.

Todini, E. (1995), 'New trends in modelling soil processes from hillslope to GCM scales', in H.R. Oliver and S.A. Oliver (eds), The Role of Water and the Hydrological Cycle in Global Change. Nato Asi Series, Series I: Global Environmental Change, Berlin: Springer Verlag, **31**, 317–47.

Todini, E. (1996), 'The Arno rainfall-runoff model', *Journal of Hydrology*, **175**, 339–82.

US Environmental Protection Agency (2004), *BASINS – Better Assessment Science Integrating Point and Non-point Sources*, http://www.epa.gov/OST/BASINS/.

Walmsley, Jay J. (2002), 'Framework for measuring sustainable development in catchment systems', *Environmental Management*, **29** (2), 195–206.

WaterStrategyMan Project (2002–2005) 'Developing Strategies for Regulating and Managing Water Resources and Demand in Water Deficient Regions', EU Contract No. EVK1-CT-2001–00098 http://environ.chemeng.ntua.gr/wsm.

WL Delft Hydraulics (2005), *RIBASIM – River Basin Planning and Management*, http://www.wldelft.nl/soft/ribasim/int/index.html.

3. Evaluation of alternative water management scenarios: case study of Ribeiras do Algarve, Portugal

Rodrigo Maia

3.1 STUDY AIMS

This chapter aims to exemplify the DSS tool application to the Ribeiras do Algarve case study. After a brief description of the river basin, various alternative water management scenarios were evaluated through the application of the referred tool.

Before analysing the different scenarios, the available and feasible management options were identified. It was then necessary to evaluate each one of them under different demand and availability scenarios. All the results obtained through the DSS allow the user to rank different options according to different indicators specified in the model.

The second phase addressed the formulation of strategies using the available options. Two different strategies were considered: one reflecting the dominant paradigm and another reflecting a new paradigm. The evaluation of the strategies performance was associated to the development of an adequate cost recovery scheme.

The main goal of the Portuguese case study was to achieve the following demand coverage percentage:

- For domestic use: 95 per cent over the year.
- For irrigation of:
    - public irrigation sites: 90 per cent over the year;
    - private irrigation sites: 80 per cent over the year;
    - golf courses: 90 per cent, during summer months.

Also, in order to promote a sustainable use of groundwater resources, a target of maximum use of 80 per cent of the aquifer recharge was envisaged.

3.2   DESCRIPTION OF THE STUDY AREA

3.2.1   General Characterization

Ribeiras do Algarve River Basin represents a total area of 3837 km^2 which occupies the southern stretch of the Portuguese territory and includes 18 municipalities (Figure 3.1).

In 2005, the Algarve has suffered deep changes in its demography due to the important development of tourism activity. In the 1980s, one could identify a productive structure based on three economic activities: agriculture, fishing and tourism.

Currently, the Algarve is the most popular tourist destination in mainland Portugal, registering a resident population in 2001 of around 370 000 inhabitants. The total population is normally increased on average by approximately 200 per cent during the summer months due to the tourist population. Figure 3.2 presents the monthly variation of the population for the year 2001 (PBHRA, 1999a).

The population is unequally distributed: while most of the inhabitants live in the littoral zone, the inland region is suffering a desertification process associated with a significant ageing of the population.

The existing pressure related to tourism activities is present throughout the year, particularly during the summer months and vacation periods, generating an imbalance between activities from different sectors. That way, tourism activity intensification adversely affects the traditional activities, leading to a more intense exploitation of natural resources.

3.2.2   DPSIR Approach

Table 3.1 describes a DPSIR (Driving Forces – Pressures – State – Impacts – Responses) approach analysis applied to the Ribeiras do Algarve River Basin.

It seems clear that in the Ribeiras do Algarve River Basin there are various and powerful reasons – namely conflicting interests on water resource uses between the tourism sector and agriculture (mainly during summer months), infrastructure deficiencies, poor groundwater quality in some areas, high values of secondary water supply network losses (16 per cent to 61 per cent) and inadequate irrigation methods – that urge the implementation of management measures.

In this context, and after consultation with the different stakeholders, the major goals of the formulation of the scenarios and strategies for the Ribeiras do Algarve River Basin are aiming to:

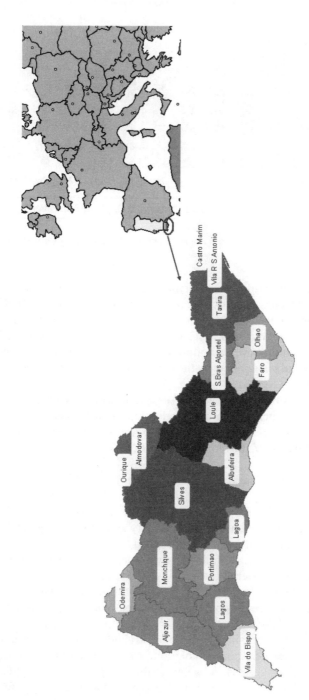

Figure 3.1   Ribeiras do Algarve River Basin location and municipalities

43

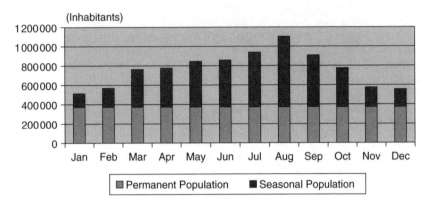

Figure 3.2   Monthly variation of permanent and seasonal population in 2001

- Implement options which enable 95 per cent of domestic demand coverage, which is currently a major issue in the west zone of the Ribeiras do Algarve River Basin, and solve localized deficits in irrigation.
- Promote options that prevent environmental resources degradation, namely aquifer overexploitation. These options shall be implemented particularly in aquifers by the sea where risk of salinization is already present.
- Promote options that enable the attainment of the economic feasibility of water use, through valuation of direct and environmental costs and of rate of cost recovery optimization, taking into account the principle of the recovery of costs.

3.2.3   Water Uses Characterization

The main water uses in the Algarve River Basin are associated with irrigation, golf courses, domestic supply, industry and animal breeding. In 2002, irrigation sites and golf courses represented 64.4 per cent of the total water demand in the river basin, followed by domestic use which accounted for 34.4 per cent of the overall river basin demand (Figure 3.3).

Traditionally, the domestic and agricultural demands were satisfied by groundwater resources, supporting their development. However the combination of natural processes and aquifer overexploitation led to groundwater salinization and water quality deterioration (Figure 3.4). Therefore aquifers progressively became a non-reliable source of water supply, causing a shift from groundwater to surface water as the major source of public water supply. This change in the supply sources enabled aquifer storage recovery.

Table 3.1   DPSIR indicators

Driving forces	Pressures	State	Impacts	Responses
• Irregular temporal precipitation distribution • Tourism development • Land use change due to tourism development • Intensive and antiquated agricultural activities with low efficiency water use • Water discharge from both urban and agriculture sectors	• High agricultural water demand • High tourist influx • High demand during summer period • Conflicting uses: irrigation vs tourist demand • High exploitation of aquifers • Increasing population density on coastal area	• Current and long-time foreseen water shortages, aggravated in the summer months during the irrigation period • High urban water supply losses (37% on average) • High irrigation water losses • Polluted surface and groundwater • Salinization in most coastal aquifers (due to overabstraction)	• Flow decrease during summer time. • Ecosystem degradation • Economic impacts due to water deficits for tourism and agriculture • Inadequate land use and water infrastructure • Poor surface and groundwater quality	Supply Enhancement • Water transfer from Guadiana's basin (Odeleite-Beliche dams) • Construction of Odelouca dam Development Policy • Improved management efficiency of reservoirs and supply networks Demand management • Use of more efficient irrigation techniques • Promotion of the reuse of treated waste water for agriculture • Significant subsidies for irrigation water

45

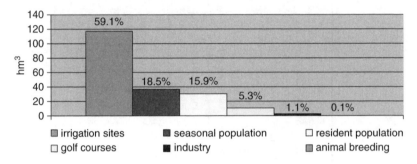

Figure 3.3   River basin water uses demand in 2002

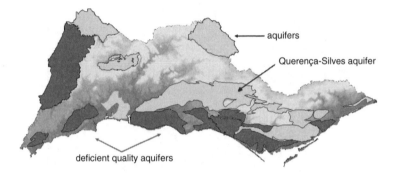

*Figure 3.4   Aquifers identified in RBP, highlighting those with good water
quality (the dark shaded), and those with quality deficiencies*

In 1995, two inter-municipal companies were created for primary urban
water supply: one for the west part of the basin, Águas do Barlavento
Algarvio, and another one for the east, Águas do Sotavento Algarvio. In
2000, the two companies merged forming the Águas do Algarve S.A.
company which has the concession of the primary water supply system,
enabling the physical connection of the two former existing water supply
pipeline systems. This connection currently (2004) allows the transference
of a maximum of 7 hm³ from one supply side of the basin to the other.

The primary water supply system supplies with surface water 29 of the
51 secondary water distribution network systems existing in the river basin,
which corresponds to more than 85 per cent of the total urban water consumption in 2002. The remaining 22 secondary network systems are supplied by groundwater under municipalities' responsibility (PBHRA,
2000a). Since 2001, Águas do Algarve S.A. has also the concession of the
primary network for wastewater drainage and treatment.

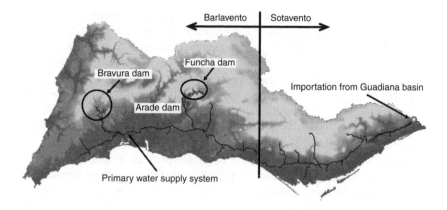

Figure 3.5   *Supply sources of the primary water supply system of Águas do Algarve S.A.*

Currently (as of 2004), the supply sources of the primary water supply system are, as shown in Figure 3.5:

- in Sotavento (east side), the Odeleite-Beliche system (located in the Guadiana River Basin from which water is imported); and
- in Barlavento (west side), the Bravura and Funcho dams (this last connects to Arade dam, water supply source for agriculture).

Nevertheless, the supply sources have abstractions limitations, dictated by concession agreements:

- for the Bravura storage reservoir, a limit of $6 \, hm^3$, in a two-year period;
- for the Funcho storage reservoir, a guaranteed minimum of 12 hm^3/year, although this volume has, since 2000, always been above that limit (about 23 hm^3/year);
- for Odeleite-Beliche the total abstraction is dictated by the correspondent water treatment plant capacity (about 69 hm^3/year), located in Tavira.

Industrial consumption is dispersed over the urban areas and represents less than 1.5 per cent (in 2004) of total urban consumption.

According to the River Basin Plan (PBHRA,1999b), the agricultural area (public and private irrigation sites) represents about 32 000 ha, that is, approximately 8 per cent of the Ribeiras do Algarve River Basin non-urbanized area, being the most important water sector user. Presently, both surface (SW) and groundwater (GW) are used for irrigation, the latter representing the main supply resource, used in 86 per cent of the irrigated area. Moreover the efficiency of irrigation methods is, on average, about 60 per cent in public irrigation sites and 80 per cent in private irrigation sites.

The main orchard and field crops cultivated in the Algarve are citrus, peaches, wine and horticulture (open air and protected culture), maize, lucerne, rice and grass. In 2000, citrus represented 35 per cent of the total irrigated area and a total water consumption of approximately 48 hm³/year, according to the River Basin Plan (PBHRA, 1999b).

In the region there are two types of irrigation sites, public and private. Public irrigation sites are mainly supplied by surface water and farmers are gathered into farmers' associations to which they pay water. By contrast private irrigation sites use mostly groundwater for irrigation and each farmer is responsible for their own irrigation site maintenance.

According to the Ribeiras do Algarve River Basin Plan, an increase of 69 per cent of the public irrigation sites area until 2006, and a growth rate of 1.3 per cent per year until 2020, for private irrigation sites is expected (PBHRA, 2001).

Due to their characteristics, golf courses were classified as a specific type of irrigated culture. By the end of 2003, about 25 golf courses already existed in the Algarve River Basin, representing approximately 41 per cent of those existing in Portugal. According to the licensing applications recently registered, about 33 new golf courses are planned to be implemented (MCOTA, 2003) mostly on the coastline, 11 of which are in Loulé Municipality. However, the implementation of these new golf courses is pending by local authorities' decision, which may eventually consider licensing criteria revision.

In fact, the fast development of golf courses, together with the idea that golf is a 'strategic product for national tourism', urges measures to be implemented in order to stop the related degradation of water quality and to assure the sustainability of existing groundwater abstractions, as the majority of golf course irrigation is supplied by groundwater. Figure 3.6 shows the location of the different public irrigation sites and golf courses.

Taking into account the present state of aquifers located on the coastal zone (namely high chloride levels and low values of the water levels), the Commission of Coordination and Regional Development of Algarve (CCDR Algarve) delimited a critical area by the coast (Figure 3.7), for which specific licensing criteria has been defined. Within that critical area any new abstractions are forbidden, except for domestic use or replacement of already existing ones. Presently, as the number of boreholes and the volume abstracted have diminished (due to the introduction of the primary water supply system of Águas do Algarve S.A.), aquifers reached more acceptable

Figure 3.6   Public irrigation sites and golf courses

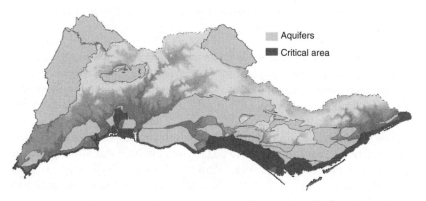

Figure 3.7   Critical area location

groundwater levels, eventually enabling CCDR Algarve to reformulate the critical area perimeter.

Animal breeding sites represent another water consumer, although of minor importance, as shown in Figure 3.3.

3.3   METHODOLOGICAL BACKGROUND

3.3.1   Demand and Availability Scenario Components

Given the importance of water consumption by the irrigation cultures and the growing importance of tourism, the formulation of demand scenarios

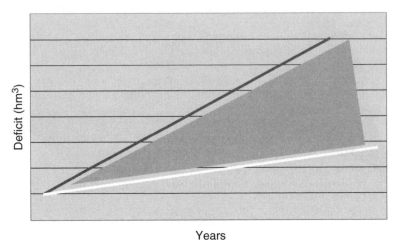

*Figure 3.8   Scheme defining extreme combinations of demand and
availability scenarios*

for the Ribeiras do Algarve River Basin was based upon assumptions about
permanent and seasonal population and agriculture growth rates. A range
of extreme combinations of low and high demand and availability scenarios
were used for the simulations, enabling the definition of a range of expected
and/or controlled deficit (Figure 3.8).

It should be emphasized that the simulation period considered began in
2000 (reference year) and ended in 2035. The year 2000 was already used as
the reference in the National Water Plan and the Ribeiras do Algarve River
Basin Plan and is also considered the starting date of infrastructural evolution of the primary water supply system.

3.3.1.1   Formulation of urban demand scenarios

For the permanent and seasonal population, a variety of data and data
estimations have been collected and analysed from several institutions and
governmental and non-governmental organisms, regarding population
evolution, consumption, network systems description, network losses,
water sources (surface and groundwater), irrigation efficiencies, types of
irrigated cultures, irrigation sites and costs associated with water distribution and drainage.

In August, 97 per cent of the seasonal population locates in the littoral
municipalities, whereas only 3 per cent locates in the inland municipalities.
These percentages indicate clearly the uneven spatial distribution of the
seasonal (tourists) population.

The population in 2000 was considered to be the same as in 2001, using the

Table 3.2   Population trends for the three scenarios

Scenario	Period	Growth rate (%)	
		Permanent population	Seasonal population
BAU	2000–2035	differentiated for each municipality*	2.3
Stabilized demand	2000–2010	differentiated for each municipality*	2.3
	2011–35	0.0	0.0
Low demand	2000–2010	differentiated for each municipality*	2.3
	2011–15	0.0	0.0
	2016–35	−0.5	−0.5

Notes:
* Albufeira: 2.01%; Aljezur: 0.19%; Almodôvar: −1.59%; Castro Marim: −0.87%; Faro: 2.01%; Lagoa: 1.07%; Lagos: 1.07%; Loulé: 1.07%; Monchique: 1.59%; Odemira: 0.87%; Olhão: 0%; Ourique: −1.59%; Portimão: 2.01%; São Brás de Alportel: 0.18%; Silves: 1.07%; Tavira: 0.18%; Vila do Bispo: 0.18% and Vila Real de Santo António: −0.87%.

results from the 2001 Census (INE, 2001). Finally, domestic consumption rates were estimated based on the real water volume delivered by Águas do Algarve S.A. to the different settlements in 2002.

Projections   Three different potential trends have been distinguished, forming the potential scenarios for domestic demand:

- a scenario where demand increases at a steady rate, equal to that currently observed, and corresponding to a 'business as usual' situation (BAU);
- a scenario where demand is stabilized ten years after the reference year (stabilized demand, SD);
- a scenario where the demand decreases 15 years after the reference year (low demand, LD).

For defining the business as usual scenario (BAU), during the period examined (2000–2035) the permanent population differentiated growth rates were defined for each municipality according to the projections presented in the Ribeiras do Algarve River Basin Plan (RBP) within 2000–2020. For seasonal population, the growth rate was set equal for all the municipalities, according to the projection from 2000–2020 of the RBP (Table 3.2) (PBHRA, 2000b). Seasonal population growth rate was higher than the

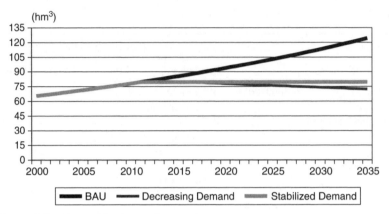

Figure 3.9   Domestic demand scenarios

growth rate set for the permanent population, due to tourism development. It should be noted that the consumption rates for the permanent and tourist populations were set according to the River Basin Plan (differentiated by municipality) and considered constant for all the period of the simulation.

The two other scenarios formulated (SD and LD) for the analysed period assumed that after a point in time the population in the Ribeiras do Algarve River Basin will reach its carrying capacity regarding the development of tourism. In one scenario, this shall be followed by a stabilization of population while a more pessimistic scenario supposes a small decrease of tourism and birth rate.

The annual growth rates for permanent and seasonal population considered for each demand scenario were set as presented in Table 3.2. The differentiation by municipality was considered equal for the three scenarios. The demand evolution corresponding to the three scenarios is presented in Figure 3.9. For industry, which represents a small contribution to urban water use, no growth rate was applied.

3.3.1.2   Formulation of irrigation demand scenarios
Concerning irrigation demand, it is important to note that it is very difficult to gather accurate data. The data introduced in the WSM DSS tool were collected from the River Basin Plan (PBHRA, 1999b). However whenever lack of information was verified, data were obtained through the consultation of different local (farmers' associations) and regional or national stakeholders, trying to follow a coherent and reliable methodology.

Projections   As for the domestic demand scenarios, according to the projections presented in the River Basin Plan for 2000–2020, the growth rates

Table 3.3   Growth rates considered for irrigation sites and golf courses

	Period	Growth rate (%)
Private irrigation site	2000–2020	1.3
	2021–35	0.0
Public irrigation sites	2000–2020	differentiated for each public irrigation site*
	2021–35	0.0
Golf courses	2000–2035	0.0

Notes:
* Silves, Lagoa and Portimão: 0.5%; Mira, Benaciate, Sotavento: 3.4%; Alcantarilha and Vale da Vila: 7.2%

considered for public and private irrigation sites and golf courses are presented in Table 3.3. A growth rate of 0.5 per cent was considered for animal breeding sites until 2020.

3.3.1.3   Formulation of availability scenarios

The climate in Ribeiras do Algarve River Basin is Mediterranean temperate, characterized by rainy winters and dry summers. The average temperature is 18°C and the average annual precipitation is around 750 mm. However there are differences between the correspondent values of the six sub-basins: a maximum of 813 mm/year in the west coast sub-basin and a minimum of 565 mm/year in the south coast ones. Those differences reflect not only spatial but also temporal different precipitation distribution.

Scenarios   The formulation of the availability scenarios (Figure 3.10) was based on the sequence of years with respect to rainfall presented by INAG (Portuguese National Water Institute) for the 13 meteorological stations considered.

According to Veiga da Cunha et al. (2002), it should be expected that climate changes will lead to a general decrease in water availability and to an increase of seasonal and spatial asymmetries in Portugal. Concerning the Algarve River Basin, projections are particularly uncertain because of a strong spatial variability of precipitation, mainly due to the mountainous range that separates the Algarve basin from the adjacent basins. The impacts are likely to be negative, namely in drier months.

The three following hydrological scenarios were considered:

- The normal scenario (Normal), representing a 35-year period defined in accordance with the historical sequence that occurred between 1970 and 2000.

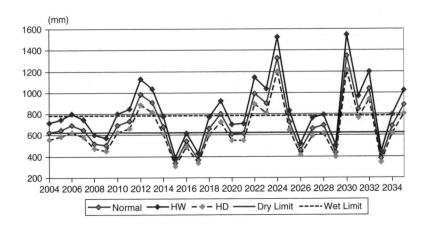

Figure 3.10   Water availability scenarios

- The high frequency of wet years scenario (HW), which was defined considering a 15 per cent increase of the Normal scenario's precipitation.
- The high frequency of dry years scenario (HD), which was defined considering a 10 per cent decrease of the Normal scenario's precipitation.

A sequence of different types of hydrological years (very wet, wet, normal, dry and very dry) was considered for each scenario. Monthly rainfall variation coefficients for each of those years, in relation to an average year, were defined for the simulation period by means of the analysis of INAG's hydrological series.

Limitations used in the WSM DSS   For modelling purposes and after analysis of this issue with Águas do Algarve S.A., some specific physical limitations to yearly abstractions were assumed for some urban supply sources:

- for Bravura storage reservoir, a limit of 4hm³/year;
- for Funcho storage reservoir, a limit of 23 hm³/year for normal and wet years, according to the abstractions verified since 2003 by the Águas do Algarve S.A., and a limit of 17 hm³/year for periods of consecutive dry years.

3.3.1.4 Combination of hydrological and demand scenarios

Besides the availability scenarios defined previously, it is important to establish different scenarios to evaluate the behaviour of the overall water system. The different management options that have been evaluated are the following:

- A combination of steady demand increase with a series of normal years (BAU + Normal), reflecting the current trends of the system in a 'business as usual' context, according to the River Basin Plan.
- A combination of steady demand increase with a high frequency of dry years (BAU + HD), reflecting a severe scenario of water shortage.
- A combination of low demand with a high frequency of wet years (LD + HW), reflecting the best-case scenario.

For each combination of demand and availability scenarios, and after preparing the database containing all the required information, one can through running the WSM DSS foresee the river basin system behaviour in terms of demand, economic and environmental sustainability for the various uses, throughout the simulation period (2000–2035), defining what will be later entitled as 'reference case'. The results for the reference case are presented in Figures 3.11 to 3.14.

As one can observe, from Figure 3.11a, the domestic deficit under the BAU + Normal and BAU + HD scenarios presents an important increase until the end of the simulation period. As said previously, most of the Ribeiras do Algarve River Basin area, namely the settlements where the permanent and seasonal population are higher, are supplied by surface water. In Sotavento the capacity of Odeleite-Beliche system is sufficient to assure the domestic demand. However in Barlavento the maximum volume available in the Funcho storage reservoir for urban supply is not enough to assure all the demand associated to the BAU scenario, significantly increasing the deficit observed. That way, as shown in Figure 3.11a, domestic deficit is higher during the dry periods as the volume that can be abstracted was smaller.

For the LD + HW scenario, the domestic deficit is always below 5 hm^3, representing on average less than 4 per cent of the domestic demand considered for this scenario.

Figure 3.11b presents the estimated domestic demand coverage under the selected demand and availability scenario combinations. As one can observe, for the BAU + Normal and BAU + HD scenarios the domestic demand coverage drops below 75 per cent by the end of the simulation period, in accordance with the results verified for the deficit. For the LD + HW scenario, the improvement of the domestic demand coverage is related to the decreasing of the population considered in the demand scenario.

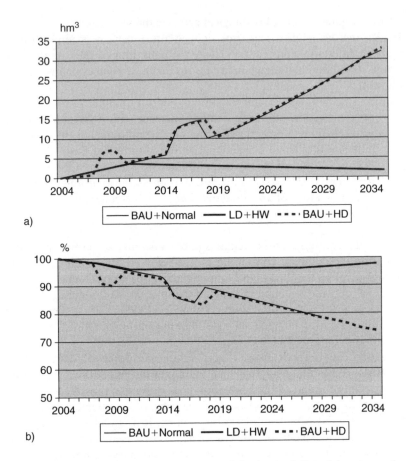

Figure 3.11   *Reference case: a) estimated domestic deficit; b) estimated*
domestic demand coverage, under the selected demand and
availability scenario combinations

As previously explained, domestic supply is mostly assured by surface water and that is also reflected in the domestic deficit associated to each type of supply source. In fact according to Figure 3.12, 99 per cent of the domestic demand deficit is due to surface water and that due to ground-water is insignificant.

It should be noted that the domestic deficit due to surface water may not only represent an effective shortage of water, but may also be a consequence of the inadequate diameter of some pipeline connections of the primary water supply system to the supplied settlements.

Almost the entire domestic demand deficit relates to Barlavento region

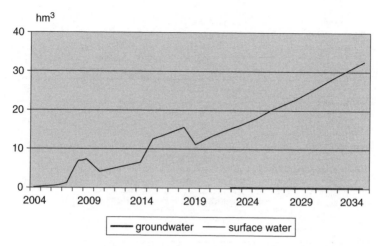

Figure 3.12   Reference case: domestic deficit according to the type of supply (BAU + HD)

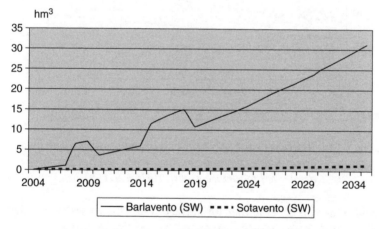

Figure 3.13   Reference case: unmet domestic demand due to surface water in Barlavento and Sotavento (BAU + HD)

(95 per cent), as a result of abstractions limitations at Funcho dam (23 hm³), which are aggravated during a dry years sequence (17 hm³) as shown in Figure 3.13.

As emphasized in section 3.2.2, secondary water supply network losses are a major issue in the Algarve region. Figure 3.14a shows the losses associated to domestic use for the BAU + HD scenario during the simulation

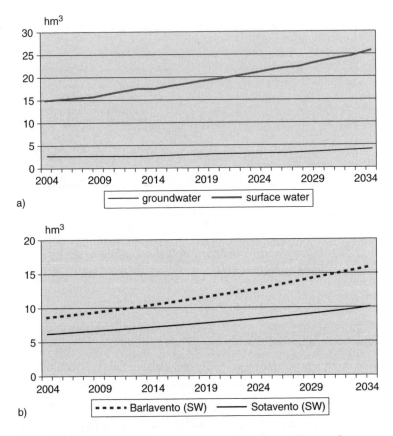

*Figure 3.14   Reference case: a) losses associated to surface and
groundwater; b) losses in Barlavento and Sotavento
associated to surface water (BAU + HD)*

period. One can observe that for surface water the losses can achieve 26
hm³ in 2034, being mostly associated to the Barlavento region (Figure
3.14b).

Contrarily to settlements, most of the irrigation sites are supplied by
groundwater and therefore dependent on its availability. The estimated irrigation deficit is consequently higher for the BAU + HD scenario and lower
for the LD + HW scenario (Figure 3.15a).

Additionally, a permanent irrigation demand deficit of 2 hm³ is observed
under all scenarios and throughout the whole simulation period. This deficit
is localized (1) in the private irrigation sites of Castro Marim and Vila Real
de Santo António, resulting from the deficient capacity of São Bartolomeu

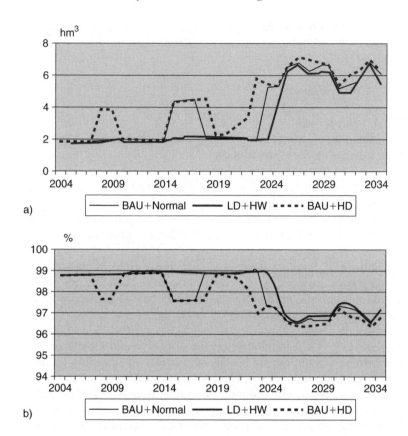

a)

b)

*Figure 3.15   Reference case: a) estimated irrigation deficit; b) estimated
irrigation demand coverage, under the selected demand and
availability scenario combinations*

aquifer to satisfy their irrigation demand; and (2) in two golf courses
(Herdade dos Salgados and Quinta do Lago – Ria Formosa), insufficiently
supplied by water treated from WWTPs.

However the peaks observed on the period 2015–17 for the BAU +
Normal scenario and on 2008–2009 and 2015–18 for the BAU + HD
scenario do correspond to surface water deficit. In fact, like domestic
demand, agriculture demand is subjected, in the Barlavento region, to limitations at the Arade dam that supplies the Silves, Lagoa and Portimão
public irrigation sites, during dry periods. The important increase of the
deficit observed from 2024 onwards is mostly due to the groundwater
unavailability in the Monchique aquifer.

Figure 3.15b presents the irrigation demand coverage under the selected demand and availability scenario combinations in accordance with what is explained above.

3.3.2   Cost Estimation

3.3.2.1   Direct costs
The estimation of direct costs specifically for the Ribeiras do Algarve River Basin is based on the evaluation of:

- Depreciation of capital costs associated to past and new investments, for both domestic irrigation and industrial uses.
- Operation and maintenance costs of new and existing infrastructures, for domestic, irrigation and industrial purposes.

Additionally, revenues from water use derive from the different water pricing values assigned to the different users. Therefore the following methodology was adopted and stakeholders consulted, according to the various users, in order to estimate direct costs.

Domestic use   The capital and specific operation and maintenance costs of the primary water supply system were estimated according to information of Águas do Algarve S.A. Concerning secondary network systems, for settlements supplied with groundwater, values were estimated according to a National Laboratory of Civil Engineering (LNEC) study (Lencastre, et al. 1994); for settlements supplied by surface water, direct costs were estimated by means of national common indicators, based on consultants' expertise.

Irrigation use   Specifically for public irrigation sites, operation and maintenance costs were set according to the River Basin Plan (PBHRA, 1999b) and to data provided by Silves, Lagoa and Portimão (SLP) and Sotavento Algarvio farmers' associations (IHERA, 2001).
   For private irrigation sites (considered as supplied by means of boreholes), capital, operation and maintenance costs for borehole construction and for irrigation methods implementation were set according to the River Basin Plan (PBHRA, 1999b).

Industrial use   Concerning industrial units using surface water, that is, supplied by Águas do Algarve S.A., network capital costs and specific operation and maintenance costs were defined similarly to domestic use costs. For industrial units using groundwater the direct costs were estimated according to a National Laboratory of Civil Engineering (LNEC) study (Lencastre et al., 1994).

3.3.2.2 Revenues from water use

Domestic pricing in Ribeiras do Algarve is volumetric, following a tariff structure where the price of water differs according to the consumed volume. There are two levels of water service supply: the first level, under Águas do Algarve S.A. responsibility, corresponds to the primary water supply system; at the second level, each municipality is responsible for providing water and sewerage services to each settlement. There is an exception to this scheme for Aljezur and Monchique municipalities, which are entirely supplied by groundwater, and where the municipality is the unique water service provider.

Currently there is a unique tariff charged by Águas do Algarve S.A. of 0.33 €/m³ to all the secondary network systems supplied. This value guarantees the total recovery of all operational costs of the service provided by that company. In contrast, there are different tariffs set by each municipality to domestic users ranging from 0.41 €/m³ in Vila do Bispo municipality to 1.04 €/m³ in Aljezur, according to the National Water Plan (PNA, 2000). These tariffs consist of a fixed element for renting the water meter and a variable element according to the amount of water consumed. According to the National Water Plan, the rate of cost recovery concerning water distribution, sewage drainage and treatment of each municipality is 30 per cent on average, varying from 60 per cent in Portimão to 16 per cent in Vila do Bispo (PNA, 2000). Therefore it can be concluded that in order to fulfil the WFD aim of 'recovery of the costs of water services, including environmental and resource costs' (WFD, 2000), municipalities urgently need to revaluate water prices and water service management.

On the other hand, irrigation pricing is only applied to public irrigation sites. Those are managed by farmers' associations that set water-selling prices according to the operational and maintenance costs. The water pricing basis for irrigation use varies according to each farmers' association, that is, while some farmers pay only a fixed fee, others pay a tariff composed of two elements, one for each irrigated hectare and the other for each cubic metre consumed. The prices vary from 0.14 €/m³ in the Silves, Lagoa and Portimão irrigation site to 0.02 €/m³ in the Sotavento public irrigation site. These amounts aim to cover operational costs but do not meet capital costs. For private irrigation sites, managed by each farmer and irrigated only by groundwater, there are no associated tariffs. Each farmer is responsible for capital, operational and maintenance costs, and no groundwater abstraction limit is imposed.

Industry revenues from water use were calculated by means of the Water National Plan data (PNA, 2000).

3.3.2.3   Environmental costs

Environmental costs for the Ribeiras do Algarve River Basin case study were defined according to WATECO Guidance Document principles (NTUA, 2003).

The analysis of the Querença-Silves aquifer behaviour, which has the highest storage capacity and is one of the few left with water quality appropriate for human consumption in the basin (Figure 3.4) – and is thus considered an alternative supply source for the region – was carried out in order to determine groundwater abstraction costs. Under a normal availability scenario, approximately 20 per cent of the annual aquifer recharge (21 hm^3) should be kept in order to assure natural discharges. Therefore the environmental cost was set equal to the construction plus operation and maintenance costs of a desalination plant, designed to assure the same volume. This estimated value (0.15 €/m^3) was applied to every abstraction from any aquifer located in the Ribeiras do Algarve River Basin.

In order to estimate surface water abstraction environmental costs, the particular case of the Funcho and Arade dams (Figure 3.5) exploitation trends, for domestic and irrigation uses, was analysed. With the purpose of satisfying domestic demand by the end of the simulation period (2035), an alternative 37 hm^3 supply source has to be provided. Two options have been considered in order to calculate environmental costs: (1) construction of a dam with an overall storage capacity of 48 hm^3; and (2) construction of two desalination plants (total capacity of 37 hm^3). An average value of 0.10 €/m^3 was adopted.

Finally, with respect to pollution originated by effluent discharges, environmental costs have been estimated as equal to the operating expenses of a secondary wastewater treatment plant (0.2 €/m^3). A secondary and tertiary treated effluent discharge bonus of 0.20 €/m^3 was estimated.

The total value of the environmental costs correspond to adding environmental costs associated to groundwater and surface water abstractions and environmental costs related to effluent disposal.

3.4   IDENTIFICATION OF AVAILABLE MANAGEMENT OPTIONS

Based on all management options mentioned by the stakeholders consulted, some options were analysed using the WSM DSS:

1.   Structural options for supply enhancement, including:
     ● Dam construction, aiming to reduce domestic demand deficit in the Algarve River Basin, in the municipalities supplied by

Águas do Algarve S.A. water company, namely in the Barlavento region.

- Network enhancements, to improve domestic demand coverage by increasing the number of municipalities supplied by the primary water supply system (currently, 29 out of 51 secondary network systems are supplied by Águas do Algarve S.A.).
- Desalination, to solve water deficit and/or water quality problems in domestic use (Aljezur and Portimão municipalities) and on golf courses (in the Campina de Faro aquifer area).
- New abstraction boreholes, referring to the construction of new boreholes in the Querença-Silves aquifer, in order to provide additional water for domestic use in settlements supplied by the primary water supply system.
- Reduction of network losses, through replacement of old and damaged pipes in all the municipal secondary water supply systems.

2. Demand management options, including:
   - Water reuse, through the reuse of treated wastewater on golf courses, for irrigation purposes, to improve water deficit and/or water quality problems in some aquifers.
   - Irrigation method improvements, for better irrigation efficiency and savings in water consumption, in all irrigation sites.

3. Socio-economic measures, more specifically the impact of new pricing structures for irrigation sites and settlements.

The selection of appropriate indicators for ranking the above options reflects the perception of the local stakeholders towards economic development and social and environmental sustainability. Since it is widely acceptable that future economic growth is to rely on tourism, the analysis of the options is to be formulated taking into account coverage of domestic use water needs.

Although agriculture is not the primary economic activity, it represents the major consumer of water in the Ribeiras do Algarve River Basin. Therefore irrigation demand coverage is also considered as an indicator of the water resource system efficiency. Aquifer overexploitation and salinization are among the key environmental problems that threaten not only the provision of supply but also the future resources of the basin. That way, environmental protection was expressed through the groundwater exploitation index.

Finally, cost analysis was taken into account through the consideration of direct costs and environmental costs, expressed in terms of present value (PV), evaluated over the period 2004–35 using a discount rate of 3.33 per cent as set for hydraulic works by law (DL, 1990).

3.5 OPTIONS DESCRIPTION

3.5.1 Structural Options

3.5.1.1 Dam construction

As previously referred to, and considering the population growth rates presented in Table 3.2, there is always a deficit in urban supply for any range of the scenarios considered. The major deficit is due to the limitation existing in the Funcho storage reservoir that is not able to guarantee the necessary volumes for urban water supply, in the Barlavento municipalities.

In order to satisfy the demand verified in Barlavento, the Portuguese National Water Institute (INAG) decided to introduce a new supply source, on which construction began in 2002. The Odelouca dam, with a capacity of 157 hm^3 and a dead volume of 23 hm^3, is intended to assure domestic demand coverage in the Barlavento region, above 95 per cent and will allow the Funcho dam to be reallocated to agriculture. However construction has been suspended, awaiting developments at the financial, environmental and social sustainability level. Figure 3.16 shows the Odelouca dam's foreseen location.

3.5.1.2 Network enhancements

Águas do Algarve S.A. water company, through the concession of the primary water supply system, has been committed to cover 95 per cent of urban water supply users. Presently, this percentage is above 90 per cent. However Alzejur and Monchique Municipalities (Figure 3.1) and some smaller settlements are not yet supplied by surface water, being still totally dependent on groundwater. As mentioned by the Águas do Algarve S.A.

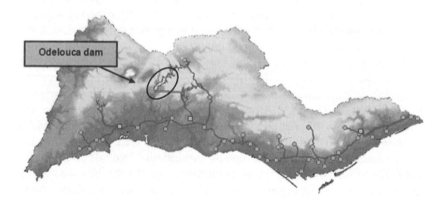

Figure 3.16   Odelouca dam location

company, two major connections are planned to be made soon, in order to benefit the two municipalities previously referred to. In addition, the replacement of one supply pipeline and the construction of new network reservoirs to reinforce the supply capacity to secondary network systems were considered, benefiting other municipalities as Loulé and Silves, increasing the urban water supply network coverage.

Moreover for the smaller settlements, the construction of new expansions represents more important investment, as the latter settlements are located further from the main pipeline.

From the application of this option, almost the entire river basin will be supplied by the primary water supply system. Nevertheless it should also be emphasized that by this option, although more municipalities are served, the available water quantity to be distributed does not change. Figure 3.17 shows the location of the new network reservoirs and pipelines considered.

3.5.1.3 Desalination
The construction of desalination units is a water supply enhancement option that has still not been used in the Ribeiras do Algarve River Basin. Two kinds of desalination units were considered for this option, with different purposes and characteristics.

For domestic use A seawater desalination unit is planned to be constructed near Portimão by 2006, in order to supply this settlement with a maximum volume of 37 043 m^3/day. The capital costs associated to the construction of this unit are 22.6 million €.

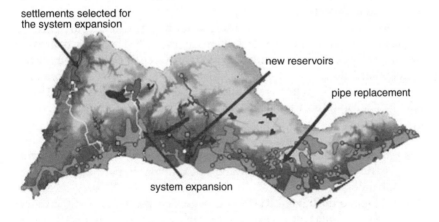

Figure 3.17 Primary water supply system: expansion, enhancements and pipe replacements

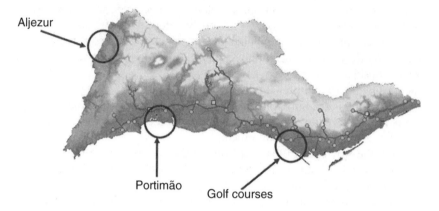

Figure 3.18   Location of the two desalination plants considered

A smaller-scale desalination plant using seawater is planned to be constructed in the Aljezur municipality in 2006 (Figure 3.18), aiming to solve current water quality problems due to groundwater supply sources. This desalination plant is designed to attain a maximum capacity of 3470 m^3/day and represents a capital cost of 2.85 million €.

For irrigation use   The construction of desalination units for the irrigation of golf courses is considered, to avoid groundwater abstraction from Campina de Faro aquifer, which presents high concentrations of nitrates and chlorines and is included in the critical area defined by CCDR Algarve as referred to in section 3.2.3.

Another unit, processing seawater, is located in Loulé municipality (Figure 3.18) and planned to start operating by 2006. The water treated in this unit will be used for irrigation purposes on four golf courses (Quinta do Lago, Quinta do Lago – São Lorenz, Quinta do Lago – Ria Formosa and Quinta do Lago – Pinheiros Altos) and its design capacity is to be 9144 m^3/day. The capital cost associated to that construction is 6.65 million €. This option enables:

- at Quinta do Lago – São Lourenz, the current connection to a wastewater treatment plant and to Campina de Faro aquifer to be abandoned;
- at Quinta do Lago – Ria Formosa golf course, to correct the water supply insufficiency based on a current connection to a wastewater treatment plant.

3.5.1.4   New abstractions boreholes

As stated in the River Basin Plan, the Algarve is the national region where groundwater assumes the most important strategic role. In fact, the intensive exploitation of these resources for different purposes led to a high density of vertical boreholes and to a high concentration of chlorines and nitrates, over the legal limit. The majority of these aquifers are located by the sea and are essentially constituted by carbonated rocks, increasing the risk of salinization.

Although the major solution adopted in Algarve to solve water supply problems in the last decade was to increase surface water exploitation through the construction of the primary water supply system, it appears that sustainable exploitation of combined surface and groundwater would be a more efficient solution, avoiding the great dependence of the region on surface water for domestic use.

Hence, analysing all the aquifers and groundwater availability, the Querença-Silves aquifer is the only one that possesses the water quantity and quality to be considered relevant for future sustainable abstraction. This aquifer is the most important in the whole region, with a storage capacity of approximately 1060 hm^3.

The construction of new boreholes in the Querença-Silves aquifer (see Figure 3.4) will enable the provision of additional water to be distributed by the primary water supply system. These new boreholes will be implemented according to a timeframe of interventions and will be located in the Vale da Vila and Benaciate public irrigation sites.

3.5.1.5   Reduction of network losses

The current estimated level of network losses in the Ribeiras do Algarve River Basin settlements ranges from 16 to 61 per cent of the total domestic water supply to each of the settlements. The option that is explored is a gradual reduction of losses (15 per cent in 15 years) for all the municipalities, in accordance with the RBP (PBHRA, 1999c). These losses reductions will be achieved through successive network interventions (upgrade, replacements, maintenance). The application of this option was made on the assumption that internal network interventions will be implemented in the different municipalities with the following schedule: 5 per cent from 2005 to 2010, 5 per cent from 2010 to 2015 and 5 per cent from 2015 to 2020. The exception is the Albufeira municipality where only the first intervention is considered, from 2005 until 2010. There, the network losses are currently already 16 per cent and therefore further interventions would not be cost-effective.

3.5.2 Demand Management Options

3.5.2.1 Water reuse

As previously referred to (see section 3.2.3), the CCDR Algarve has delimited a critical area where aquifers, as a result of the proximity to the sea, are subjected to or in risk of salinization (Figure 3.7). Thus the construction of new abstraction boreholes is not allowed except if employed for domestic use. The water reuse option aims to protect and/or reduce the pressure on these aquifers' use.

This option is being considered by Águas do Algarve S.A. after the recent enlargement of its water supply concession also to include water drainage, treatment and exploitation. Nevertheless no criteria have been disclosed to the public so far. Since the distance from the WWTP to golf courses is a major issue for this option, for simulation purposes only golf courses situated within the critical area and less than 2000 metres from a WWTP were considered.

In 2006, six golf courses were selected to adopt this type of water supply: three in the Loulé municipality (Vilamoura – Millennium, Vilamoura – Laguna Course, Vale do Lobo – Ocean Golf Course) and three in the Albufeira municipality (Balaia Village, Herdade dos Salgados and Pine Cliffs).

Currently, five of these six golf courses abstract water from aquifers included within the critical area and presenting high concentrations of nitrate and chlorines: The Vilamoura – Millennium and Vilamoura – Laguna courses from Quarteira aquifer; Balaia Village and Pine Cliffs from Albufeira-Ribeira de Quarteira aquifer; and Vale do Lobo – Ocean Golf Course from Campina de Faro aquifer. Moreover Herdade dos Salgados golf course is already currently connected to two WWTPs but those, although working in sequence and trying to complement each other, are unable to meet the required demand.

As the majority of the WWTPs in Algarve incorporate secondary treatment, this option will imply tertiary treatment implementation. For simulation purposes, the capital cost associated to this tertiary treatment, although most probably making part of a general improvement of the sewerage and WWTPs network required (not considered in the simulation), will be by the golf courses benefiting from this option.

3.5.2.2 Irrigation method improvements

Agriculture represents the most important water consumer in the Algarve region. Irrigation sites represent almost 124 hm^3 (approximately 65 per cent) of the total water consumption. Almost 97 hm^3 correspond to groundwater consumption. The foreseen irrigated area growth (as in Table

Table 3.4a *Irrigation methods application extent (% area), for public irrigation sites*

Public irrigation sites	2004		2006	
	Furrow	Sprinkler	Furrow	Sprinkler
Silves, Lagoa and Portimão	100%	0%	0	100%
Mira	100%	0%	0	100%
Alvor	100%	0%	100%	0%

Table 3.4b *Irrigation methods application extent (% area), for private irrigation sites*

	2006		2012		2020	
	Furrow	Sprinkler	Furrow	Sprinkler	Furrow	Sprinkler
Private irrigation sites	20%	80%	15%	85%	10%	90%

3.3), will cause an increase in water need and therefore an enhancement of the irrigation water deficit. Moreover it is predicted that an area of 10 650 ha of public irrigation sites is to be implemented by 2006.

In order to fight the lack of water and reduce losses in agriculture, which represented a maximum of about 27 hm³ (22 per cent of the supply volume used for irrigation) for the BAU + Normal scenario in 2000, an irrigation method improvement was implemented, replacing furrow irrigation by the drip irrigation method. The replacement was for both public and private irrigation sites. Hence the area percentage of furrow irrigation method implementation decreases whereas the drip implementation area percentage increases. Tables 3.4a and 3.4b present the application percentage (% area) change from furrow to drip irrigation for public and private irrigation sites.

As part of the option, the efficiency of furrow and sprinkler irrigation methods were enhanced, for example by means of repairing (Table 3.5).

3.5.3 Socio-economic Measures

3.5.3.1 Domestic and irrigation pricing
This simulation intends to achieve recovery of direct costs from water services and to reduce domestic and irrigation unmet demand through a direct

Table 3.5   Irrigation method efficiency improvements, for public and private irrigation sites

	2006		2012		2020	
	Furrow	Sprinkler	Furrow	Sprinkler	Furrow	Sprinkler
Public and private irrigation sites	65%	85%	65%	85%	70%	85%

decrease in demand. The domestic water pricing scheme examined is a gradual increase of, on average, 5 per cent every year in Aljezur, Albufeira, Monchique and Portimão municipalities and 10 per cent per year for the remaining municipalities, from 2005 to 2010. These price alterations imply yearly increases that range from 0.04 €/m^3 to 0.14 €/m^3.

Concerning irrigation, a price increase of 2 to 15 per cent per year from 2005 to 2010 is applied simultaneously to some selected public irrigation sites and golf courses that did not meet operational costs and/or where unmet irrigation demand is observed. In Alcantarilha and Vale da Vila public irrigation sites, the price increase is applied only from 2006 to 2010 because their exploitation only starts in 2006. These price alterations imply yearly increases that range from 0.01 €/m^3 to 0.08 €/m^3.

In both cases and in the absence of any specific studies for the Algarve River Basin, a value of −0.5 for demand elasticity is assumed, in accordance with Águas do Algarve S.A. water company.

3.6   RESULTS ANALYSIS

Each option was analysed using the WSM DSS tool and compared with the reference case (see section 3.3.1.4). A large number of results were obtained, related to the different issues previously focused on, from hydrological and demand scenarios to economic aspects.

Comparison of the main achievements on deficit reduction and demand improvement (based on effectiveness and on unmet demand ratios), economic analysis values and performance indicators of the (9) options simulated under the three different scenarios, regarding domestic and irrigation use, are presented hereafter. Effectiveness is defined as the ratio between the supply delivered and the demand required for each purpose.

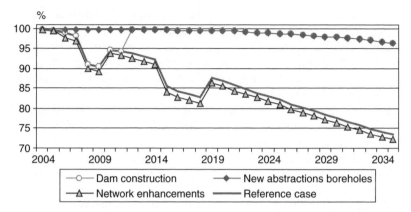

Figure 3.19   Effectiveness for domestic use: comparison between the reference case and three options simulated (BAU + HD)

3.6.1 Domestic Use

Two main kinds of behaviour regarding the effectiveness in deficit reduction are found when comparing the reference case with the simulated options, for the most severe hydrological and demand scenario (BAU + HD): the first, in which a similar trend to the reference case is observed, namely maintaining marked shortage in some sequence of dry periods; and the second, in which all or some of these periods disappear, the demand deficit following a continuous trend and being markedly reduced compared to the reference case.

Figure 3.19 exemplifies this, using only three of the simulated options compared to the reference case, for the BAU + HD scenario.

The 'dam construction' case and the 'new abstractions boreholes' case do show a different behaviour when compared with the reference case, with effectiveness reaching values above 95 per cent, achieving the domestic unmet demand goals.

The two marked dry periods with aggravated unmet demand shown in the reference case are solved by the 'new abstraction boreholes' option; the dam construction does not solve the shortage in the first of these periods only because it corresponds to a date when it is still not implemented. As explained in section 3.3.14, those demand deficit peaks are due to the Funcho dam's limitations and affect mostly the Barlavento region.

Also in Figure 3.19, the 'network enhancements' option's behaviour is similar to the reference case, indicating the fact that this option is not directly related to the lack of water at the Funcho dam (affecting only the Barlavento region). This is also the case of all the other options shown hereafter in Figure 3.20a2, which plots the effectiveness of the full set of simulated options. This means that all the options that do not introduce additional water into the primary water supply system cannot solve the major demand deficit in the dry periods and can even aggravate it (as shown in Figure 3.19 for the 'network enhancements' option).

Figure 3.20 presents effectiveness and unmet demand improvement for the simulated options (9), under the three different scenarios, in order to compare the results obtained.

Comparison of results for the BAU + Normal (Figures 3.20a1 and 3.20b1) and BAU + HD (Figures 3.20a2 and 3.20b2) scenarios shows that those are similar, translating an effectiveness behaviour of the first similar to the second, already described, but with shorter and/or less frequent (dry) periods of increased deficit. In both scenarios, 'dam construction' and 'new abstractions boreholes' are the only options reaching values above 95 per cent upto the end of the simulation period, achieving the domestic unmet demand goals.

Otherwise, and under the LD + HW scenario (Figures 3.20a3 and 3.20b3), the behaviour of each option is totally different when compared with the two scenarios previously analysed. In fact, under this scenario, availability is greater and water demand is lower, and so no significant water demand problems are detected, compared to the two other scenarios analysed. As one can observe, all the options, except the 'network enhancements' option, present an effectiveness value above 95 per cent throughout the simulation period. The 'domestic pricing' and 'desalination' options present the highest effectiveness values, reaching almost 100 per cent during the whole simulation period, mainly due to the low demand scenario. As the domestic demand is already lower, the increase in price is enough to guarantee high values of effectiveness. Regarding the 'desalination' option, the increase in population which caused the overall decrease in the effectiveness associated to this option, namely after 2010, in the whole basin for both BAU + Normal and BAU + HD scenarios, does not exist under the LD + HW scenario. Therefore the decrease in effectiveness is basically eliminated under the LD + HW scenario. In contrast to what is observed under BAU + Normal and BAU + HD scenarios for the 'irrigation method improvements', 'water reuse', 'irrigation pricing' and 'network enhancements' options, effectiveness increased slightly under the LD + HW scenario. This increasing trend could also be justified by the population growth rate stabilization previously referred to.

As stated before, the domestic water supply relies mostly on surface water and the irrigation supply mostly on groundwater. Therefore specifically for the 'irrigation method improvements', 'water reuse' and 'irrigation pricing' options, the irrigation demand decrease originated by the implementation of these options does not have any visible influence on the effectiveness for domestic use under the three analysed scenarios (Figures 3.20b1, 3.20b2 and 3.20b3). Furthermore, one specific remark has to be made related with the 'network enhancements' option on the negative improvement originated by the implementation of the latter (Figures 3.20b1 and 3.20b2): as the available water volume is not increased by the implementation of the option, the improvement verified is always below 0 per cent, reaching a minimum of -98 per cent in the implementation year, hence this option is less effective.

3.6.2 Irrigation Use

Similarly to what happened for domestic use, two kinds of behaviour are verified up to 2024. As one can see in Figure 3.21, options such as 'dam construction' are able to increase the lower effectiveness observed for the reference case between 2015 and 2018, under the BAU + HD scenario. On the other hand, most of the other options, similarly to those figured for the 'network enhancements' and 'new abstractions boreholes' options, do not have that same impact on effectiveness. The observed peak in 2023 for the 'network enhancements' option translates into more water left for irrigation purposes in the Monchique aquifer. However the decrease in effectiveness existing after 2024 due to this aquifer is not compensated for by the implementation of either of these options.

Figures 3.22a1 and 3.22a2 do show that the effectiveness under the BAU + Normal and BAU + HD scenarios, not only for the 'dam construction' but also for the 'irrigation method improvements' and 'irrigation pricing' options, present a similar behaviour. These options are the only ones that allow for keeping the effectiveness constant until 2023. Moreover neither of the options analysed is able to improve effectiveness from 2024 onwards.

Regarding improvements of the unmet irrigation demand, one can observe that the implementation of the three above-mentioned options diminish the unmet irrigation demand, due to water shortage in the Arade storage reservoir (see section 3.3.1.4), foreseen for the 2008–2009 and 2015–18 periods for the BAU + HD scenario and between 2015 and 2017 for the BAU + Normal scenario. It is important to note that for the 'dam construction' option, and according to its implementation (in 2012) under the BAU + HD scenario, only the unmet demand existing in the second dry period (2015–18) is solved.

In 2024–25, the existing irrigation unmet demand due to Monchique aquifer overexploitation is clearly mitigated by the 'network enhancements' and the 'irrigation method improvements' options. Nevertheless after 2025

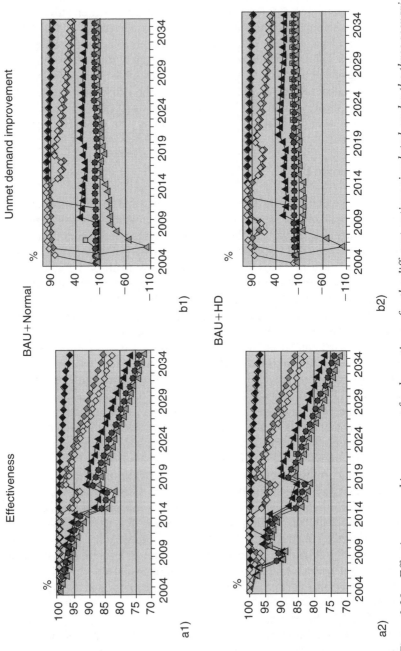

Effectiveness   Unmet demand improvement

BAU+Normal

a1)   b1)

BAU+HD

a2)   b2)

Figure 3.20   Effectiveness and improvement for domestic use for the different options simulated, under the three scenarios

74

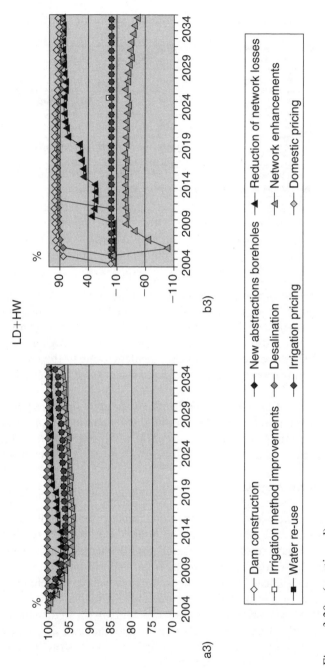

LD+HW

a3)

b3)

- ◇ Dam construction
- □ Irrigation method improvements
- ■ Water re-use
- ✦ New abstractions boreholes
- ◇ Desalination
- ✦ Irrigation pricing
- ▲ Reduction of network losses
- ◭ Network enhancements
- ◇ Domestic pricing

Figure 3.20 (continued)

75

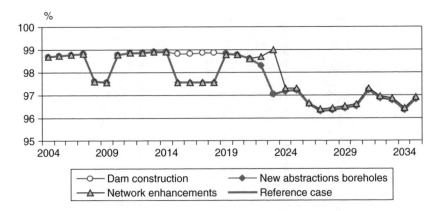

Figure 3.21   Effectiveness for irrigation use: comparison between the reference case and three options simulated (BAU + HD)

and up to the end of the simulation period, only the last option, and this only in a limited way, is able to mitigate Monchique's irrigation deficit, through the decrease of the amount of water consumed for irrigation purposes. The 'water reuse' option is the one presenting the highest improvement from 2025 on, effectively reducing the deficit due to the golf courses involved, enabling an extra volume of groundwater to be available for other purposes.

Finally, for the LD + HW scenario, all the options simulated present a similar behaviour as referred to for the other two scenarios, emphasizing the fact that, due to the less demanding scenario and higher water availability, no shortages are verified during the dry periods mentioned previously.

3.6.3   Economic Analysis

In this section, the main results addressing direct costs and environmental costs are discussed. Firstly, it should be pointed out that different options are analysed regarding direct costs and environmental costs. In fact the results hereafter discussed (Figure 3.23) correspond only to the options which present significant result changes comparatively to the reference case. For all the other options, only brief comments are made.

Under all the scenarios, the options which involve a higher increase in present value (PV) direct costs relative to the reference case are, in descending order: 'irrigation method improvements', 'dam construction', 'desalination' and 'new abstraction boreholes'.

Compared to the reference case, under the BAU + Normal scenario, the increase in PV direct costs associated to 'irrigation method improvements' (28 per cent, based on values of Figure 3.23a1 corresponds to both capital and specific operation and maintenance costs (specific O&M costs) increase. Also, 'dam construction' represents an increase in terms of present value of 12 per cent under the BAU + Normal and BAU + HD scenarios (Figures 3.23a1 and 3.23b1) not only due to the correspondent 75 million € capital costs but also to extra specific O&M costs. Under all the three scenarios, the construction of the desalination plants to supply Aljezur and Portimão municipalities and golf courses in Quinta do Lago represents a 10 per cent increase in PV direct costs under BAU + Normal and BAU + HD and a 5 per cent increase under LD + HW (Figures 3.23a1, 3.23b1 and 3.23c1). In fact, the construction of desalination plants, although each of them is aimed to be a localized measure rather than a global one, is included within the measures causing a higher increase in PV direct costs, due to desalination units' high specific operation and maintenance (O&M) costs. More specifically, if one focuses only on the analysis of the settlements and the golf courses covered by this measure, the present value presents an 83 per cent increase under the BAU + Normal and BAU + HD scenarios (88 and 87 million € respectively) and a 52 per cent (54 million €) increase under the LD + HW scenario. Finally, the 'new abstraction boreholes' option represents an 8 per cent increase in PV direct costs under BAU + Normal and 7 per cent under BAU + HD scenarios, which correspond mainly to extra specific O&M costs associated to the extra groundwater volume abstracted.

Among the water management options which present minor variations (less than 1 per cent) comparatively to the reference case, in terms of present value, there are: 'network enhancement', 'water reuse' and 'reduction of network losses'. Specifically for the 'network enhancement' option, the slight decrease of PV direct costs is due to two factors: firstly, the unmet demand increase verified in some Barlavento municipalities, particularly in Albufeira, Portimão and Lagoa, which contributes to a decrease in specific O&M costs; and secondly (although new infrastructures have to be built), the O&M costs associated to surface water transport, that are approximately 68 per cent lower than for groundwater, which applies to Caldas de Monchique, Monchique and Marco Sul settlements.

Finally, the options which present a clear decrease in PV direct costs relative to the reference case are 'domestic pricing' and 'irrigation pricing'. Concerning the increase of water price for domestic use, the decrease observed in PV direct costs corresponded to a yearly decrease in demand in settlements of 22 per cent (21 hm³) on average under all scenarios. Therefore the specific O&M costs decrease is reflected in a decrease of PV direct costs: 9 per cent under BAU + Normal, 7 per cent under BAU + HD

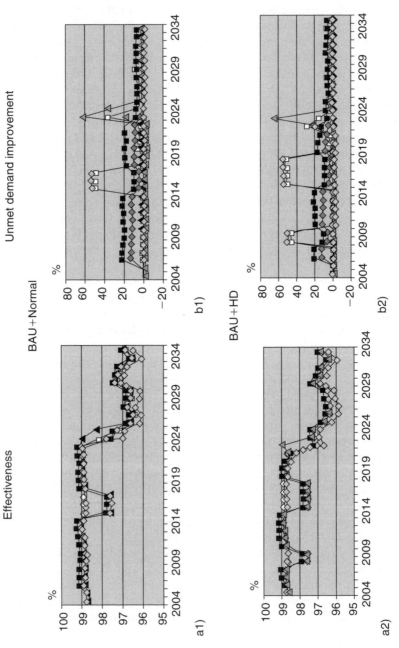

Figure 3.22   Effectiveness and improvement for irrigation use for the different options simulated, under the three scenarios

78

LD+HW

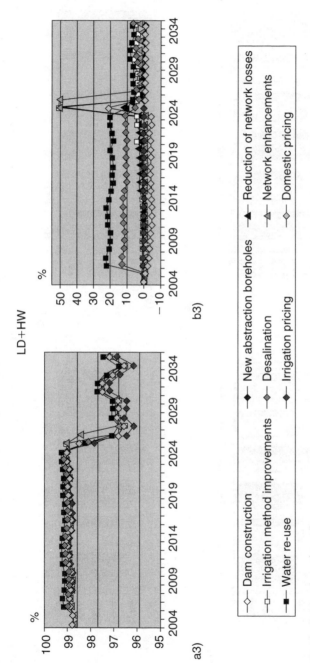

a3)

b3)

—◇— Dam construction
—□— Irrigation method improvements
—■— Water re-use
—◆— New abstraction boreholes
—◇— Desalination
—◆— Irrigation pricing
—▲— Reduction of network losses
—◁— Network enhancements
—◇— Domestic pricing

Figure 3.22 (continued)

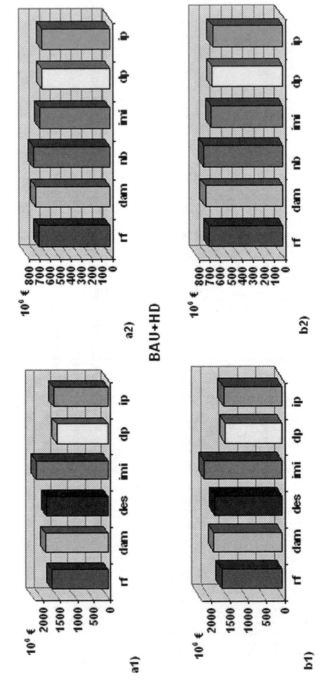

Figure 3.23   Cost for the different options under the three scenarios (present value, million €): a1) b1) c1) total direct cost; a2) b2) c2) total environmental cost

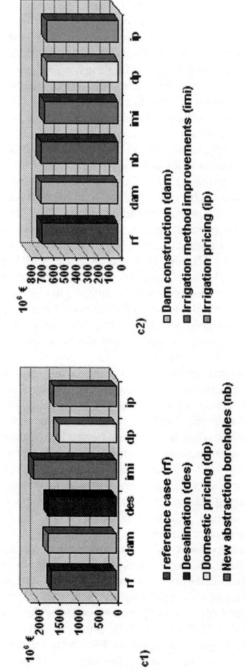

LD+HW

Figure 3.23 (continued)

and 10 per cent under LD + HW (Figures 3.23a1, 3.23a2 and 3.23a3). Similarly regarding the 'domestic pricing' option, there is a decrease in demand but this time in the irrigation sites covered by this measure. The specific O&M costs decrease is reflected in a 3 per cent decrease of PV direct costs, under all the scenarios (Figures 3.23a1, 3.23a2 and 3.23a3).

In terms of PV environmental costs, the water management options for which their application resulted in a present value increase are 'dam construction' and 'new abstraction boreholes'.

The 'dam construction' option represents an increase in PV environmental costs of approximately 5 per cent under both BAU + Normal and BAU + HD scenarios and less than 1 per cent increase under the LD + HW scenario (Figures 3.23a2, 3.23b2 and 3.23c2), due to more surface water being abstracted from the Odelouca storage reservoir and more water being treated in wastewater treatment plants (WWTPs). Similarly, the overall PV environmental costs increase in the basin associated to the introduction of the 'new abstraction boreholes' option (7 per cent under BAU + Normal and BAU + HD and 1 per cent under LD + HW) (Figures 3.23a2, 3.23b2 and 3.23c2), corresponds to the extra amount of water volume abstracted from the Querença-Silves aquifer – plus, on average: 15 per cent (14 hm^3) under the BAU + Normal scenario; 21 per cent (17 hm^3) under the BAU + HD scenario; and 4 per cent (3 hm^3) under the LD + HW scenario – and to additional pollution costs due to water consumed in settlements covered by this measure.

The 'network enhancements', 'desalination' and 'reduction of network losses' options contribute to small increases (less than 1 per cent) of environmental costs under all the scenarios. Specifically, and taking as an example the 'desalination' option, there are two components varying in opposite directions: while the surface water and groundwater environmental costs decrease, due to a decrease in both groundwater and surface water abstracted to supply the Portimão municipality, the volume of wastewater treated in Portimão WWTP increases, therefore increasing pollution costs. Finally, a 1 per cent decrease is observed for the 'water reuse' management option, but this time due to a decrease in the groundwater volume abstracted for irrigation purposes.

The two socio-economic measures implemented, 'domestic pricing' and 'irrigation pricing', due to the corresponding demand decrease referred to previously, contributed to a decrease in surface water and groundwater environmental costs, and also in pollution costs. A decrease in PV environmental costs between 4 per cent and 5 per cent under all the scenarios is verified (Figures 3.23a2, 3.23b2 and 3.23c2). Similarly, the 'irrigation method improvements', cause a decrease in PV environmental costs between 2 per cent and 3 per cent, under all the scenarios (Figures 3.23a2, 3.23b2 and 3.23c2), due mainly to the decrease in surface water and groundwater consumption.

3.6.4 Evaluation of Management Options Feasibility Regarding the Indicators

The selection of appropriate indicators for ranking the above options reflected the attitude of the local stakeholders towards economic development, and social and environmental sustainability. The effectiveness of each option was approached through the evaluation score obtained, based on the behaviour with respect to domestic and irrigation demand coverage. Environmental sustainability was expressed through the performance of the groundwater exploitation index.

Finally, economic efficiency was expressed through the evaluation score obtained by the WSM DSS, from the performance with respect to total direct cost and environmental cost, expressed in present value terms.

The satisfactory range of values and the weights assigned to the chosen indicators are presented in Table 3.6.

Concerning PV direct cost and PV environmental cost, only the final value obtained for each option will be used in order to assess the option performance.

Tables 3.7a and 3.7b, Tables 3.8a and 3.8b and Tables 3.9a and 3.9b present the final results of the option evaluation for the Ribeiras do Algarve case study under BAU + Normal, in numerical values and normalized form, respectively.

Although considered, the scores for the evaluation of the groundwater exploitation index were not included in the tables because under all the scenarios, and for all the options, its value was zero. A justification for that may be the similar value pattern for the groundwater exploitation index under all options whenever dry periods occurred, that is, when values higher than the upper limit occur. That caused no distinction between the values of one of the evaluation parameters (duration), although differences were observed in terms of average values and of the extent of the deviations.

Table 3.6 Satisfactory range of values and weights for the indicators of the Ribeiras do Algarve case study

Indicator	Satisfactory range of values	Weight
Domestic demand coverage	95–100%	0.40
Irrigation demand coverage	80–100%	0.30
Groundwater exploitation index	0–80%	0.30

Table 3.7   Option performance matrix and normalized option performance matrix under BAU+Normal

Table 3.7a   Option performance matrix (BAU+Normal)

Option	Effectiveness	Economic efficiency	
	(relative performance index for demand coverage)	Environmental cost PV, million €	Direct cost PV, million €
Reference case (BAU+Normal)	0.300	692.5	1690.1
Dam construction	0.475	722.3	1885.4
Network enhancement	0.300	687.3	1676.0
Desalination	0.307	689.3	1846.9
New abstraction boreholes	0.493	735.5	1808.4
Reduction of network losses	0.300	689.9	1690.5
Irrigation method improvements	0.300	673.8	2143.9
Water reuse	0.300	685.2	1680.0
Domestic pricing	0.305	661.9	1536.2
Irrigation pricing	0.300	656.4	1632.4

Table 3.7b   Normalized option performance matrix (BAU+Normal)

Option	Effectiveness	Economic efficiency	
	(relative performance index for demand coverage)	Environmental cost (PV)	Direct cost (PV)
Reference case (BAU+Normal)	–	***	****
Dam construction	*****	*	**
Network enhancement	–	***	****
Desalination	–	***	**
New abstraction boreholes	*****	–	***
Reduction of network losses	–	***	****
Irrigation method improvements	–	****	–
Water reuse	–	***	****
Domestic pricing	–	*****	*****
Irrigation pricing	–	*****	****

Table 3.8   Option performance matrix and normalized option performance matrix under BAU+HD

Table 3.8a   Option performance matrix (BAU+HD)

Option	Effectiveness	Economic efficiency	
	(relative performance index for demand coverage)	Environmental cost PV, million €	Direct cost PV, million €
Reference case (BAU+HD)	0.300	686.9	1664.9
Dam construction	0.353	719.2	1875.1
Network enhancement	0.300	683.4	1661.3
Desalination	0.308	686.8	1837.8
New abstraction boreholes	0.490	736.9	1801.1
Reduction of network losses	0.300	685.7	1675.0
Irrigation method improvements	0.300	670.2	2129.9
Water reuse	0.300	681.2	1665.4
Domestic pricing	0.306	659.6	1553.8
Irrigation pricing	0.300	651.3	1607.9

Table 3.8b   Normalized option performance matrix (BAU+HD)

Option	Effectiveness	Economic efficiency	
	(relative performance index for demand coverage)	Environmental cost (PV)	Direct cost (PV)
Reference case (BAU+HD)	–	***	****
Dam construction	**	*	**
Network enhancement	–	***	****
Desalination	–	***	***
New abstraction boreholes	*****	–	***
Reduction of network losses	–	***	****
Irrigation method improvements	–	****	–
Water reuse	–	***	****
Domestic pricing	–	*****	*****
Irrigation pricing	–	*****	*****

Table 3.9　Option performance matrix and normalized option performance matrix under LD+HW

Table 3.9a　Option performance matrix (LD+HW)

Option	Effectiveness	Economic efficiency	
	(relative performance index for demand coverage)	Environmental cost PV, million €	Direct cost PV, million €
Reference case (LD+HW)	0.305	680.4	1634.8
Dam construction	0.311	683.0	1733.0
Network enhancement	0.300	677.5	1635.9
Desalination	0.700	665.7	1716.2
New abstraction boreholes	0.700	689.0	1657.5
Reduction of network losses	0.419	677.0	1637.4
Irrigation method improvements	0.305	662.8	2098.5
Water reuse	0.305	674.6	1635.3
Domestic pricing	0.700	644.3	1462.0
Irrigation pricing	0.305	643.8	1576.4

Table 3.9b　Normalized option performance matrix (LD+HW)

Option	Effectiveness	Economic efficiency	
	(relative performance index for demand coverage)	Environmental cost (PV)	Direct cost (PV)
Reference case (LD+HW)	–	*	****
Dam construction	–	*	***
Network enhancement	–	*	****
Desalination	*****	***	***
New abstraction boreholes	*****	–	***
Reduction of network losses	**	*	****
Irrigation method improvements	–	***	–
Water reuse	–	**	****
Domestic pricing	*****	*****	*****
Irrigation pricing	–	*****	****

Under BAU + Normal and BAU + HD scenarios, among all the management options and in terms of the Relative Performance Index for Demand Coverage (RPIDC), the options which present a better performance are 'dam construction' and 'new abstraction boreholes' (Tables 3.7a and 3.8a). If comparing the values obtained for this performance index under BAU + Normal and BAU + HD, with the variation of effectiveness: (1) for domestic use (Figures 3.20a1 and 3.20a2), under the same scenarios, one can observe that throughout the simulation period the 'dam construction' and 'new abstraction boreholes' options perform better; and (2) for irrigation use, the 'dam construction' option presents higher values of effectiveness between 2015 and 2017. The component associated to the domestic use of the RPIDC determines the overall indicator value. Therefore although differences are verified in the behaviour in terms of effectiveness for irrigation between 'dam construction' and 'new abstraction boreholes' (Figure 3.21), the overall value for RPIDC remains high for both options (Table 3.8a). Under the same two scenarios, 'desalination' and 'domestic pricing' options perform worse than the latter two options, but slightly better than the remaining options in terms of effectiveness (Figures 3.20a1 and 3.20a2). Nevertheless because the scoring process for the RPIDC for the 'desalination' and 'domestic pricing' options leads to score values similar to the value corresponding to the reference case (Tables 3.7a and 3.8a), only the normalized scores of 'dam construction' and 'new abstraction boreholes' present relevant normalized performance values (Tables 3.7b and 3.8b). Concerning the 'network enhancement', 'reduction of network losses', 'irrigation method improvements' and 'water reuse' options, the scores for RPIDC are equal to the reference case, reflecting what is shown in Figures 3.20a1 and 3.20a2 and Figures 3.22a1 and 3.22a2 in which similar variation trends of effectiveness among these options are observed. The same value is also obtained for the 'irrigation pricing' option, although there are differences in the variation trend of the effectiveness for irrigation use when compared with the reference case (Figures 3.22a1 and 3.22a2). This can possibly be explained by the fact that only public irrigation sites and golf courses were considered in this option, since farmers exploring private irrigation sites do not pay a real tariff for the water consumed. The decrease in demand, caused by the price increase, in public irrigation sites and golf courses, combined with no improvement of unmet irrigation demand in private irrigation sites, resulted in a similar trend of the irrigation coverage variation during the analysed period for this option and the reference case (Figures 3.22a1 and 3.22a2).

Under the LD + HW scenario (Table 3.9a), the highest scores of RPIDC are verified for the 'new abstraction boreholes', 'desalination' and 'domestic pricing' options whereas 'dam construction', in contrast to what is verified under BAU + Normal and BAU + HW (Tables 3.7a and 3.8a, now presents a lower score than the two last options. Concerning 'desalination', the higher score verified for the last option under the LD + HW scenario is the result of the combination of high values of effectiveness for domestic use (Figure 3.20a3) with the implementation of the 'desalination' option before the 'dam construction' option.

Concerning PV environmental costs, the socio-economic measures ('domestic pricing' and 'irrigation pricing' options) present the most favourable values, that is, lower ones, followed by the 'irrigation method improvements' option. Nevertheless the latter option presents the highest value in terms of PV direct costs whereas the socio-economic measures still present lower values. More specifically, the 'domestic pricing' option shows itself to be the most favourable concerning PV environmental costs and PV direct costs for all the scenarios considered, since it originates a decrease in demand and therefore a decrease in specific operation and maintenance costs and environmental costs (Tables 3.7a, 3.8a and 3.9a).

3.7   STRATEGIES FORMULATION

Conflicting interests in water resources coexist between the tourism sector and agriculture, which is still the most important water sector user (about 65 per cent in 2000), and localized water shortages occur mainly during summer months. Infrastructure deficiencies, poor groundwater quality in some areas, high values of secondary water supply network losses (16 per cent to 61 per cent) and inadequate irrigation methods call for management measures in order to solve and prevent conflicts between users.

Therefore, and following the evaluation of the results and taking into account the different management options, two alternative strategies, each based on a different paradigm, could be formulated and compared between them and against the reference case. While strategy 1 (dominant paradigm) is based on the implementation of structural measures and the exploitation of surface water, strategy 2 (new paradigm) does not represent a radical shift from structural to non-structural options but reflects the need to consider: (1) other alternatives to conventional water supply sources, namely desalination; (2) implementation of small-scale, localized management measures as an alternative to the application of measures at a regional scale; and (3) sustainable combination of surface and groundwater water resources exploitation, therefore increasing the extent of demand satisfaction.

To evaluate the performance of these two strategies, one has chosen to consider a combination of a steady demand increase scenario (BAU), reflecting the expansive scenario presented in the River Basin Plan, and a hydrological scenario (Normal), representative of the series of years observed in the last decades and in accordance with the data provided by INAG. Figure 3.24 shows the tentative time-frame of interventions for both strategies.

As previously explained, strategy 1 (dominant paradigm) is based on the implementation of structural measures. According to this, the implementation of the Odelouca dam in 2010 is the most important option in this strategy, as a regional measure relying on surface water. Moreover the introduction of this option is the global and conventional structural option that strategically distinguishes strategy 1 from strategy 2. The 'new abstraction boreholes' option is only implemented in order to satisfy the demand until the Odelouca dam operation starts.

On the other hand, strategy 2 reflects the need to implement localized measures and to achieve the sustainable use of surface water and groundwater. That way, 'desalination' for domestic and irrigation purposes and 'water reuse' for golf courses, although being structural measures, are far from the conventional options normally implemented. As in strategy 1, the 'new abstraction boreholes' option is also introduced, but now with an increased importance as a more important volume of water is abstracted, intending to diminish the dependence on surface water for domestic supply. The small-scale measures implementation is also accentuated by the introduction of some system enhancements in strategy 2.

Furthermore, one should emphasize that the 'irrigation method improvements' and 'losses reduction' options are used in both strategies as they are defined in the River Basin Plan (RBP).

3.7.1 Result Analysis

3.7.1.1 Domestic use
With respect to domestic use, the reference case was compared with both strategies.

For the reference case, the domestic demand coverage by the end of the simulation period is 73 per cent, whereas for strategy 1 it is 98 per cent and for strategy 2 it is 96 per cent (Figure 3.25). In fact, only a slight difference can be observed between the two strategies' application from 2030, reaching a maximum of 2 per cent in 2035, related to the fact that the Odelouca dam is more effective.

In terms of domestic deficit improvement (Figure 3.26), the abovementioned difference represents a variation of 6.5 per cent in 2035 between the two strategies.

Moreover, analysing in more detail the results obtained for strategy 1 (dominant paradigm) (Figure 3.27a), one can point out the improvement of

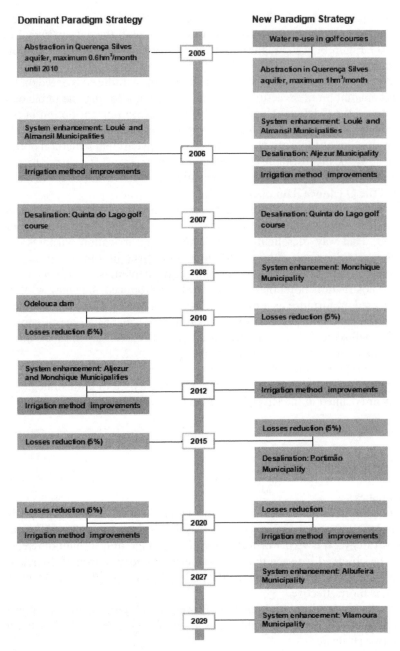

Figure 3.24   Tentative time-frame of interventions within dominant and new paradigm strategies

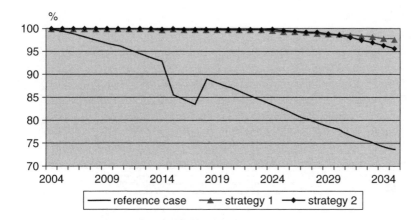

Figure 3.25   Domestic demand coverage

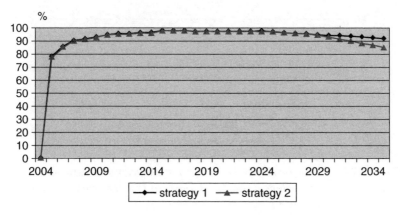

Figure 3.26   Domestic deficit improvement between strategy 1 and strategy 2

domestic demand coverage on 14.5 per cent, on average for the simulation period, observed for surface water, mostly associated to the application of the structural options, essentially the Odelouca dam construction. With the application of this strategy, the main goal of 95 per cent of domestic demand coverage is globally achieved in the overall region, as aimed for by Águas do Algarve S.A., hence also in the Barlavento region (Figure 3.27b), but there only after an improvement of 23 per cent on average for the simulation period, attaining a maximum of 42 per cent in 2035.

Regarding the domestic demand coverage supplied by groundwater, a marginal improvement of 0.4 per cent, on average, is verified over the

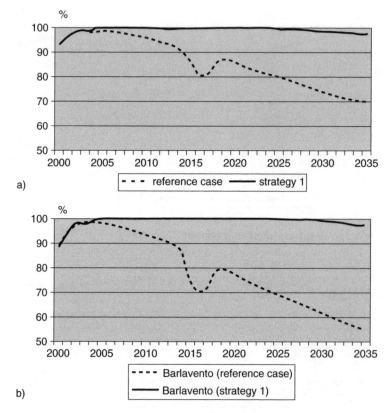

Figure 3.27   *Domestic demand coverage for surface water associated to:*
a) the whole basin; b) Barlavento (for reference case and
strategy 1)

simulation period, predominantly associated to the application of the 'losses reduction' option.

With the application of strategy 2 (new paradigm), the results are similar to strategy 1 showing that the absence of regional strong structural options (that is, the Odelouca dam) can be counterbalanced by smaller options, solving problems at the local level.

3.7.1.2   Irrigation use
Regarding irrigation use, some differences can be observed between the two strategies analysed and the reference case. The two strategies increase the irrigation demand coverage in the period 2015–17, solving the shortage verified in the reference case due to the previously existent deficit in the

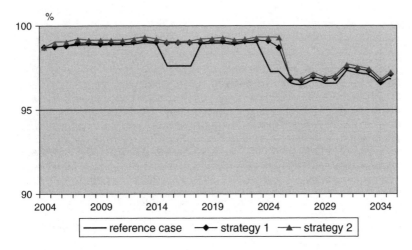

Figure 3.28   Irrigation demand coverage

Silves, Lagoa and Portimão public irrigation sites. Moreover, as concerns the Monchique private irrigation site, with the application of both strategies, not only the decrease observed in 2024 for the reference case is shortly delayed but also the deficit is minimized up to the end of the simulation period, although only by 1.5 to 2 per cent.

It should be emphasized that strategy 2 presents the highest irrigation demand coverage during the simulation period and both the reference case and the two strategies present an irrigation demand coverage always above 95 per cent, even in dry periods (Figure 3.28).

Figure 3.29 presents the irrigation deficit improvement for strategies 1 and 2.

In accordance with the previously referred for Figure 3.28, two peaks are observed for irrigation deficit improvement between 2015–17 and 2024–25. For the first peak, strategy 2 presents an improvement of 62 per cent on average, more than that verified for strategy 1 (58 per cent), and for the second peak, an improvement of 75 per cent on average occurs for strategy 2, which is approximately 14 per cent better than strategy 1. This last difference can be explained by the application of the 'system expansion' option to Monchique in strategy 2 (2008), anticipating the corresponding option in strategy 1 (2012), leaving more water quantity available in Monchique aquifer for irrigation purposes.

Furthermore, as one can observe, the irrigation deficit improvement achieved with strategy 2 is always above that verified for strategy 1 (almost 13 per cent on average during the simulation period). Nevertheless the major

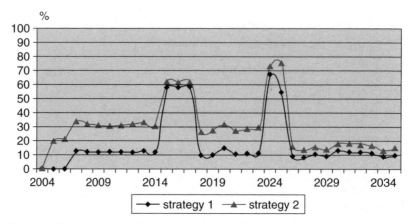

*Figure 3.29   Irrigation deficit improvement between strategy 1 and
                strategy 2*

differences are verified between 2005–14 (20 per cent on average) and 2018–23 (17 per cent on average), due to the Herdade dos Salgados golf course that in strategy 2 benefits from the 'water reuse' option implemented in 2005.

Figures 3.30 and 3.31 present, for both strategies, the irrigation demand coverage and the demand deficit improvement differentiating public and private irrigation sites and golf courses.

With the application of strategy 1, the irrigation demand coverage in public irrigation sites is always equal to 100 per cent (Figure 3.30a) mostly due to the Odelouca dam implementation that allows an increase of water volume in the Arade dam. The peak in the corresponding irrigation deficit improvement (Figure 3.30b), between 2015 and 2017, illustrates the efficiency of strategy 1, solving the irrigation deficit in Silves, Lagoa and Portimão public irrigation sites, as previously mentioned. Regarding private irrigation sites, one can observe a decrease of 3 per cent in irrigation demand coverage in 2026, essentially due to the unmet irrigation demand located in Monchique. Nevertheless after 2026, about 9 per cent of irrigation deficit improvement is attained, on average, until the end of the simulation period, as shown in Figure 3.30b. The irrigation demand coverage in golf courses is 96 per cent on average during the whole simulation period. Regarding the corresponding deficit improvement, one can emphasize the increase in 2007, achieving 37.5 per cent, due to the application of the 'desalination' option to Quinta do Lago golf course and a peak during the dry period (2015–17), reaching 50 per cent, related to two golf courses supplied by surface water, consequently benefiting from the increase of water available in the Arade dam.

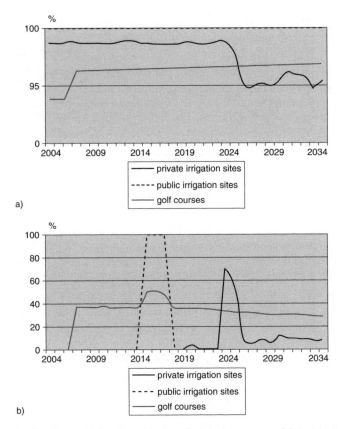

Figure 3.30   *Strategy 1: a) irrigation demand coverage; b) irrigation deficit improvement, for private, public irrigation sites and golf courses*

In strategy 2, the same value for irrigation demand coverage in public irrigation sites is achieved (Figure 3.31a), due to the application of the 'irrigation method improvements' option, which contributes to total demand satisfaction. Regarding private irrigation sites, the results are similar to those obtained for strategy 1. The improvement of the irrigation deficit verified in golf courses is substantially greater as it achieves 100 per cent after 2007, except during the dry period (2015–17) when it drops to 78 per cent. This fact is directly related to the two golf courses which are supplied by the Arade dam, which is incapable of satisfying the demand during this period (Figure 3.31b).

For both strategies, some structural and non-structural options were implemented in order to decrease groundwater abstractions and

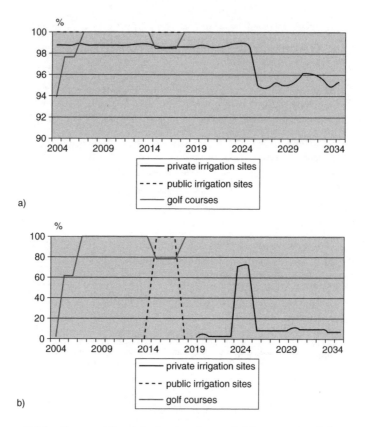

Figure 3.31   Strategy 2: a) irrigation demand; b) irrigation deficit
improvement, for private, public irrigation sites and golf
courses

consequently decrease the groundwater exploitation index when compared
with the reference case. Considering an average for the whole simulation
period, the groundwater exploitation index for the reference case is around
67 per cent. As expected, with the implementation of strategy 1, this index is
lower (2 per cent less). As regards strategy 2, the creation of new abstraction
boreholes in the Querença-Silves aquifer together with the application of the
'irrigation method improvements' and 'losses reduction' options, still allows
a slight decrease in the groundwater exploitation index for the whole basin
comparative to the reference case (1 per cent less).

As regards the Querença-Silves aquifer, the sustainable use of surface
and groundwater resources achieved with strategy 2 permits reaching
95 per cent of domestic demand coverage without a significant increase in

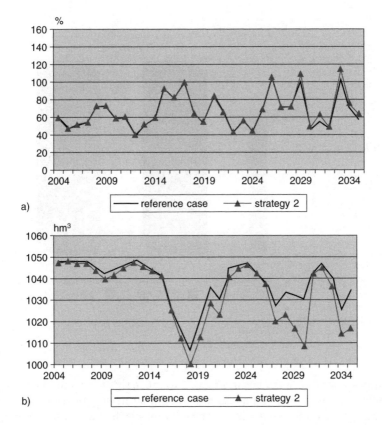

Figure 3.32   Querença-Silves aquifer: a) groundwater exploitation index; b) storage

the groundwater exploitation index of this aquifer. Observing its behaviour in detail (Figure 3.32a), on average, an increase of only 3 per cent on this index is verified after the application of the 'new abstraction boreholes' option which creates a small decrease of the volume stored in the aquifer until the end of the simulation period (Figure 3.32b).

3.7.2   Economic analysis and strategy evaluation

Owing to the enormous amount of investment in the Ribeiras do Algarve River Basin, the application of strategies 1 and 2 imply an increase of PV direct costs relative to the reference case (41 per cent and 37 per cent respectively) (Figure 3.33). Moreover the difference in the PV direct costs between strategy 1 and strategy 2 is about 3 per cent (67 million €). The

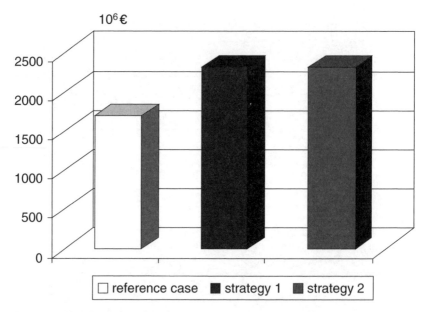

*Figure 3.33   Present value direct costs associated to reference case,
             strategy 1 and strategy 2*

major investment in the basin is related to the 'irrigation method improvements' option, which is applied under both strategies. In strategy 2, the
investment in dam construction is mostly replaced by the investment in the
construction of desalination units, the latter presenting higher values of
specific O&M costs, approximately 0.50 €/m^3 against 0.05 €/m^3 for dam
construction.

Concerning strategy 2, and in comparison to the reference case and strategy 1, a decrease of 1.5 per cent (10.2 million €) and 2.3 per cent (15.8
million €) respectively in PV environmental costs is observed (Figure 3.34).
The main reasons for this decrease are the substitution of the Odelouca dam
construction (strategy 1) by the implementation of options ('desalination',
'water reuse' and 'losses reduction' options) that though increasing the
amount of effluent discharged into the water bodies and possibly increasing pollution costs, cause a decrease in both surface and groundwater
abstraction costs.

Table 3.10 collates the performance indicators of the two strategies and
the reference case.

Concerning the effectiveness in terms of demand coverage of domestic
and irrigation uses (Table 3.10), strategy 1 performs better mainly due to

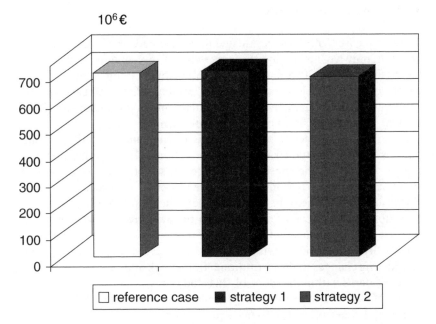

Figure 3.34 *Present value environmental costs associated to reference case, strategy 1 and strategy 2*

Table 3.10 *Strategy evaluation table (BAU+Normal)*

Option	Effectiveness	Economic efficiency		Benefits
	(relative performance index for demand coverage)	Environmental cost PV, million €	Direct cost PV, million €	PV, million €
reference case	0.3	693	1690	16 786
strategy 1	0.57	698	2377	17 231
strategy 2	0.42	682	2310	17 248

the construction of the Odelouca dam, specifically by the end of the simulation period. In terms of PV environmental costs, a better performance of strategy 2 is observed as explained above (see Figure 3.34). Moreover it is fairly obvious that the investments needed, in order to carry out the implementation of both strategies 1 and 2, cause these strategies to be less favourable than the reference case in terms of PV direct costs, to which add the higher consumption and operational and maintenance costs due to the increase of water availability to the users.

3.7.3 Cost Recovery Strategy

The cost recovery strategies, evaluated under the BAU + Normal scenario, are set mainly having in mind the large value of investments to be made in the basin between 2005 and 2020, pointing out: (1) for strategy 1, the construction of Odelouca dam; (2) for strategy 2, the construction of desalination plants, namely the high capacity one in Portimão; and (3) for strategy 1 and 2, irrigation method improvements.

Although the impact of both 'domestic pricing' and 'irrigation pricing' options have been studied individually (section 6.4), only the 'domestic pricing' option will be considered in order to structure the cost recovery strategies. Two main reasons may be given in order to justify this choice: (1) the agricultural sector has been long dependent on subsidies; and (2) no irrigation use fees have been charged to private irrigation sites although they are already defined within the legal framework. Moreover the inclusion of 'irrigation pricing' within the cost recovery strategies would imply considering changes to the institutional framework and/or policy which are not considered within the scope of this study.

Therefore, the cost recovery targets, planned to be achieved through the increase of water prices for domestic users, are:

- a 100 per cent recovery of direct costs from 2020 onwards;
- a targeted minimum cost recovery of 70 per cent associated to environmental costs by 2025.

As already stated in section 3.5.3.1, in the absence of any specific studies for the Algarve River Basin and in accordance with the Águas do Algarve S.A. water company, demand elasticity is estimated to be -0.5.

An iterative process was initiated in order to find a water price that would enable the achievement of the rate of cost recovery targets set for both strategies. Therefore a differentiated increase in water prices for domestic users, concerning each strategy, is planned to take place every two years from 2005 to 2015. Currently, the average weighted price for domestic supply in the Ribeiras do Algarve River Basin is, according to data from the Water National Plan (PNA, 2000), 0.68 €/m³, varying among the different municipalities from 0.41 €/m³ at the Vila do Bispo municipality to a maximum price of 1.04 €/m³ in the municipality of Aljezur.

As a result of the process, the final water prices calculated for domestic use in the year 2035 are on average:

- 1.21 €/m³ for strategy 1 (varying from 0.65 €/m³ in the Vila do Bispo municipality to 1.56 €/m³ in the Aljezur municipality);

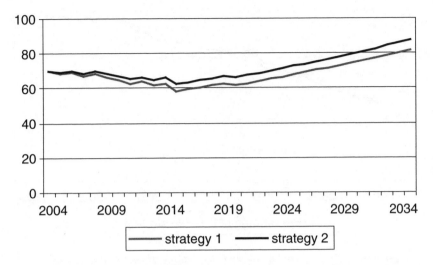

Figure 3.35 Domestic demand (million m³) (under cost recovery strategy)

- 1.12 €/m³ for strategy 2 (varying from 0.62 €/m³ in the Vila do Bispo municipality to 1.56 €/m³ in the Aljezur municipality).

Moreover and as shown in Figure 3.35, the increase in the domestic use water price causes domestic demand to decrease. Comparing domestic demand before and after the application of the cost recovery strategy, domestic demand decreases 27.5 per cent for strategy 1 and 22.3 per cent for strategy 2, a severe decrease of demand that is an effect of the assumed demand elasticity value.

More specifically, the adjustment in water tariffs for domestic use causes a decrease in domestic demand between 2005 and 2015 of 15 per cent under strategy 1 and 9 per cent under strategy 2 (Figure 3.35). An inflection in this trend is observed after 2015 as a result of both water pricing stabilization and population growth. The demand decrease between 2005 and 2015 is higher for strategy 1 as a result of a higher price increase.

The optimized price increase enables the accomplishment of an overall rate of cost recovery, under both strategies, of 89 per cent by 2020, corresponding to a 100 per cent recovery of direct costs. Moreover an overall rate of cost recovery of 97 per cent is achieved in 2025, corresponding to the aimed recovery goal of approximately 100 per cent of direct costs and 70 per cent of environmental costs (Figure 3.36).

Following this process, the two strategies are re-evaluated against each other and against the reference case (Table 3.11). The values between

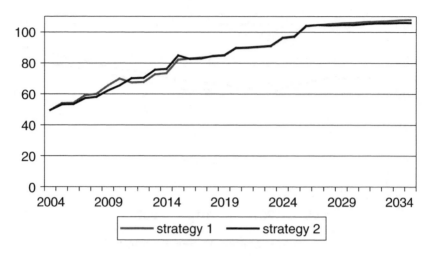

Figure 3.36   Rate of cost recovery (%) – domestic use (under cost recovery strategy)

Table 3.11   Strategy evaluation table (under cost recovery strategy) (BAU+Normal)

Option	Effectiveness (relative performance index for demand coverage)	Direct cost PV, million €	Environmental cost PV, million €	Benefits PV, million €
reference case	0.3	1690	693	16 786
strategy 1	0.7 (0.57)	2153 (2377)	645 (698)	16 709 (17231)
strategy 2	0.7 (0.42)	2129 (2310)	640 (682)	16 829 (17248)

brackets correspond to the strategies' results before the application of the cost recovery strategy.

As stated earlier, the water tariffs adjustment in domestic use causes a decrease in domestic demand, resulting into an increase in demand coverage after recovery strategies are applied. Consequently, compared to what happened before the cost recovery strategy was applied, PV environmental costs decrease (7.5 per cent for strategy 1 and 6 per cent for strategy 2), mainly due to lower surface and groundwater abstractions in order to supply domestic users. Similarly, the decrease observed in terms of PV direct costs (9.4 per cent for strategy 1 and 7.8 per cent for strategy 2) is due to a decrease in specific operation and maintenance costs associated to water treatment and conveyance. Finally, a decrease in domestic demand

and therefore in water supplied to domestic users causes a decrease in the total benefits drawn from users for water use (Table 3.11). The obtained results reflect a cost recovery strategy under established targets based on the assumption of a demand elasticity for the region. This analysis would benefit from a more rigorous definition of this value.

3.7.4 Conclusions

The main goal of the water management options analysed within this study is to eliminate the existing deficit in urban and irrigation supply, in the Algarve region. With both strategies, which combine different water management options, the main goals defined in section 1 are achieved.

Strategy 1 (dominant paradigm strategy) is based on stakeholders' consultation, and relies on regional-scale conventional and structural options, Odelouca dam being the most representative. On the other hand, the application of strategy 2 (new paradigm strategy) comprises localized non-conventional measures such as 'desalination' for domestic and irrigation purposes and 'water reuse' for golf courses, aiming to achieve the sustainable exploitation of both surface and groundwater water resources.

While strategy 1 accompanies what is foreseen in the River Basin Plan (RBP) concerning domestic use, using essentially surface water, strategy 2 diminished the dependence on surface water sources, returning to groundwater abstractions which were the most important supply sources until the end of the 1990s. Under both strategies, regarding irrigation use, the 'irrigation method improvements' option, according to what is defined in the RBP, is the most representative measure and the one which mostly influences the irrigation demand coverage and the direct and environmental costs.

Finally, a simple exercise was performed in order to determine the optimal domestic water pricing values which enable the achievement of cost recovery targets. The outcome of this iterative process resulted in an increase in domestic demand coverage and a decrease of both direct and environmental costs within the Ribeiras do Algarve River Basin. The impact of a cost recovery strategy addressing the recovery of direct and environmental costs for irrigation use could also be evaluated, but would imply changes to the current institutional framework and/or policy. Moreover it should be pointed out that: (1) the cost recovery targets were set to common sense rather than institutionalized values which are presently non-existent; and (2) the demand elasticity values for Ribeiras do Algarve are unavailable and therefore more precise studies addressing this subject must be carried out. One should emphasize that this exercise is only an example of how to use the WSM DSS tool in order to establish possible cost recovery strategies aiming to achieve economical sustainability, according to the Water Framework Directive cost recovery goals.

REFERENCES

DL (1990), Decree Law nb 2/90 (Decreto Regulamentar no 2/90 de 12 de Janeiro, Diário da República – I Série 144–159), Ministério das Finanças.

IHERA (2001), 'Estimation of the water costs in the public irrigation site of Sotavento' (in Portuguese), Instituto de Hidráulica, Engenharia Rural e Ambiente (IHERA).

INE (2001), CENSOS, http://www.ine.pt/prodserv/censos/index_censos.htm.

Lencastre, A., J. Carvalho, J. Gonçalves and M. Piedade (1994), 'Construction and exploitation costs, support tool for a sustainable development policy in urban water systems', Vol. 9 (in Portuguese). Laboratório Nacional de Engenharia Civil (LNEC).

MCOTA (2003), 'Golf courses in Algarve' (in Portuguese), Ministério das Cidades, Ordenamento do Território e Ambiente.

NTUA (2003), 'WSM Decision Support System' (version 2.10), Economic Analysis Manual.

PBHRA (1999a), 'Urban and industrial supply' (in Portuguese), Plano de Bacia Hidrográfica das Ribeiras do Algarve (River Basin Plan of the Ribeiras do Algarve), 1st phase, Annex 6, Vol 6B, Part 1. Ministério das Cidades, Ordenamento do Território e Ambiente.

PBHRA (1999b), 'Water use economic analysis' (in Portuguese), Plano de Bacia Hidrográfica das Ribeiras do Algarve (River Basin Plan of the Ribeiras do Algarve), 1st phase. Annex 13. Ministério das Cidades, Ordenamento do Território e Ambiente.

PBHRA (1999c), 'Urban and industrial supply' (in Portuguese), Plano de Bacia Hidrográfica das Ribeiras do Algarve (River Basin Plan of the Ribeiras do Algarve), 1st phase. Annex 7, Vol. 7A. Ministério das Cidades, Ordenamento do Território e Ambiente.

PBHRA (2000a), 'Hydrological water balance' (in Portuguese), Plano de Bacia Hidrográfica das Ribeiras do Algarve (River Basin Plan of the Ribeiras do Algarve), 1st phase, Annex 3, Vol. 3C, Ministério das Cidades, Ordenamento do Território e Ambiente.

PBHRA (2000b), 'Socio-economic development prospective analysis' (in Portuguese), Plano de Bacia Hidrográfica das Ribeiras do Algarve (River Basin Plan of the Ribeiras do Algarve), 2nd phase. Volume II. Ministério das Cidades, Ordenamento do Território e Ambiente.

PBHRA (2001), 'Evaluation of water uses and needs' (in Portuguese), Plano de Bacia Hidrográfica das Ribeiras do Algarve (River Basin Plan of the Ribeiras do Algarve), 3rd phase, Annex 1, Ministério das Cidades, Ordenamento do Território e Ambiente.

PNA (2000), 'Water economy of the Portuguese National Water Plan' (in Portuguese), Economia da Água do Plano Nacional da Água (Anexos). Instituto da Água.

Veiga da Cunha, L., R. Oliveira and V. Nunes (2002), 'Water resources' in F.D. Santos, K. Forbes and R. Moita (eds), *Climate Change in Portugal Scenarios, Impacts and Adaptation Measures*, Lisbon; Gravida, pp. 137–71.

WFD (2000), Directive 2000/60/EC, Water Framework Directive, OJ L 327, 22. 12. 2000, pp. 1–72.

PART III

A participatory approach to addressing
conflicting demands and varying hydrological
conditions for the sustainable use of water on
Mediterranean islands: the MEDIS project

4. Climate change and vulnerabilities to drought on Mediterranean islands

Manfred A. Lange, Antonia Alkistis Donta and the MEDIS consortium[1]

BACKGROUND AND INTRODUCTION

Global changes, that is, changes in Earth system parameters largely caused by human activities, will have a number of consequences or impacts with varying magnitudes for different parts of our globe. In general, global climate change will lead to an intensification of the water cycle with enhanced frequencies of floods and extreme precipitation events in regions traditionally prone to this threat and with increased water scarcity in already water-deficient regions of the world (Alcamo et al., 2000; Arnell et al., 2001; Gleick, 2000). Changes in the availability of water through shifts in precipitation patterns and reduced precipitation volumes as a consequence of altered climate conditions thus represent a threat, particularly to present arid or semi-arid regions. Given current projections of climate change on a scale of 50 to 100 years (Houghton et al., 2001), it seems likely that the availability of water in large parts of Southern Europe will be further reduced, thus enhancing the water stress[2] in this region (Alcamo et al., 2000; Lehner et al., 2001). This will result in increased vulnerabilities of communities and ecosystems to water scarcity[3] and will threaten the well-being and the future development of societies and countries in the Mediterranean Basin, the region that this chapter will focus on. The rationale for focusing mainly on the Mediterranean stems from the fact that this region is already – and is likely to remain – an area of enhanced water scarcity relative to other parts of Europe as well as in a global context (Alcamo et al., 2000).

The problems to be faced are exacerbated on islands of the Mediterranean for a number of reasons. Islands by their very nature are isolated. This implies that the use of trans-boundary water to compensate for temporal or seasonal water shortage, which is frequently practised in continental situations, is virtually impossible. The transport of water from the nearest mainland by either pipelines or ship transport is excessively expensive and has been utilized in only a few exceptional cases (for example Mallorca and Cyprus during years of severe droughts). Thus the precipitation that falls on the island remains the only immediate source of water for the recharge of reservoirs and for consumption.

Islands are largely dependent on the availability, timing and amount of precipitation. At least in some parts of the Mediterranean, the amount of precipitation has steadily decreased and the main precipitation period has shortened over the last 40 years (see below). This trend may continue and lead to further diminished water resources as a result of regional climate change, thus exacerbating the problem (Bolle, 2003b; Xoplaki, 2002).

Because in many cases, the natural reservoirs on the islands have been utilized to the point where they can not be consumed as potable water any more, alternative sources of water have to be exploited. This includes foremost the desalination of sea water, which also represents a costly alternative to regular surface or groundwater use.

Another common characteristic, not only for the islands but for the Mediterranean in general, is the predominance of agriculture as the major consumer of ground- and surface water. Water for irrigation usually comprises more than 60 per cent of the total water consumption on Mediterranean islands (see below). This fact and the lack of – or the neglect of – stringent regulations and policies on water use and extraction has in many cases led to the overexploitation of natural reservoirs. However as long as the (often subsidized) price of irrigation water remains as low as it does in many cases (for instance, the price for irrigation water in one of the Local Farmers's Irrigation Organizations in western Crete amounts to no more than 0.07 €/m^3), farmers may continue to utilize the existing reservoirs to their depletion.

Near-coastal aquifers are particularly prone to overexploitation. This is due to the relatively high concentration of human settlements as well as of tourist operations along the islands' coasts. However extraction of water beyond the natural recharge potential often leads to the intrusion of seawater into the aquifer, rendering its water useless for human consumption.

This by no means complete list of issues highlights some of the challenges to be met in achieving or maintaining a sustainable use of water on Mediterranean islands. However there are additional problems, typical for the Mediterranean in general, that will also have to be considered when addressing water management and water policies on islands of the Mediterranean. These problems are more of a socio-economic nature and include unresolved conflicts between different users, deficits and inefficiencies in institutional water management, and non-compliance with existing rules and regulations, to name just a few (see below).

In addition to these considerations, another factor should be taken into account: the vulnerability to water scarcity on Mediterranean islands. In dealing with vulnerability in the context of water management, the emphasis in the past has been on minimizing risks and on adapting to changing or existing circumstances. Given the concept of vulnerability (for a definition of the terminology used, see below), planned adaptation has to be viewed as an essential strategy to reduce vulnerability, given that sensitivities of the considered system are relatively robust and remain virtually unchanged, specifically with regard to possible change in climatic conditions.

With regard to adaptation to water scarcity, three different dimensions of water management will have to be considered: a physical and environmental dimension, an economic and regulatory dimension, and a social, institutional and political dimension (Figure 4.1). As can be seen, there are mutual relationships between these dimensions. This implies that they will have to be considered holistically, when deriving effective adaptive

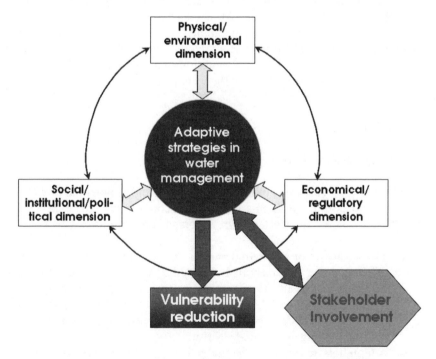

Figure 4.1   Schematic depiction of different vulnerability/adaptation dimensions to water scarcity

strategies that will result in overall reductions in vulnerability to water stress in a given region.

The overriding characteristic that governs most of the problems mentioned above lies in their complex and multifaceted nature, which requires a holistic approach involving the integration of the natural and human sciences. Thus in considering water availability and use to derive strategies for a sustainable and equitable distribution of water, interdisciplinarity is a necessary prerequisite.

Moreover lasting solutions to sustainable water management in the Mediterranean as well as effective adaptation strategies (Figure 4.1) will only be found through recommendations and/or regulations that are based on mutually agreed principles between the stakeholders involved. This requires a stakeholder-based participatory process that builds on the results of scientific investigations on the one hand and on the consent of major stakeholders on the other (Lange et al., 1999).

Before addressing these issues in more detail, we will briefly describe some of the aspects and foundations of integrated assessments, which are central to a vulnerability analysis. This will be followed by a brief description of the MEDIS project. The remaining part of the chapter will be devoted to the characteristics of each of the vulnerability dimensions, the challenges for water management on Mediterranean islands associated with each of them under present and future climatic conditions, and some thoughts on possible adaptive strategies addressing these challenges.

INTEGRATED ASSESSMENT

Background and Motivation

In addressing water scarcity in the Mediterranean and its potential threat to societies and natural ecosystems, three central concepts have to be specified (IPCC, 2001; Parry and Carter, 1998; Scheraga and Grambsch, 1998):

- The sensitivity of a system describes the degree to which a system is affected, either adversely or beneficially, by climate-related stimuli. The effect may be direct (for example a change in crop yield in response to a change in the mean, range or variability of temperature) or indirect (for example damage caused by an increase in the frequency of coastal flooding due to sea-level rise).
- Adaptation to climate change refers to adjustments in natural or human systems in response to actual or expected climatic stimuli or their effects, which moderates harm or exploits beneficial

opportunities. Various types of adaptation can be distinguished, including anticipatory and reactive adaptation, private and public adaptation, and autonomous (that is, intrinsic to the system under consideration) and planned adaptation (that is, adaptation measures initiated through human activities).

- Vulnerability represents the degree to which a system is susceptible to, or unable to cope with, adverse effects of climate change, including climate variability and extremes; vulnerability is a function of the character, magnitude and rate of climate variation to which a system is exposed, its sensitivity and its adaptive capacity.

Having clarified these important concepts, we need to define two other terms before proceeding:

- The adaptability or the adaptive capacity[4] of a system depicts the ability or potential of a system to adjust through changes in its characteristics or behaviour to climate change (including climate variability and extremes), to moderate potential damage, to take advantage of opportunities, or to cope with the consequences of climate change (see below); in the context of this chapter, we will concentrate on planned adaptability.
- Resilience describes the amount of change a system can undergo without changing state, that is, without altering its main characteristics.

Finally, water scarcity α is defined as:

$$\alpha = \frac{\text{water withdrawal}}{\text{availability of renewable resource}}.$$

The above given definitions can be formalized through the following simple equations:

$$S = f(S_i, CeC, E) \tag{4.1}$$

where S stands for the overall sensitivity of the system considered, f for an (a priori) unknown functional relationship between the quantities considered (to be defined), S_i for sensitivities of each component i of this system, CeC for the change in external condition (for example climate change) and E denotes the exposure of the system to these changes. In looking at multiple stressors (that is, changes in external conditions), the issue of cumulative effects, that is, the fact that individual stressors may interact with each other in various ways, comes into play. However this represents an extremely complex process that will not be considered here.

Likewise, one can write for the adaptability A:

$$A = f(AC_i, CeC) \qquad (4.2)$$

with AC_i depicting the adaptive capacity or adaptability of each component i of the system and finally for the vulnerability, V, of the system:

$$V = f(S, A) \qquad (4.3)$$

If we assume that S is constant for a given change in external conditions CeC, then equation (4.3) reduces to:

$$V \cong f(A) = f(AC_i, CeC) \qquad (4.4)$$

Thus for a given CeC, the overall vulnerability depends approximately only on the adaptive capacities of the components of the system under consideration (see above). Reducing vulnerability under these conditions will mainly be achieved through the enhancement of the adaptive capacities AC_i of the system under consideration.

Basic Concepts and Methods of an Integrated Assessment

Integrated assessments (IAs) provide a conceptual framework that enables the integration of knowledge from a wide variety of disciplines and sources and strives to reach the following goals (Weyant et al., 1996):

- a comprehensive and coordinated exploration of future projections of human and natural systems;
- the provision of information and background to key questions of policy formulation;
- a specification of priorities on research needed to enhance the ability to specify robust policy options.

Integrated assessments of climate change represent a fairly well-established research field. First assessment studies were carried out in the 1970s and 1980s. However at that time their conceptualization was ill-defined and such studies were therefore not widely accepted (Rotmans and van Asselt, 1996; Weyant et al., 1996). With climate change more recently gaining increasing attention and importance, the scope and objectives of IA have been formulated more precisely. Rotmans and van Asselt (1996) describe a framework for IAs that is rooted in a cyclical, iterative process that involves participation and consensus-building among scientific, policy and societal stakeholders (Yarnal, 1998). The characteristics and requirements of an IA have been summarized as (for a detailed description, see Lange, 2000):

- a multi- or interdisciplinary approach;
- an attempt to address multiple stressors and their cumulative impacts; and
- a striving to derive information that assists in policy- and decision-making, rather than in the sole advance of knowledge for its intrinsic value (cf., Weyant et al., 1996; Yarnal, 1998).

Various methods for an IA have been introduced in the literature (Janssen, 1998; Lange, 2000), including the IPCC approach (Carter et al., 1996; Parry and Carter, 1998). A schematic depiction of major elements of an integrated assessment is given in Figure 4.2.

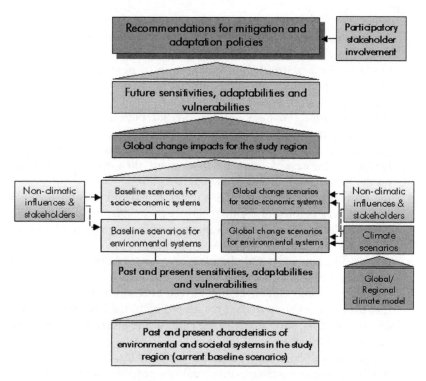

Figure 4.2 Schematic depiction of major elements of an integrated assessment study

Aside from the already introduced quantities and terms, there are two more concepts that need to be briefly described:

- Baseline scenarios: depict the development of environmental or societal systems or components in the absence of climate change, that is, they represent a projection of the future development based on determinants other than climate change (that is, political, societal, economic).
- Global change scenarios: depict the development of environmental or societal systems or components in the presence of climate change, that is, they represent a projection of the future development based on climate change as well as on other determinants (political, societal, economic).

With these definitions in mind, the methodology of an IA (either on a global or a regional spatial scale) can be summarized by the following steps:

1. an assessment of past and present climate variability and climate change, respectively;
2. based on this assessment, the specification of past and present sensibilities, adaptabilities and vulnerabilities of environmental and socio-economic (societal) system;
3. the specifications of baseline scenarios for both environmental and socio-economic (societal) systems; this involves considerations and projections of future non-climate-driven developments as well as, particularly in the case of a regional assessment, the view of stakeholders on the future development of the study region;
4. the provision of climate scenarios (on a global and possibly regional scale) through global or regional climate modelling; these models will be driven by scenarios for atmospheric greenhouse gas concentrations, which are linked to the baseline scenarios (3);
5. the specification of global change scenarios for both environmental and socio-economic (societal) systems; this involves projections that take into account climate change-driven alterations in these systems that evolve in addition to changes according to the baseline scenarios of (3) as well as, particularly in the case of a regional assessment, the view of stakeholders;
6. baseline and global change scenarios depict (at least, depending on the number of climate scenarios involved) two possible 'futures'; the comparison between these two future developments reveals the impacts of climate change for the study region under consideration;

7.   based on this assessment as well as on results in (2) above, future sensibilities, adaptabilities and vulnerabilities can be derived; and
8.   against the background of a desirable future which preserves environmental integrity and human welfare, the vulnerability estimates to global change of environmental and socio-economic systems under considerations will lead to recommendations for political mitigation and adaptation strategies (Parry and Carter, 1998) as the ultimate goal of an IA.

The temporal scale of an IA typically comprises a few decades up to a century.

To carry out an IA, various techniques have been devised. In recent years, integrated assessment modelling has become one of the more prominent tools. However in this chapter, we will not go into any more detail on IA methodologies, which have been described elsewhere (Alcamo and Image Project, 1994; Dowlatabadi and Morgan, 1993; Janssen, 1998; Lange, 2001; Nordhaus, 1992; Rayner and Malone, 1998; Rosenberg et al., 1993; Rotmans, 2000; Rotmans and Dowlatabadi, 1998; Rotmans and van Asselt, 1996; Weyant et al., 1996; Yarnal, 1998).

Before addressing vulnerabilities to water scarcity in the Mediterranean, we will briefly describe the objectives of the MEDIS project.

THE MEDIS PROJECT

The requirements and strategies for an integrated assessment and for addressing vulnerabilities to water scarcity outlined above are central to the EU-funded research project MEDIS ('Towards sustainable water use on Mediterranean islands: addressing conflicting demands and varying hydrological, social and economic conditions').

The overall goal of MEDIS is to 'contribute towards the sustainable use of water on Mediterranean islands where conflicting demand for water is combined with a wide range of hydrological, social and economic conditions'. This is to be achieved through a set of recommendations for the implementation of sustainable, equitable water management regimes on each island that reflect the current and possible future (climatic) conditions on each island. These recommendations will be in compliance with the WFD, and be built on the experiences and conclusions reached in consultation between stakeholders from all five islands involved. In so doing, work in MEDIS:

●   concentrates on a synthesis of results from previous studies and the integration of information from various disciplines;

- seeks to develop an infrastructure for a participatory stakeholder involvement, which will enable the establishment of water management practices that are both sustainable and equitable;
- considers (possibly drastically) altered conditions that may arise due to changed climatic conditions through a set of 'what-if' scenarios;
- is carried out at a catchment scale on major islands of the Mediterranean extending from the west to the east: Mallorca, Corsica, Sicily, Crete and Cyprus (in the project and in this chapter, we refer exclusively to the southern part of Cyprus, that is, the Republic of Cyprus);
- concentrates on agriculture as the predominant consumer of water on Mediterranean islands; and
- undertakes comparative analyses between each island in order to derive generic conclusions and to utilize possible common solutions to water management problems in compliance with the WFD.

MEDIS is carried out by a consortium of 12 institutions from seven countries[1].

Further detail on the project, the methodology employed and first results can be found elsewhere (Lange and MEDIS consortium, 2004).

ADAPTIVE CAPACITY AND VULNERABILITY REDUCTION ON MEDITERRANEAN ISLANDS

As pointed out before, in considering vulnerabilities to enhanced water scarcity in general requires consideration of at least three dimensions, which have been graphically depicted in Figure 4.1. Despite their complex interrelatedness, which was also mentioned above, we will in the following consider each of the three dimensions separately and try to come to some integrated aspects in the concluding part of this chapter as well as throughout the following sections. In so doing, we will concentrate on islands of the Mediterranean with some reference to the Mediterranean Basin at certain points.

A Few Basic Concepts

Before embarking on the concrete issues of vulnerability reduction to water scarcity on Mediterranean islands, we will once more consider some basic concepts, here related to adaptive capacities. Enhancing or utilizing adaptive capacity as a means of adaptation serves to enhance a system's coping capacity and increase its coping range. This leads ultimately to a reduction in its vulnerability with respect to a particular type of climate hazard, for example water scarcity, as mentioned above.

The mobilization of adaptive capacities depends critically on the resources available for adaptation, the ability of those who need to adapt to deploy these resources effectively, and their readiness or willingness to do so. Resources that may be utilized to enhance the adaptive capacity of a human system include natural resources, human and financial capital, knowledge of risks and appropriate social institutions geared to managing these risks as well as appropriate technologies and methods.

The ability to develop stringent strategies and plans can be considered as an essential prerequisite for the development of adaptation strategies. Such a development requires a comprehensive assessment of the (climate-related) risks and hazards the system is exposed to and the knowledge of possible adaptation options. The next steps are comprised of the design of adaptation strategies and their effective implementation.

The decision-making processes related to adaptation require the incorporation of sustainable development principles. The processes themselves need to be legitimate, that is, within the limits of any legal requirement and acceptable to those involved, and open to scrutiny by stakeholders and the general public. These are three very important requirements which have to be fulfilled in order to derive sustainable adaptations that meet the need of the communities involved and are supported by major stakeholders and the general public.

Vulnerability and Adaptation: Physical and Environmental Dimensions

As mentioned before, we consider the Mediterranean Basins and its islands. Table 4.1 provides some basic characteristics of these islands with regard to the physical conditions and the availability and replenishment of water resources.

With regard to the supply of water, it has already been mentioned that there is a singular dependence on precipitation as the sole (natural) (re-)supply mechanism. The current situation, particularly with regard to the eastern Mediterranean, can be described by two factors: a decline in precipitation for the last century (Bolle, 2003a; Xoplaki, 2002) and a persistently large evaporation due to high surface temperatures particularly during the summer months (Figure 4.3). The precipitation trend as shown in Figure 4.3, though specifically for Cyprus and the eastern Mediterranean, is in agreement with general trends seen throughout the entire Mediterranean Basin (see for example Xoplaki et al., 2004).

Strongly influenced by large-scale circulation patterns such as the North Atlantic Oscillation (NAO), precipitation for the wet season (October to

Table 4.1 Basic characteristics related to water management on Mediterranean islands

Parameter		Mallorca	Corsica	Sicily	Crete	Cyprus
Regional context	Climate type	Mediterranean temperate	Mediterranean	Mediterranean	Mediterranean sub-humid	Mediterranean semi-arid
	Aridity index		0.87	0.388 (semi-arid)	0.48 (semi-arid)	0.3–0.5 (semi-arid)
	Total area	3 640 km²	8 682 km²	28 000 km²	25 706 km²	9 251 km²
	Permanent population	609 000	260 196	55 329	5 076 700	793 100
	Annual tourist arrivals	210 000 (max.: 405 000)[6]	2 Mill.		> 4 Mill. (1999)	2.7 Mill.
Water availability	Mean yearly precipitation	650 mm/a	900 mm/a	500–1 000 mm/a	300–1 600 mm/a	500 mm/a (182–759); 477 mm/a²
	Total annual water supply	2 400*10⁶m³	8 000*10⁶m³	14 000–28 000*10⁶m³	7 690*10⁶m³	4 015*10⁶m³
	Annual Evapotransp-iration		2 500*10⁶m³		5 380*10⁶m³ (3 550–7 230)	2 918*10⁶m³ (72%)
	Total water resources/availability		1 500*10⁶m³	2 472*10⁶m³	2 310*10⁶m³ (1 520–3 100)	1 097*10⁶m³
Water resources	● Surface water	12*10⁶m³ (21.2%)	10 500*10⁶m³	27%	924*10⁶m³ (40%)	250*10⁶m³ (23%)
	● Groundwater	37.4*10⁶m³ (66.1%)	1 900*10⁶m³	71%	1 386*10⁶m³ (60%)	634*10⁶m³ (58%)
	● Storage/dams/reservoirs	7.2*10⁶m³ (12.7%)		2%	23.37*10⁶m³ (infrastructure)	183*10⁶m³ (16%)
	● Desalination				0	30*10⁶m³ (3%)

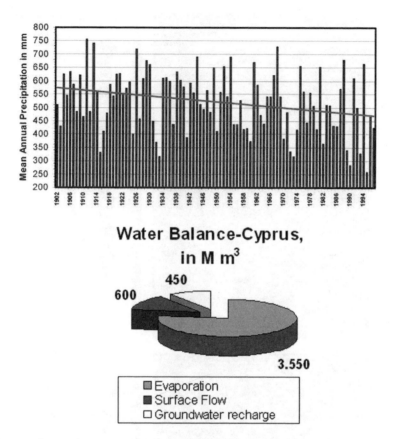

Source: Constantinou, pers. comm.

*Figure 4.3   Mean annual precipitation and overall trend for 1902–1997
           (a) and relation between evaporation, surface flow and
           groundwater recharge of precipitated water (b) on Cyprus*

March) over much of the Mediterranean has steadily decreased by 2.2 mm
month^{-1} decade^{-1} during the second half of the twentieth century after a
general increase since the middle of the nineteenth century (Xoplaki et al.,
2004).

Given current projections of global climate development (Houghton
et al., 2001), this trend is likely to continue. Dedicated regional climate
models based on IPCC general climate model results have confirmed this
hypothesis (Figure 4.4). As can be seen, the model results suggest a
substantial increase in summer temperatures and a significant decrease in

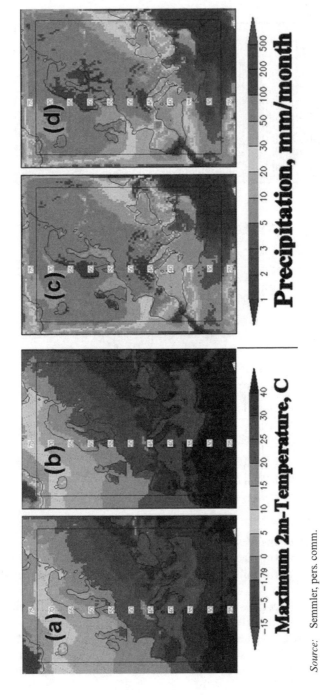

Maximum 2m-Temperature, C

−15 −5 −1.79 0 5 10 15 20 25 30 40

Precipitation, mm/month

1 2 3 5 10 20 30 50 100 200 500

Source: Semmler, pers. comm.

Figure 4.4   Maximum 2m-temperatures for 1960–90 (a) and 2070–2100 (b) and summer precipitations for 1960–90 (c) and 2070–2100 (d) derived from the regional climate REMO 5.1 and based on the Hadley-Centre-GCM HadAM3H

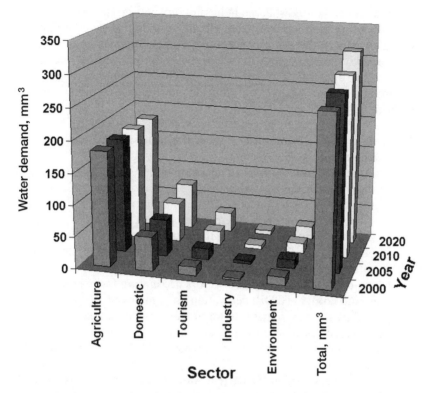

Source: Constantinou, pers. comm.

Figure 4.5 Projected water demand in $10^6 m^3 year^{-1}$ for various sectors on Cyprus up to the year 2020

summer precipitation over most of the Mediterranean Basin for the period 2070 to 2100 compared to the present situation. The summer months (June, July, August) are the time when demand both from agriculture and tourism is highest, thus leading to enhanced water scarcity.

When considering projections of future water demand for various sectors, the prospects are equally discouraging. Again, looking at Cyprus (Figure 4.5), there is a steady increase in water demand. This projection represents a conservative estimate given that the demand for agriculture is assumed to remain at the present level. However in light of the aforementioned climate development, this appears to be a rather unrealistic assumption, considering that agricultural production will likely be maintained at current levels.

Given this situation, what might possible adaptation strategies look like? In considering such strategies, we will again underline the fact that even though we are at this point concentrating on environmental and physical aspects, adaptive strategies will include measures that address one or both of the other dimensions described above. With this in mind, the following list presents only a first and surely incomplete attempt at summarizing such strategies:

1. Reduce water consumption – under this heading, the most promising strategies embrace:
    a. Water pricing, that is, an increase in consumer prices, possibly differentiated between different user groups; alternatively or additionally quotas on water extraction may be imposed, again possibly differentiated between different user groups.
    b. An important option will be to create incentives for reduced water consumption, for example subsidies for water saving, not – as has often been the case – for water consumption.
2. Change in water allocation – sectors accounting for maximum gross domestic product (GDP) generation and employment should be supported by the government; however care should be taken in avoiding possible one-sided economical advantages for specific sectors; thus incentives to save water for water-intensive sectors should be introduced in parallel.
3. Reduce losses – given the current water scarcity in many parts of the Mediterranean, it is hard to understand that drinking and irrigation water is being lost in large volumes. While this water is not 'lost' (that is, it is often fed back into groundwater aquifers), such losses of valuable potable water should be avoided. More specifically:
    a. Loss of water to the sea either as riverine discharge or through sub-sea groundwater discharge (SGD) should at least be reduced (Burnett et al., 2003). However in devising appropriate measures, care should be taken to avoid adverse impacts on bio-geochemical cycles and on marine ecosystems in near-coastal waters.
    b. Reduce losses and contamination of water in distribution networks. On Cyprus, annual losses of drinking water in the distribution network account for $40*10^6 m^3$, corresponding to 15 per cent of the total demand and 23 per cent of the total domestic demand on Cyprus. An improvement and renewal of distribution networks, even though an investment of substantial quantity, should be pursued where appropriate.
4. Increase utilization of additional water resources – while largely neglected for a long time, there is now increasing attention being paid

to this possible remedy. In particular, potable or irrigation water can be obtained through:

a. waste water recycling;
b. utilization of brackish water; and
c. rainwater harvesting.

Vulnerability and Adaptation: Economic and Regulatory Dimensions

As mentioned above, water is an indispensable commodity when it comes to economic and social development in a region. However each economic sector requires different amounts of renewable resources to thrive. In the case of water, we find an extreme situation with agriculture and irrigation accounting for a substantial fraction of the available water (Figure 4.6). The predominance of agriculture as the main consumer is a widespread characteristic of the Mediterranean Basin and for many arid and semi-arid regions of the world.

Given this situation, it is somewhat surprising to realize that the contribution of these sectors to the GDP and the employment on the island is contrary to its water demand (Figure 4.7).

As can be seen, while the water demand is highest for agricultural activities, the contribution of this sector to the GDP and to employment is relatively small. The situation is reversed when the tourism industry is considered (because of lack of data, we were forced to group tourism, the services industry and private households into one category), an industry which is largely responsible for economic growth and well-being on most of the islands considered.

As mentioned before, despite the relatively low water demand of tourism on the islands, peak needs arise during the summer months, when water requirements for irrigation also reach maximum values. This has led in some instances to significant unrest, if not conflicts, between farmers and tourism operators. However the tourism industry has in some cases reverted to ensuring their water supply through other means, for example dedicated water desalination plants or use of waste water recycling for satisfying grey-water needs, thus at least partly avoiding this problem.

However as mentioned above, global change and the accompanying changes in climatic parameters (Figure 4.4) are likely to affect both sectors adversely.

Before addressing possible adaptation strategies, an additional point with regard to agriculture will be briefly described. As a result of traditional practices and/or certain agricultural policies, crops grown on the islands are often quite water demanding (Figure 4.8) and/or are at the same time difficult to sell on the export or the domestic market. A particular point in

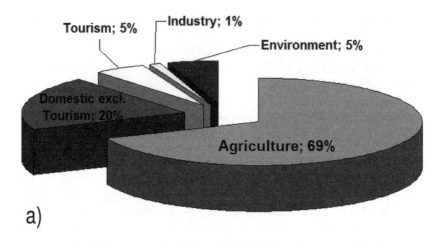

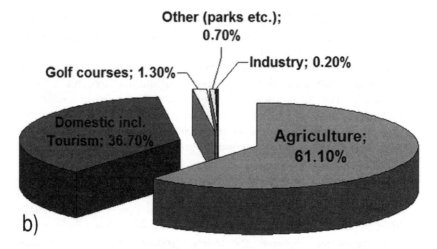

Sources: (a) Iacovidis and Glekas, pers. comm. (b) Candela, et al., pers. comm.

Figure 4.6 Current water demands for Cyprus (a) and for Mallorca (b)

case is the cultivation of bananas on Cyprus. The species grown, while not characterized by a particularly high specific water demand, nevertheless account for the highest total water consumption of crops grown on Cyprus. However the bananas harvested are not suitable for the European market as they do not adhere to European agricultural norms. Thus they are difficult to sell on the European market and the capacity of the domestic market is not sufficient to absorb the harvested products. Consequently,

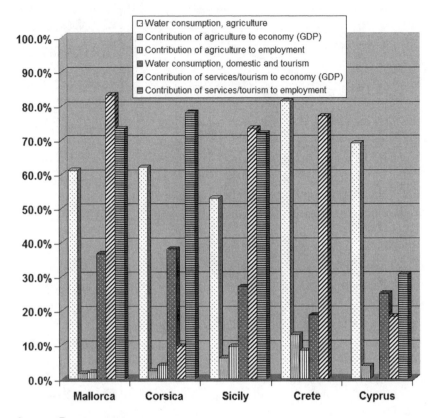

Source: Donta, pers. comm.

*Figure 4.7   Comparison between water consumption, contribution to GDP
and employment of agriculture versus tourism/service industry
on the five islands under consideration*

large quantities of the harvest has in the past been discarded, resulting not
only in the waste of the produce but also in the waste of the water needed
to grow it.

Practices like the one just described are to be avoided. This brings us to
a brief summary on possible adaptation strategies with regard to the economic and regulatory dimension of vulnerability reduction:

1. Support sectors with high economic potential and small water needs.
    This refers somewhat to point (2) of the previous section. However we
    would like to stress again that such measures will have to be applied

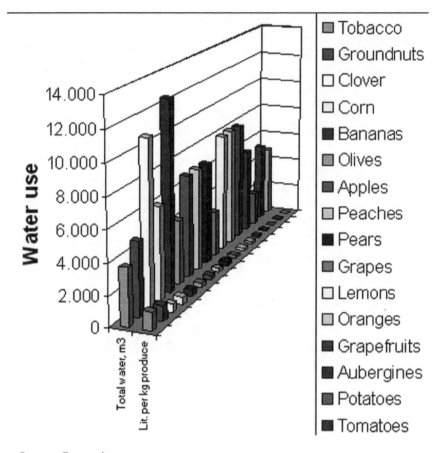

Source: Constantinou, pers. comm.

Figure 4.8   Total water used and water need in litres per kilogram of produce for various crops grown on Cyprus

with great care, ensuring that one-sided measures that do not account for the overall importance of other, apparently less favourable sectors are being avoided.

2. Change agricultural practices (quantity, quality of water). Under this heading, we make a plea for at least two alternatives to present practices:
    a. The first refers to the crops cultivated on each island. Stakeholders should be consulted and informed about possible alternatives to currently practised cropping patterns, particularly with regard to the water requirement of plants but also related to watering schedules and the amount of irrigation water applied per plant (for a summary

on possible alternatives, see Olesen and Bindi, 2002). Furthermore care should be taken to optimize tillage systems as well as weeding and harvest controls with the aim of minimizing irrigation needs.

b. The second recommendation or strategy refers to the application of fertilizers as well as pesticides. Excess amounts of agrochemicals often leach into the soil where they often enter the groundwater bodies. This leads to a deterioration of water quality to the point where the water becomes unsuitable for human consumption. Thus the application of agrochemicals should also be optimized in order to avoid adverse effects on groundwater quality. In fact the use of agrochemicals and the aforementioned changes in agricultural techniques should be considered jointly in order to arrive at best practices that not only maximize yield but also minimize water use and the possible impact on groundwater quality.

3. Eliminate or reduce subsidies for water prices. Subsidies of various kinds have in the past contributed either to excessive water use and/or – in the case of agriculture – to cropping patterns that are economically and environmentally unsustainable (see above). Eliminating subsidies for water prices for any sector is not only desirable with regard to healthy and just economic development, it is also required with regard to the EU-WFD's principal objective of achieving full cost recovery (see above).

4. Promote cultivation of crops that have a high potential on the domestic and the foreign market (eliminate wasting products and water). This refers to the case described above of the Cyprus banana and to similar practices on other islands. Farmers need to be informed about possible alternatives and should be encouraged to pursue these, possibly with the help of government agencies or – preferentially – with stakeholder-controlled initiatives (for example farmers' marketing organizations).

5. Provide assistance in capacity-building of farmers and for investments in modern irrigation technology. Providing information and assistance in rational and careful water consumption as part of the capacity-building of stakeholders on the islands is a particularly important strategy to enable enhanced adaptation and to reduce vulnerability to water scarcity. This can take place on various levels and in any sector with sizeable water needs. As mentioned above, the agricultural industry is a particularly pertinent point in case.

6. Provide economic incentives for rational water use in all sectors. This measure refers to some of the strategies already mentioned (for example points 1 and 4, above). Incentives may be provided through for example specific water tariffs and or relaxation of quotas and limitations on water consumption for those sectors that strive for a more rational use of potable water.

The MEDIS project

Vulnerability and Adaptation: Social, Institutional and Political Dimensions

Vulnerability to water scarcity under this dimension relates to a number of issues that are either of a social, institutional or political nature. More specifically, the following issues should be taken into account.

With regard to the social component of the problem, the prevalence of inadequate or even false perceptions of the water issue by many stakeholders (often summarized by the statement: 'water is only a problem when it is scarce') has in many instances rendered initiatives for a more rational use of water unsuccessful. This is an issue that is hard to 'quantify' or even understand as it is often rooted in long-standing traditions and customs that are hard to break.

A problem often related to this issue has to do with traditional ownerships of wells and other water sources. It is often impossible to convince stakeholders to give up or share what they consider their property which has belonged to their family for many generations. Thus cultivating an understanding for a more just and equitable distribution of water among the various user groups is mostly considered intrusive and consequently rejected. Both issues lead not only to water use beyond an acceptable level, but they also make it extremely difficult to establish appropriate water management practices aimed at a controlled and equitable distribution of water to all user groups.

Also along the lines of social patterns and traditions is the widespread practice of extracting water from wells that are not registered, let alone metered. Such practices, which have evolved over centuries, sometimes even encouraged by government directives or recommendations, are considered quite legitimate and are hard to change. However they contribute not only to a lack of appropriate and sufficient data for water management planning but also to an uncontrolled and often excessive exploitation of already stressed reservoirs.

Against this background of a traditional and often inadequate problem awareness lies the issue of competition for water resources on an island that is not only prevalent between different sectors, as mentioned above. Competition for existing resources, that are often quite plentiful when considered integratively for the entire island, takes place on all levels, from individuals to municipalities to prefectures or regions. The overall effect of such competition is often an unsustainable if not a wasteful use of water by those consumers who claim to have the rights on the water resource in their sphere of interest. It also creates problems when larger-scale, harmonized management schemes are being envisioned and implemented, such as the EU-WFD.

With regard to institutional and legal issues, one is often surprised to learn that comprehensive and fairly sufficient regulations, directives and laws exist that could potentially ensure an appropriate water management on the islands and avoid some of the scarcity and water stress experienced today. However this requires that these regulations are properly monitored and enforced. As mentioned above, traditional ownership and the extraction of water from unmetered wells represents but one of the problems in that regard.

In addition, what is also observed in some instances is the fact that violations of laws and directives are not penalized. Thus, even if an infringement of a law is being recognized, local authorities often refrain from imposing the associated penalty, hence undermining the value of these laws and their usefulness for an effective and equitable water management regime.

Effective water management also hinges on an understandable and acceptable regulatory and administrative structure. However what is often observed is a network of complex, diverse and overlapping responsibilities (Figure 4.9), that not only limits acceptance by local stakeholders but also prevents the introduction of harmonized management regimes according to the requirements of the EU-WFD.

Moreover being part of a larger country (except for Cyprus), whose capital lies usually on the mainland creates a typical situation of the island being on the periphery of the respective country. This implies that most of the laws that govern water management pay only minor attention to the specific situations prevailing on the islands. This in turn results in reduced acceptance and in difficulties imposing these laws on the island. Regulations from outside the country such as the EU-WFD meet even more opposition, or at least negligence, by the inhabitants of the islands.

Being decided outside the islands, political decisions on new laws and regulations often lack a sufficient factual basis or are even based on false information about relevant facts. This has in some instances led to laws that are counter-productive with regard to a sustainable water management regime on the islands. Along the same lines, some policies and recommendations, often related to agricultural practices, have proven to be inadequate and have contributed to wasteful use of water resources (see above).

What are possible adaptive strategies to address these problems and shortcomings? Again, we will introduce a number of recommendations that are by no means exhaustive and should only be viewed as indicative of possible solutions to be pursued:

1. Public awareness campaign (water use, ownership, conflicts); capacity building. This recommendation seems to be particularly pertinent in light of the aforementioned problems. Again, this measure should be

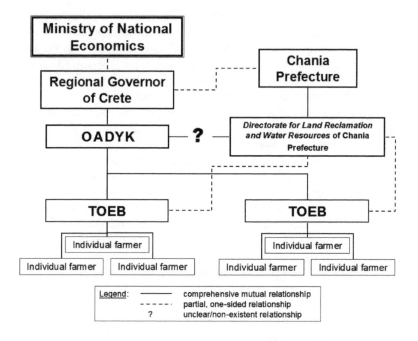

Note: OADYK stands for Organization for the Development of Western Crete; a TOEB is
a Local Farmers' Irrigation Organization

Figure 4.9   *Schematic depiction of the major elements of the water*
management regime in Chania Prefecture, Crete, Greece

geared specifically to particular stakeholder groups and should enable
a more adequate problem awareness as well as an enhanced capacity to
deal with water scarcity problems.

2. Implement a more complete monitoring of water extraction. As men-
    tioned before, the legal and regulatory instruments to enable an ade-
    quate water management regime on the islands is often already in
    existence. However to utilize such regulations, proper instruments for
    comprehensive monitoring need to be established and/or maintained.

3. Improve enforcement of existing rules and regulations. Equally impor-
    tant are adequate, and consequently executed, enforcement mecha-
    nisms. This also relates to the penalties that are imposed in cases of
    violation and that need to be followed through consequently and
    coherently.

4. Simplify and enhance efficiency of water administration. Administrative
    structures that are hard to comprehend and understand are prone to be

ineffective. Thus there should be attempts to simplify and reduce the administrative mechanisms and structures related to water management, in order to improve acceptance by the stakeholders and water consumers.

5. Transfer of power to regional and local decision-makers. A particularly effective way to increase administrative efficiency is the transfer of power from central (distant) government institutions to local or regional authorities. The aforementioned TOEBs (Figure 4.9) are a particularly positive case in point. However care should be taken to ensure that such institutions do not become an obstacle to harmonized and larger-scale water management regimes such as the EU-WFD. In making this statement, we are well aware that what we are proposing what constitutes a fine balance to be struck between local or regional autonomy and national or international jurisdiction by the political decision-makers. However we are convinced that institutions such as the TOEBs are much better suited to become partners in the EU-WFD than individual users or single municipalities.

6. Encourage stakeholder-controlled water management structures. This recommendation follows directly from what has been said above. Again, we are convinced that the encouragement of stakeholder-driven water management practices prepares the islands much better for dealing with water scarcity but also for the implementation of the EU-WFD than individual stakeholders or stakeholder groups.

7. Ensure/improve adequate factual basis for political decision-making. This is a plea for a more extensive and more adequate alliance between political decision-makers and the scientific community. We are convinced that science has to play a major role in devising new strategies for sustainable water management on Mediterranean islands. However as has been stressed throughout this chapter, we are equally convinced that such strategies need the input from and the consent of all relevant stakeholders on the islands.

CONCLUSIONS

The availability of water in sufficient quantities and of adequate quality on Mediterranean islands is a problem of significant importance. The EU Water Framework Directive aims to address water management in a comprehensive and harmonized manner. However implementing the EU-WFD meets a number of major challenges, not the least on the islands of the Mediterranean. The EU-funded research project MEDIS aims to address the specific problems on the islands, strives towards common solutions through a process of systematic comparison of answers that have been found on each island, and intends to derive recommendations for a sustainable, equitable and stakeholder-driven water management regime on the islands. In so doing, emphasis lies on a holistic, interdisciplinary research strategy that strives to involve stakeholders in each phase of the project.

Such a holistic research approach is also pertinent when addressing the problem of current and future water scarcity on the islands. In considering water scarcity, we focus on three vulnerability dimensions: the physical and environmental dimension; the economic and regulatory dimension; and the social, institutional and political dimension. We present brief summaries on current and future challenges to be faced for each of the aspects. This presents the basis for a set of recommendations and strategies that serve both goals: the formulation of recommendations for improved water management and the reduction of vulnerabilities to water scarcity on Mediterranean islands.

While not to be considered exhaustive or complete, we are convinced that these recommendations will serve to alleviate some of the problems currently faced with regard to water availability and to prepare Mediterranean islands better for future water problems and a swift and effective implementation of the EU-WFD.

ACKNOWLEDGEMENTS

We acknowledge support of MEDIS by the European Commission under contract number EVK1-CT-2001-00092 and would like to thank Dr Panagiotis Balabanis, the responsible officer at the Commission, for his support. We would also like to thank all individuals who have contributed to MEDIS at the partner institutions and particularly those colleagues who have contributed data and information for the present publication, most notably my colleague at the Centre for Environmental Research, Dr Antonia Donta.

NOTES

1. The MEDIS consortium consists of the following institutions: Centre for Environmental Research, University of Münster, Germany; Institute for Geoinformatics, University of Münster, Germany; Institute for Geophysics, University of Münster, Germany; Centre for Ecology and Hydrology, National Environmental Research Council, UK; Department of Political and Social Sciences, University of Cyprus, Cyprus; Institute of Electronic Structure and Laser, Foundation for Research and Technology, Hellas, Greece; NAGREF, Subtropical Plants and Olive Tree Institute, Greece; Regional Governor of Crete, Water Resources Management Department, Greece; Dipartimento di Costruzioni e Tecnologie

Avanzate, University of Messina, Italy; Système Physique de l'Environement – URA CNRS 2053, Université de Corse, France; Dep. de Ingenieria del Terreno, Universitat Polytecnica de Catalonya, Spain; Balearic Island University, Spain. For further details see: http://www.uni-muenster.de/Umweltforschung/medis/index.html.
2. The term 'water stress' describes pressures on water resources quantity and quality, resulting in the inability to meet human and environmental needs and generating conflicts and negative impacts.
3. The term 'water scarcity' depicts an imbalance between availability of (renewable) water resources and water demand for different uses and also embraces water quality aspects (see below).
4. Here and in the remainder of this chapter, we follow the approach taken by the Intergovernmental Panel on Climate Change (IPCC) and use the terms 'adaptability' and 'adaptive capacity' synonymously.

REFERENCES

Alcamo, J., T. Henrichs and T. Rösch (2000), 'World Water in 2025 – Global modeling and scenario analysis for the World Commission on Water for the 21st Century', Center for Environmental Systems Research, University of Kassel, Germany; http://www.usf.uni-kassel.de/usf/archiv/dokumente/kwws/kwws.2.pdf.
Alcamo, J. and Image Project (1994), *IMAGE 2.0: Integrated Modelling of Global Climate Change*, Dordrecht and Boston: Kluwer Academic Publishers.
Arnell, M., C. Liu, R. Compagnucci, L. da Cunha, K. Hanaki, C. Howe, G. Mailu, I. Shiklomanov and E. Stakhiv (2001), 'Hydrology and water resources', in J.J. McCarthy, O.F. Canziani, N.A. Leary, D.J. Dokken and K.S. White (eds), *IPCC, 2001: Climate Change 2001: Impacts, Adaptation and Vulnerability. Contribution of Working Group II to the Third Assessment Report of the Intergovernmental Panel on Climate Change*, Cambridge, UK and New York, USA: Cambridge University Press, pp. 191–234.
Bolle, H.-J (2003a), 'Climate, climate variability, and impacts in the Mediterranean area: an overview', in *Mediterranean Climate – Variability and Trends*, Volume 1 in *Regional Climate Studies*, Berlin, Heidelberg and New York: Springer-Verlag, pp. 5–86.
Bolle, H.-J. (ed.) (2003b), *Mediterranean Climate – Variability and Trends*; Volume 1 in *Regional Climate Studies*, Berlin, Heidelberg and New York: Springer-Verlag, 372.
Burnett, W.C., H. Bokuniewicz, M. Huettel, W.S. Moore and M. Taniguchi (2003), 'Groundwater and pore water inputs to the coastal zone', *Biogeochemistry*, **66**, 3–33.
Carter, T., M. Parry, S. Nishioka and H. Harasawa (1996), 'Technical guidelines for assessing climate change impacts and adaptations', in R.T. Watson, M.C. Zinyovera, R.H. Moss, and D.J. Dokken (eds), *Climate Change 1995: The Science of Climate Change. Contribution of Working Group II to the Second Assessment Report of the Intergovernmental Panel on Climate Change*, Cambridge: University of Cambridge Press, UK, pp. 823–33.
Dowlatabadi, H. and M.G. Morgan (1993), 'Integrated assessment of climate change', *Science*, **259** (5103), 1813, 1932.
Gleick, P.H. (2000), 'The changing water paradigm – a look at twenty-first century water resources development', *Water International*, **25** (1), 127–38.

Houghton, J.T., Y. Ding, D.J. Griggs, M. Noguer, P.J. van der Linden, X. Dai, K. Maskell and C.A. Johnson (eds) (2001), *IPCC, 2001: Climate Change 2001: The Scientific Basis. Contribution of Working Group I to the Third Assessment Report of the Intergovernmental Panel on Climate Change*, UK and New York, USA: Cambridge University Press.

IPCC (2001), 'Annex B. Glossary of Terms', http://www.ipcc.ch/pub/syrgloss.pdf.

Janssen, M. (1998), *Modelling Global Changes. The Art of Integrated Assessment Modelling*, Cheltenham, UK and Lyme, USA, Edward Elgar Publishing.

Lange, M.A. (2000), Integrated global change impact assessments, in M. Nuttal and T.C. Callaghan (eds) *The Arctic: Environment, People, Policy*, Amsterdam: Harwood Academic Publishers, pp. 517–53.

Lange, M.A. (2001), 'Global changes and their impacts: basic concepts and methods', in M.A. Lange (ed.), *IRISEN. Integrated Regional Impact Studies in the European North. Proceedings of an Advanced Study Course at Abisko Research Station, Sweden, on July 4–16, 1999*, Institute for Geophysics, University of Münster, Germany, pp. 57–88.

Lange, M.A., S.J. Cohen and P. Kuhry (1999), 'Integrated global change impacts studies in the Arctic: the role of the stakeholders', *Polar Research*, **18** (2), 389–96.

Lange, M.A. and MEDIS consortium (2004), 'Water management on Mediterranean islands: current issues and perspectives', in *Proceedings of IDS Water 2004*, http://www.idswater.com/Admin/Images/Paper/Paper_47/ Manfred%20Lange-Paper. pdf, May 10–28.

Lehner, B., T. Henrichs, P. Döll and J. Alcamo (2001), 'EuroWasser – model-based assessment of European water resources and hydrology in the face of global change', Center for Environmental Systems Research, University of Kassel, Germany, http://www.usf.uni-kassel.de.

Nordhaus, W.D. (1992), 'An optimal transition path for controlling greenhouse gases', *Science*, **258** (5086), 1315–19.

Olesen, J.E. and M. Bindi (2002), 'Consequences of climate change for European agricultural productivity, land use and policy', *European Journal of Agronomy*, **16**, 239–62.

Parry, M. and T. Carter (1998), *Climate Impact and Adaptation Assessment*, London: Earthscan.

Rayner, S. and E.L. Malone (eds) (1998), *Human Choice and Climate Change. Volume 3 – Tools for Policy Analysis*; Columbus, OH: Battelle Press.

Rosenberg, N.J., P.R. Crosson, K.D. Frederick, W.E. Easterling, M.S. McKenny, M.D. Bowes, R.A. Sedjo, J. Dramstadter, L.A. Katz and K.M. Lemon (1993), 'The MINK Methodology: background and baseline', *Climatic Change*, **24**, 7–22.

Rotmans, J. (2000), 'Integrated assessment: a birds eye view', FIRMA.

Rotmans, J. and H. Dowlatabadi (1998), 'Integrated assessment modeling', in S. Rayner and E.L. Malone (eds), *Human Choice and Climate Change. Volume Three: The Tools for Policy Analysis*, Columbus, OH: Battelle Press, pp. 291–377.

Rotmans, J. and M. van Asselt (1996), 'Integrated assessment: a growing child on its way to maturity', *Climatic Change*, **34**, 327–36.

Scheraga, J.D. and A.E. Grambsch (1998), 'Risks, opportunities, and adaptation to climate change', *Climate Research*, **10**, 85–95.

Weyant, J., O. Davidson, H. Dowlatabadi, J. Edmonds, M. Grubb, E.A. Parson, R. Richels, J. Rotmans, P.R. Shukla, R.S.J. Tol, W. Cline and S. Fankhauser (1996), 'Integrated assessment of climate change: an overview and comparison of approaches and results', in J.P. Bruce, H. Lee and E.F. Haites (eds), *Climate Change 1995 – Economic and Social Dimensions of Climate Change. Contribution of Working Group III to the Second Assessment Report of the Intergovernmental Panel on Climate Change*, Cambridge: University of Cambridge Press, pp. 367–96.

Xoplaki, E. (2002), 'Climate variability over the Mediterranean', PhD, Universität Bern and University of Thessaloniki, Bern, Switzerland and Thessaloniki, Greece, 213.

Xoplaki, E., J. Gonzalez-Rouco, J. Luterbacher and H. Wanner (2004), 'Wet season Mediterranean precipitation variability: influence of large-scale dynamics and trends', *Climate Dynamics*, **23**, 63–78.

Yarnal, B. (1998), 'Integrated regional assessment and climate change impacts in river basins', *Climate Research*, **11**, 65–74.

5. Water use in agriculture on Mediterranean islands: present situation and future perspective

Kostas Chartzoulakis and Maria Bertaki

INTRODUCTION

Water is considered as the most critical resource for sustainable development in most Mediterranean countries. It is essential not only for agriculture, industry and economic growth, but also it is the most important component of the environment, with significant impact on health and nature conservation. Currently, the rapid growth of population, together with the extension of irrigation and industrial development, are stressing the quantity and quality aspects of the natural system. Because of the increasing problems, man has begun to realize that he can no longer follow a 'use and discard' methodology with either water resources or any other natural resource. As a result, the need for a consistent policy of rational management of the water resources has become evident.

Global agriculture now accounts for 70 per cent of water used, with many parts of the world using even more. The global irrigated area has increased more than sixfold over the last century, from approximately 40 million hectares in 1900 to more than 260 million hectares in 1999 (Postel, 1999; FAO, 1999). Today 40 per cent of the world's food comes from the 18 per cent of the cropland that is irrigated. Irrigated areas increase almost 1 per cent per year and the irrigation water demand will increase by 13.6 per cent by 2025 (Rosegrant and Cai, 2002). On the other hand, 8–15 per cent of fresh water supplies will be diverted from agriculture to meet the increased demand of domestic use and industry. Furthermore, the efficiency of irrigation is very low, since only 55 per cent of the water is used by the crop (Figure 5.1). In developed agriculture, losses due to poor nutrition and plant health are greatly reduced, to the extent that crop losses relating to water availability continue to exceed those from all other causes (Passioura, 2002). To overcome water shortages for agriculture is essential to increase water use efficiency and to use marginal waters (reclaimed, saline, drainage) for irrigation.

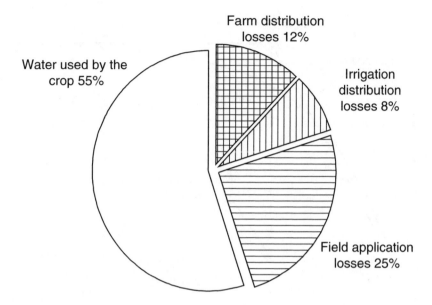

Figure 5.1   *Water losses in agriculture*

The sustainable use of water is a priority for agriculture in water-scarce areas. Imbalances between availability and demand, degradation of surface and groundwater quality, inter-sectorial competition and inter-regional conflicts often occur in these places. So under scarcity conditions considerable effort has been devoted over time to introduce policies aiming to increase water efficiency, based on the assertion that more can be achieved with less water through better management. Better management usually refers to improvement of allocative and/or irrigation water efficiency. The former is closely related to adequate pricing, while the latter depends on the type of irrigation technology, environmental conditions and on scheduling of water application. It is well known that crop yield increases with water availability in the root zone, until 'saturation level', above which there is little effect (Hillel, 1997). The yield response curve (Figure 5.2) of specific crops depends on various factors, such as weather conditions and soil type as well as the reduction of agricultural inputs like fertilizers and pesticides. Therefore it is difficult for a farmer to tell at any given moment whether there is a water deficit or not. Since overabundant water usually does not cause harm, farmers tend to 'play safe' and increase the irrigation amount, especially when associated costs are low.

Specialists on water resources in the Mediterranean are becoming more and more convinced that growing scarcity and misuse are the major threats

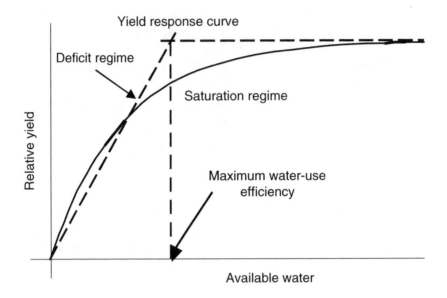

Figure 5.2   Plant yield response to water

not only for sustainable agricultural development, which accounts for up to 80 per cent of the water consumption, but also to the other water use sectors. The situation has worsened during recent decades due to the occurrence of occasional droughts, explosive urban growth and water quality degradation.

On Mediterranean islands, due to the technical and financial constrains of transporting water from mainland, the situation is even worse. In most countries the percentage of agricultural contribution to GDP has been declining over recent decades, reflecting the relative decrease in importance of agriculture in comparison to other economic sectors. Although the contribution of agriculture to GDP is low, ranging from 13 per cent in Crete to 1.5 per cent in Mallorca (Figure 5.3), agricultural water use is an essential element not only for crop production but also for the environment and the tourism industry.

The overall objective of this chapter is to describe briefly the existing situation and problems of water resources used for agriculture on Mediterranean islands, as well as the different measures that should be applied to secure the availability of water and to reduce water pollution.

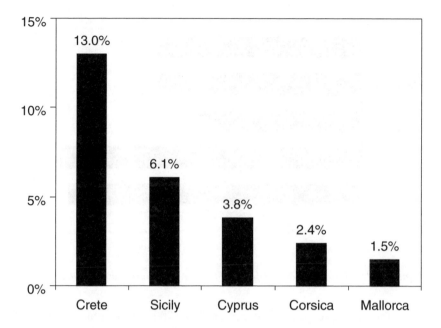

Figure 5.3   Contribution of agriculture to island economy

WATER RESOURCES AND AGRICULTURE

Climate

Climate variability is one of the many factors influencing water resources availability in the Mediterranean islands. The mean average rainfall ranges from 500 mm/year in Cyprus up to 900 mm/year in Crete and Corsica (Figure 5.4). However this amount has uneven distribution in time and space in each island. In eastern Mediterranean islands, like Cyprus and Crete, about 70–80 per cent of total rainfall occurs in three to four months (November to February) while summers are usually long and dry.

Cyprus has the lowest mean annual rainfall rate among the islands but shows substantial variation from 300 mm in the plains to over 1000 mm on the Troodos Mountains. Rainfall in Cyprus has reduced about 15 per cent during the last 100 years. Average annual precipitation is low in Mallorca and Sicily (about 600 mm/year). However in Mallorca it varies from 1400 mm/year in the Tramundana Range to 400 mm/year in the southern part of the island. The annual rainfall in Crete ranges from 300 to 700 mm

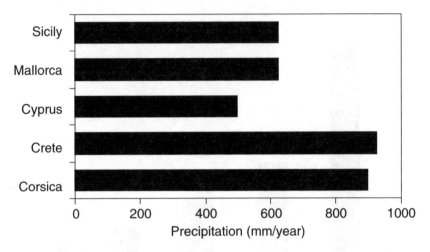

Figure 5.4   Mean annual precipitation in the Mediterranean islands

in the low areas and along the coast, and from 700 to 1000 mm in the plains of the mainland, while in the mountainous areas it reaches up to 2000 mm (Chartzoulakis et al., 2001). Long series of rainfall data all over Crete do not show any significant change in precipitation over the years (Markou-Iakovaki, 1979; Macheras and Koliva-Machera, 1990).

The global change will definitely affect the climate of Mediterranean islands. According to the Intergovernmental Panel on Climate Change (IPCC), there will be a global surface temperature increase of 1.7–4.0°C by 2100 (IPCC, 2001a). Predictions for the future indicate that annual temperature for the coastal areas of the eastern Mediterranean will be increased by about 1.5°C by 2050 (Ragab and Prudhomme, 2002). Furthermore, there is a decreasing trend in annual precipitation in Southern Europe and the Mediterranean region (Hurrell and van Loon, 1997). Data for the area of Heraklion, Crete show that despite the fact that annual precipitation was not clearly reduced during the second half of the twentieth century, a significant reduction of summer precipitation over the last 20 years was observed (Figure 5.5). This is a general trend in the Mediterranean region since summer rainfall is now 20 per cent less in the area than at the end of the nineteenth century, while predictions for 2050 indicate that annual precipitation will be reduced from 5–20 per cent in Greece, with higher percentages of reduction during summer (Ragab and Prudhomme, 2002).

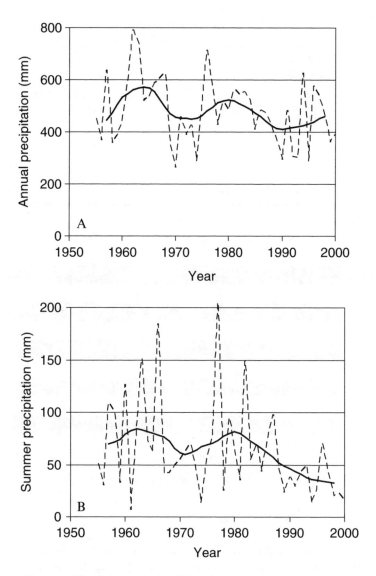

Source: European Climate Assessment and Dataset.

*Figure 5.5   Changes in the sum of annual (A) and summer (B)
            precipitation during the second half of the twentieth century in
            the area of Heraklion*

Table 5.1   Total water used (Mm³) and origin of the water

Island	Total water used (Mm³)	Origin of water			
		Ground-water	Surface water	Recycled water	Desalinated water
Corsica	61	30	70	–	–
Crete	372	93	7	–	–
Cyprus	266	46	38	1	15
Mallorca	253	83	3	7	7
Sicily	1875	78	21	–	1

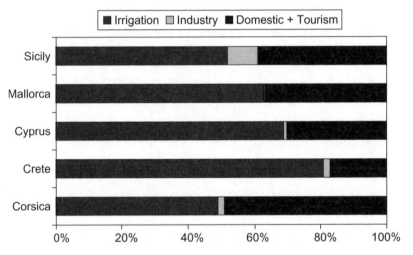

Figure 5.6   Water allocation among the different sectors in the islands

Water Resources and Irrigation

The total available water resources in Mediterranean islands participating in MEDIS are shown in Table 5.1. Agriculture is by far the main user, consuming more than 50 per cent of available water resources (Figure 5.6), ranging from 55 per cent in Corsica up to 82 per cent in Crete. It is also the sector least efficient in water use, since irrigation efficiency is estimated at only 55 per cent. Agriculture creates pressures on water resources through direct abstraction for agricultural uses such as irrigation and watering of livestock and by potentially polluting activities such as the overuse of fertilizers and pesticides.

Table 5.2   Origin of irrigation water in Mediterranean islands

	Cyprus	Mallorca	Crete	Corsica	Sicily
Groundwater	55%	91%	92%	–	68%
Surface water	44%	–	8%	100%	32%
Recycled water	1%	9%	–	–	–

Groundwater is the main source of irrigation water in most islands (Table 5.2), except Corsica, where 100 per cent of the irrigation water comes from surface reservoirs. Although treated wastewater is a valuable irrigation water resource, its use is very low. Cyprus is the only island where the contribution of treated wastewater for irrigation is 1 per cent. In Mallorca treated wastewater is used for the irrigation of golf courses, which is not considered as irrigated agriculture. However the reuse for irrigation of the effluent from existing treatment plants may increase the irrigated areas in the islands; for example in Crete irrigated area could be increased by 5.3 per cent. The high cost of desalination water limits its use for irrigation.

In Crete the main source of irrigation water is groundwater, with 87 per cent of the total water used coming from subterranean sources. In Cyprus the main source of irrigation water is groundwater with 55 per cent of water used for agriculture coming from groundwater, 44 per cent from surface water and 1 per cent from recycled water. In Mallorca 91 per cent of the irrigation water for agricultural production comes from groundwater sources whilst urban treated wastewater is used mainly for the irrigation of golf courses and city parks. In Sicily the origin of irrigation water is mostly groundwater (68 per cent) whereas in Corsica, essentially all irrigation water comes from surface waters.

AGRICULTURE AND CROPS

The area used for agriculture varies a lot among the islands, ranging from 16 per cent in Cyprus up to 47 per cent in Sicily (Figure 5.7). In most of the islands there is a slight trend in reducing agricultural land; in Crete agricultural land reduced by 7 per cent in the period 1961–2001 whereas the reduction in Cyprus was 1 per cent in the period 1995–2000. In Sicily, even though agriculture contributes only by 6 per cent in GDP, almost half of the island area is used for agriculture. In Mallorca and Crete the percentage of the agricultural land is also high (more than 35 per cent) whereas in Corsica and Cyprus it is below 20 per cent.

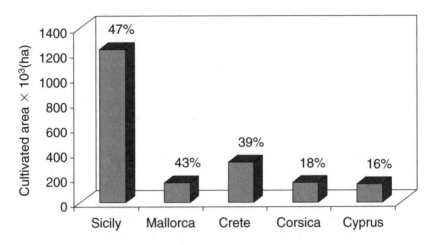

Figure 5.7   Area used for agriculture in Mediterranean islands

Although the crops grown on Mediterranean islands are mainly the same due to similar climatic conditions, there are significant differences in the importance of each crop among the islands. The main groups of crops grown on Mediterranean islands and their percentage are shown in Figure 5.8.

Tree crops are the main group of crops in Crete and Cyprus, while row crops dominate in Sicily, Mallorca and Corsica. Tree crops include citrus, olives, nuts, kiwi and cherries, while row crops include grain cereals, edible pulses, fodder crops and seeds and industrial plants. Of tree crops, olives occupy 60 per cent of the total cultivated area in Crete, while citrus is the dominant tree crop for Sicily and Cyprus occupying 41.65 and 20 per cent of the total cultivated area respectively. In Cyprus vegetable crops like tomatoes, potatoes and melons are very important, covering more than 40 per cent of the agricultural land. Of row crops, grain cereals occupy 38.8 per cent of the total cultivated area in Mallorca, wheat occupies 40.5 per cent in Sicily while fodder crops (maize, lucerne) occupy 67 per cent in Corsica. Grapevines are an important crop in Corsica, covering more than 30 per cent of the agricultural land, while their cultivation in Sicily and Crete covers 22.8 and 9.6 per cent respectively.

The demand for irrigation is high on all islands even though only a small percentage of agricultural land is irrigated (ranging from 8.8 per cent in Mallorca up to 33.4 per cent in Crete). Although Mallorca has the lower percentage of irrigated agriculture (8.8 per cent), the water allocated to agriculture is more than 60 per cent of the total water consumption, indicating that the cultivated crops (mainly row crops) are high water-demanding crops.

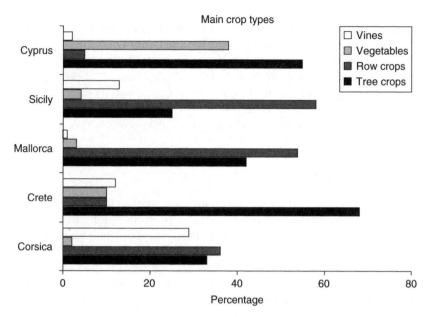

Figure 5.8   Main crop groups cultivated in Mediterranean islands

Table 5.3   Cultivated and irrigated area in Mediterranean islands

	Cultivated area %	Cultivated area ha	Irrigated area %	Irrigated area ha
Crete	39.0	322 230	33.4	107 909
Cyprus	15.5	145 000	25.0	36 000
Mallorca	42.7	155 450	8.8	13 748
Corsica	18.0	155 890	14.3	22 330
Sicily	47.0	1 226 253	17.6	216 072

In Crete 91 per cent of vegetables, 34 per cent of row crops, 36.3 per cent of fruit trees and 45 per cent of grapevines are irrigated. There has been an increase of more than 30 per cent in the irrigated area during recent decades in the island. Of fruit trees, olives occupy the largest percentage (68 per cent) of the irrigated area.

In Cyprus tree crops, and citrus specifically, consume the highest amount of water (32 per cent) followed by deciduous crops (apples, peaches, cherries, pears, plums, figs, walnuts, pecan nuts and pomegranates) and olives

(11 and 5 per cent respectively). In Mallorca, the largest part of the irrigated area is occupied by fodder crops (51.2 per cent) followed by vegetables (19.7 per cent). Consequently the biggest water consumers are fodder crops, consuming 60.8 per cent of the total irrigation water, followed by vegetables (17.5 per cent), potatoes (9.4 per cent) and citrus trees (8.3 per cent). In Corsica fruit trees (of which 32.5 per cent are citrus) occupy the largest part of the irrigated land (53 per cent) while olives represent 22.8 per cent of the tree crops. In Sicily irrigated land is occupied by vineyards, olive and citrus trees.

Crop Water Requirements

It is difficult to find and interpret data on water applied for each crop, since the amount of water used depends on the weather conditions, the soil type, the method of irrigation used and the effectiveness of water management. Although the amount of water actually applied to each crop is measured in most cases, because it is obligatory, data are not available. In some islands (Crete, Cyprus) quotas or suggestions on the seasonal irrigation water amount have been applied by local authorities for public operated irrigation networks.

In order to identify the high water-demanding crops grown in Mediterranean islands, an estimation of potential evapotranspiration (ETo) has been made using the Penman–Monteith method (FAO, 1998), or that of Hargreaves (Hargreaves and Samani, 1985; Hargreaves 1994) in the case of lack of meteorological data. With the Penman–Monteith method ETo is estimated by the formula:

$$ETo = \frac{0.408\Delta(R_n - G) + \gamma\frac{900}{T+273}u_2(e_s - e_a)}{\Delta + \gamma(1 + 0.34u_2)}$$

where:
ETo	reference evapotranspiration [mm day^{-1}]
Rn	net radiation at the crop surface [MJ m^{-2} day^{-1}]
G	soil heat flux density [MJ m^{-2} day^{-1}]
T	air temperature at 2m height [°C]
u_2	wind speed at 2m height [m s^{-1}]
es	saturation vapour pressure [kPa]
ea	actual vapour pressure [kPa]
$es-ea$	saturation vapour pressure deficit [kPa]
Δ	slope vapour pressure curve [kPa °C^{-1}]
γ	psychrometric constant [kPa °C^{-1}]

With Hargreaves method ETo is estimated by the formula:

$$ETo = 0.0023 \; Ra \; (T_{aver} + 17.8)(T_{max} - T_{min})^{0.5}$$

where: Ra extraterrestrial radiation [MJ m^{-2} day^{-1}]

T_{aver} average daily temperature defined as the average of the mean daily maximum and mean daily minimum temperature [°C]

T_{max} mean daily maximum temperature [°C]

T_{min} mean daily minimum temperature [°C]

Crop water requirements were then estimated in each island using crop coefficients and effective rainfall. Figure 5.9 illustrates the crop water requirements of main crops in each island. Estimated values of course do not depict the actual water used by farmers, which in most cases exceed by far the calculated values.

Taking into account the estimated crop water requirements, citrus is the high water-demanding crop for Cyprus, Crete and Sicily, followed by fodder crops (lucerne, maize) and vegetables (tomatoes, potatoes and so on). It is notable that Colocasia, a local open field vegetable of Cyprus, is an extremely water-demanding crop, so that the local authorities made efforts – and partially succeeded – to reduce its cultivation during recent decades. Olive is the least water-demanding crop in the Mediterranean islands. The crop water requirement must be taken into consideration in scheduling agricultural reforms and water management policies.

Irrigation Systems and Scheduling

Modern irrigation systems have been widely used in recent decades (drip, sprinkler, micro-irrigation) on all islands. Localized (drip or mini-sprinklers) irrigation systems are mainly used for tree crops (olives, citrus and deciduous trees), while sprinkler irrigation is dominant for fodder crops and some vegetables (potatoes in Mallorca and Cyprus). For vegetable crops and greenhouses, advanced drip irrigation systems are used on all islands, including fertilizer application through the system. Traditional surface irrigation (furrows, basins, flooding) are still used in some cases, but have generally been replaced by modern irrigation systems.

Irrigation scheduling is another aspect of the utmost importance for the appropriate irrigation of horticultural crops. It consists of a set of procedures which allow, for a given crop, the farmer to find out when and how much to irrigate. Irrigation scheduling methods are based on environmental, physiological and soil parameters. The continuous technical progress in

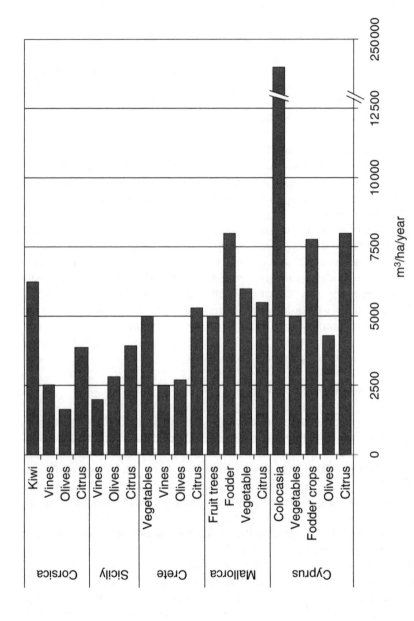

Figure 5.9 Crop water requirements in the islands

the irrigation scheduling methods using plant physiological indices (leaf water potential, stomata opening, changes in diameter of selected organs, infrared thermometry, refractometry of the sap, and so on), although showing important innovations, involve measurements that are complex, time-consuming and difficult to integrate and require highly qualified farmers. Furthermore the cost of such methods is very high, besides other difficulties, and the majority of the farmers on the Mediterranean islands do not use them at all.

For tree crops, irrigation scheduling is mainly empirical, although in some cases it is based on meteorological parameters (mainly Class A pan-evaporation and Reference evapotranspiration ETo) provided to farmers by local authorities (Crete, Cyprus) or co-operatives. For vegetables, especially in greenhouses, the monitoring of soil moisture (by tensiometers, gypsum blocks or gravimetrically) is the most common method used for irrigation scheduling, since it assures a low-cost, simple operation and reliable estimation of soil water status.

PRICE OF IRRIGATION WATER

The price of irrigation water varies greatly among the islands due to different pricing structure and policies. Furthermore, water prices vary among different areas in the same island or even among catchments.

In Crete, the price of water per cubic metre varies greatly between catchment areas and even within the same catchment area, depending mainly on the managing agency. In publicly developed and operated irrigation projects the price of water does not fully cover operation and maintenance (O&M) or capital replacement costs. So in the large publicly operated irrigation projects the price of water is as low as 0.07–0.08 € per m³, whereas in community or municipality operated projects it reaches 0.10–0.15 € and in some private projects it reaches 0.23–0.35 €. The price of irrigation water in Cyprus is on average 0.10 €/m³, in Mallorca it varies between 0.18 and 2.4 €/m³, while in Corsica the average price is 0.50 €/m³.

SUSTAINABLE WATER MANAGEMENT IN AGRICULTURE: RECOMMENDATIONS

Sustainable water management in agriculture has the basic goal of matching water availability and water needs in quantity and quality, in space and time, at reasonable cost and with acceptable environmental impact. The adoption of sustainable water management on Mediterranean islands is not only a technological problem but involves many other considerations relative to the social behaviour of rural communities, the economic constraints, or the legal and institutional framework that may favour the adoption of some measures and not others. The implementation of a sustainable water management programme in agriculture for achieving the above-mentioned goal requires developments in the following areas.

A. Adoption of Best Irrigation Practices

In most Mediterranean islands irrigation efficiency can be maximized by the best irrigation practices being adopted by farmers or water authorities. Such practices include:

Reduction of water losses   Water leakages in the conveyance, distribution and application networks should be detected via advanced technologies, for example telemetry systems, GIS or remote sensing. Old water projects experiencing considerable water losses should be rehabilitated and modernized.

Improve the efficiency of the irrigation system used   Improvements in surface irrigation methods include land levelling and reduced widths and/or shortened lengths.
For on-farm water distribution, use the following:

1.   grated pipes and lay flat pipes,
2.   buried pipes for basin and borders,
3.   lined on-farm distribution canals,
4.   construction of on-farm earth canals,
5.   control of discharges and seepages.

For improvements in sprinkler irrigation systems do the following:

1.   adopt or correct sprinkler spacing,
2.   design pressure variation so that it does not exceed 20 per cent of the average sprinkler pressure,
3.   use pressure regulators in sloping fields,
4.   use monitoring and pressure adjustment equipments,
5.   apply irrigation during non-windy periods,
6.   for windy areas adopt larger sprinkler drops,
7.   adopt water application rates that are smaller than the infiltration rate of the soil,
8.   adopt a careful system of maintenance.

Improvements in localized irrigation systems aiming to reduce the volumes of water applied and increase the water productivity include the use of a single dripline for a double-row crop, the use of micro-sprayers in high-infiltration soils, the adjustment of the duration of water application and timing to soil and crop characteristics, the control of pressure and discharge variations, the use of appropriate filters for the water quality and the characteristics of the emitter used, and the adoption of careful maintenance and automation.

Increase water use efficiency This can be achieved with the obligatory use of localized irrigation systems by the farmers (with or without subsidies), the establishment of a system for advising farmers on irrigation, and proper irrigation scheduling. Irrigation scheduling requires knowledge of: (1) the crop water requirements and yield response to water: (2) the constrains of each irrigation method and type of irrigation equipment: (3) the crop sensitivity to salinity when water of inferior quality is used: (4) the limitations relative to the water supply system; and (5) the financial and economic implications of irrigation practice.

Adoption of innovative irrigation techniques. In water-scarce regions irrigation approaches not necessarily based on full crop water requirements like regulated deficit irrigation (RDI) or partial root drying (PRD) must be adopted. Fertigation (efficient fertilizer application) and chemigation (easy control of weeds and soil-borne diseases) should also be promoted.

Regulated deficit irrigation (RDI) is an optimizing strategy under which crops are allowed to sustain some degree of water deficit and yield reduction. During regulated deficit irrigation the crop is exposed to a certain level of water stress either during a particular period or throughout the growing season. The main objective of RDI is to increase the water use efficiency (WUE) of the crop by eliminating irrigation that has little impact on yield (Table. 5.4), and to improve control of vegetative growth (improve fruit size and quality). The resulting yield reduction may be small compared with the benefits gained through diverting the saved water to irrigate other crops for which water would normally be insufficient under conventional irrigation practices. The application of fertilizers through the irrigation system (fertigation) has become a common practice in modern irrigated agriculture. Localized irrigation systems, which could be highly efficient for water application, are also suitable for fertigation. Thus the soluble fertilizers at concentrations required by crops are applied through the irrigation system to the wetted volume of the soil. The potential advantages of fertigation are the delivery of precise amounts of fertilizer to the root system of the crop, optimum conditions for the use of fertilizer by the

*Table 5.4   Water use and yield of 'Fino' lemon under control and RDI
              irrigation*

Irrigation system	Applied water (mm)	Yield (kg/tree)	Number of fruit per tree
Control	690.5	208.1 a[*]	1839 a
RDI	485.7	199.5 a	2069 a

Note: * Different letters within the same column indicate significant differences
at a = 0.05 (LSD-test)

Source: Domingo et al. (1996).

crop, high fertilization efficiency, flexibility in timing of fertilizer application in relation to crop demand, environmental friendly fertilization
(control of nutrient losses) and increased yield and improved quality of the
products.

B. Adoption of Best Soil and Crop Management Practices

There is a large variety of traditional and modern soil and crop management practices for water conservation (run-off control, improvement of soil
infiltration rate, increase of soil water capacity, control of soil water evaporation) and erosion control in agriculture, some of which apply also for
weed control (Pereira et al., 2002). Effort should be made in the rational use
of chemicals for pest and weed control in order not to further pollute the
environment.

Soil management

Soil surface tillage – which concerns shallow tillage practices to produce an
increased roughness on the soil surface permitting short-time storage in
small depressions of the rainfall in excess of the infiltration.

Contour tillage – where soil cultivation is made along the land contour and
the soil is left with small furrows and ridges that prevent run-off. This technique is also effective to control erosion and may be applied to row crops
and small grains provided that field slopes are shallow.

Bed surface profile – which concerns cultivation of wide beds and is typically used for horticultural row crops.

Conservation tillage – including no-tillage and reduced tillage, where residuals of the previous crop are kept on the soil at planting. Mulches protect the soil from the direct impact of raindrops, thus controlling crusting and sealing processes. Conservation tillage helps to maintain high levels of organic matter in the soil; thus it is highly effective in improving soil infiltration and controlling erosion.

Mulching – with crop residues on the soil surface which shades the soil, slows water overland flow, improves infiltration conditions, reduces evaporation losses and also contributes to control of weeds and therefore of non-beneficial water use.

Increasing or maintaining the amount of organic matter in the upper soil layers – because organic matter provides for better soil aggregation, reduced crusting or sealing on the soil surface and increased water retention capacity of the soil.

Addition of fine material or hydrophilic chemicals to sandy or coarse soils – this technique increases the water retention capacity of the soil and controls deep percolation. Thus water availability in soils with low water-holding capacity is increased.

Control of acidity – by liming, similarly to gypsum application to soils with high pH. This treatment favours more intensive and deep rooting, better crop development and contributes to improved soil aggregation, thus producing some increase in soil water availability.

Adoption of appropriate weed control techniques – to alleviate competition for water and transpiration losses by weeds.

Crop management
Several techniques have been designed to minimize the risks of crop failure and to increase the chances for beneficial crop yield using the available rainfall, such as:

Selection of crop patterns – taking into consideration the seasonal rainfall availability and the water productivity of the crops and crop varieties.

Adoption of water stress-resistant crop varieties – instead of high-productive but more sensitive ones

Use of short-cycle crops or varieties – reduces the overall crop water requirements

Rational use of fertilizers – fertilizer type and amount should be applied according to crop needs (based on leaf and soil analysis). Use of slow-release fertilizers is desirable.

Reducing the fertilizer rates – when a low yield potential is predicted; this not only reduces costs but also minimizes the effects of salt concentration in the soil.

C. Water Pricing

Although Mediterranean islands have to follow the WFD (2000/60) of the EU, the most important recommendation we can make at present is that irrigation water tariffs must cover the O&M cost of water use and services. For proper water pricing, volumetric water metering and accounting procedures are recommended. Progressive, seasonal and overconsumption water tariffs as well as temporary drought surcharge rates contribute to water savings and should be promoted. Furthermore an increasing block tariff charging system, that discourages water use levels exceeding a crop's critical water requirements, must be established. It will be the basis for promoting conservation, reducing losses and mobilizing resources. Furthermore it could affect cropping patterns, income distribution, efficiency of water management, and the generation of additional revenue which could be used to operate and maintain water projects.

D. Reuse of Marginal Waters (Reclaimed or Brackish) for Irrigation

Reclaimed waters can be used under some restrictions for the irrigation of tree, row and fodder crops. In addition to water, they provide the soil with nutrients, minimizing the inorganic fertilizer application. Usage of treated sewage is regarded with scepticism by farmers. They prefer instead to use surface and/or groundwater. Special effort should be given to educating farmers to accept treated sewage. In addition, the tariff for this source of water should be lower than the tariff of the primary sources. This may not be difficult to achieve because the primary and secondary levels of treatment are regarded as sunk costs since they are required by the new WFD. When using low-quality water, for example brackish or saline water, an integrated approach for water, crops (salt-tolerant varieties), field management (suitable tillage) and irrigation systems (adequate leaching, suitable devices) should be considered.

E. Wider and more Effective Participation of Farmers in Water Management

Participation of farmers in the preparation of the plans, in decision-making, in monitoring the implementation and generally in the operation and management of irrigation schemes has proven very beneficial in improving irrigation efficiency in many parts of the world. The participation of farmers in the above processes safeguards the acceptability of the plans by the general public, raises support on the part of the body politic and promotes success in possible conflict resolutions.

F. Strengthening Capacity

The goal of agricultural water demand management on Mediterranean islands cannot be achieved without strengthening the capacity of the irrigation sector to improve the efficiency of institutions in charge of irrigation and to upgrade the scientific and technical knowledge of the staff involved. It includes:

Education and training – of professional and technical staff, decision-makers and others, including farmers, on a wide range of subjects related to sustainable agricultural water management.

Manpower build-up – Institutions to be staffed with qualified manpower (managers, engineers, technicians, social scientists) that should be adequately compensated.

Facilities and procedures – Water authorities at all levels of management should be equipped with technologically advanced devices and programs, for example computers and software for the application of new techniques such as GIS, remote sensing and so on. These advanced techniques facilitate multi-sectoral information availability and use, and help water managers in their decision- making.

Legislative changes – to the fragmented and antiquated legislation should be promoted. The changes should be conducive to Water Directive WFD60/2000.

CONCLUSIONS

Agriculture is by far the main water user in Mediterranean islands, ranging from 55 per cent in Corsica up to 82 per cent in Crete. On all islands, water for agriculture comes mainly from groundwater sources, while only in Corsica is surface water the sole source of irrigation water. Although being a valuable irrigation water resource, the contribution of treated wastewater to irrigation is very low (1 per cent in Cyprus and 7 per cent in Mallorca). Although modern irrigation systems are used in most cases, the efficiency of irrigation is still low (55 per cent).

Socio-economic pressures and climate change impose restrictions on water allocated to agriculture. The adoption of sustainable water management on Mediterranean islands is not only a technological problem, but involves many other considerations relative to the social behaviour of rural communities, the economic constraints, and the legal and institutional framework that may favour the adoption of some measures and not others. Sustainable water management in agriculture can be achieved by adopting improvements in irrigation, soil and plant practices, water pricing, reuse of treated wastewater, and farmers' participation in water management and capacity-building.

REFERENCES

Chartzoulakis, K.S., N.V. Paranychianakis and A.N. Angelakis (2001), 'Water resources management in the island of Crete, Greece, with emphasis on the agricultural use', *Water Policy*, **3**, 193–205.

Domingo, R., M.C. Ruiz, M.J. Blanco and A. Torrecillas (1996), 'Water relations, growth and yield of Fino lemon trees under regulated deficit irrigation', *Irrigation Science*, **16** (3), 15–123.

FAO (1998), 'Crop evapotranspiration: Guidelines for computing crop water requirements', Irrigation and Drainage Paper no 56, Rome.

FAO (1999), 'Land and Water Digital Media Series no 6', www.fao.org

Hagreaves, G.H. (1994), 'Defining and using reference evapotranspiration', *Journal of Irrigation and Drainage Engineering ASCE*, **120** (6), 1132–9.

Hargreaves, G.H. and Z.A. Samani (1985), 'Reference crop evapotranspiration from temperature', *Transactions of the ASAE*, **1** (2), 96–9.

Hillel, D. (1997), 'Small-scale irrigation for arid zones: principles and options', FAO Technical Paper 2, Rome.

Hurrell, J.W. and H. van Loon (1997), 'Decadal variations in climate associated with the North Atlantic oscillation', *Climatic Change*, **36**, 301–26.

IPCC (2001a), 'Overview of impacts, adaptation and vulnerability to climate change; in J.J. McArthy, O.F. Canziani, N.A. Leary, D.J. Dokken and K.S. White (eds), *Climate Change 2001: Impacts, Adaptation and Vulnerability*, Cambridge: Cambridge University Press.

Macheras, P. and F. Koliva-Machera (1990), 'Rainfall statistical characteristics of

Iraklio area during this century', in A.N. Angelakis and I. Ganoulis (eds), *Proceedings of the 4th Greek Congress of the Hellenic Hydrotechnical Union*, Vol. 4, 51–60, (in Greek), Thessaloniki, Greece: Giahoudis-Giapoulis.

Markou-Iakovaki, M. (1979), 'Atmospheric precipitation in the island of Crete', PhD. Thesis, School of Physics and Mathematics, University of Athens, Greece.

Passioura, J.B. (2002), 'Environmental biology and crop improvement. *Functional Plant Biology*, **29**, 537–46.

Pereira, L.S., I. Cordery and I. Iacovides (2002), 'Coping with scarcity', IHP-VI *Technical Document in Hydrology*, **58**, Paris: UNESCO.

Postel, S. (1999), *Pillar of Sand: Can the Irrigation Miracle Last?*, New York: W.W. Norton & Co.

Ragab, R. and C. Prudhomme (2002), 'Climate change and water resources management in arid and semi-arid regions: prospective and challenges for the 21st century', *Biosystem Engineering*, **81**, 3–34.

Rosegrant, M.W. and X. Cai (2002), 'Global water demand and supply projections: results and prospects to 2025', *Water International*, **27**, 170–82.

Tsagarakis, K.P., P. Tsoumanis, K.S. Chartzoulakis and A.N. Angelakis (2001), 'Water resources status, including wastewater treatment and reuse in Greece: related problems and perspectives', Water International, **26** (2), 252–8.

PART IV

An economic approach to integrated and
sustainable water resources management in
arid and semi-arid regions: a group of
environmental economists from the ARID
cluster

6. A typology of economic instruments and methods for efficient water resources management in arid and semi-arid regions

Katia Karousakis and Phoebe Koundouri

6.1 INTRODUCTION

Water scarcity issues are a cause for serious concern in arid and semi-arid regions and existing water shortages are predicted to escalate in both frequency and duration over the next century (UNEP, 2003). Global water consumption grew sixfold between 1900 and 1995, more than double the rate of population growth, and continues to rise with growing farming, industry and domestic demand. By 2025, the number of countries qualifying as water-scarce is anticipated to rise to 35 (from 20 in 1990). Given that water provides one of the most important life-support functions, ensuring food security through agricultural production and enabling the existence of all ecosystems, the allocation of scarce surface and groundwater resources in an efficient manner is of paramount importance. The significance of groundwater resources should not be underestimated as this resource represents around 90 per cent of the world's readily available freshwater resources and some 1.5 billion people depend upon it for drinking water. In addition to the quantitative shortages of water resulting from demand and supply imbalances, water scarcity in arid and semi-arid regions is further exacerbated by deteriorating water quality caused by point and non-point source pollution.

In Europe, industry accounts for 54 per cent of total water consumption, agricultural water use accounts for about 33 per cent, while 13 per cent is used for domestic purposes. The driving forces of water demand are strongly linked with national and international social and economic policies, and additional forces of water shortages are due to natural variability in water availability (rainfall) and changes in Europe's climate. These cases are most pronounced in the Mediterranean and as can be seen from the case studies provided in previous chapters in this book (Cyprus, Crete, Sicily, Corsica and Mallorca), in many areas conflicting demands for water in different sectors is resulting in unsustainable water use or the risk of overextraction. Water scarcity problems can constitute a threat to sustainable development and have major environmental, social, economic and political repercussions. Typical consequences associated with water scarcity include surface water exploitation, reservoir and lake eutrophication, aquifer exploitation, minimum and ecological flow, and desertification and erosion in basins, among other things (EEA, 1996).

The need for an integrated approach to water resources management has thus become increasingly evident over the past years. In response to this, EU legislation has striven to develop a more comprehensive approach culminating in the EU Water Framework Directive (WFD). The Directive establishes a framework for the protection of all water bodies (including inland surface waters, transitional waters, coastal water and groundwater). The key objective is to achieve 'good water status' for all waters by 2015.

This chapter provides the economic perspective to implementing integrated water resources management and describes the valuation techniques and economic instruments that have been developed and are available to help price water efficiently, and allocate it to its highest-valued user.

6.2   A MANUAL FOR IMPLEMENTING INTEGRATED WATER MANAGEMENT: THE ECONOMIC PERSPECTIVE

The implementation of an integrated water management framework from an economic perspective can be described in a three-step approach consisting of:

1. The economic characterization of water in the region;
2. The assessment of the recovery of the costs of water services; and
3. The economic assessment of potential measures for balancing water demand and supply.

A comprehensive economic characterization of water in the region requires first of all that its economic significance is evaluated. This involves an assessment of the residential, industrial, agricultural and tourism water needs in the area. This will include information on the population connected to the public water supply system vs those with self-supply, the total cropped area, cropping patterns, gross production and income of the farming population for the agricultural sector, and the total number of tourist days, and employment and turnover in the tourism sector. The key economic drivers influencing pressures and water uses need to be determined including: (1) the general socio-economic indicators such as population growth, income and employment; (2) the key sector policies that significantly influence water use (for example agricultural and environmental policies); (3) the development of planned investments likely to affect water availability; and (4) the implementation of future policies (environmental and other) that are likely to affect water use. These economic drivers will need to be accounted for in a dynamic perspective, that is, to determine how these are likely to evolve over time. The final component of the economic characterization of water in a region is the application of appropriate methodologies to assess sector-specific water demand. This involves deriving the marginal value of water in consumption and production, the price and income elasticity of demand, the marginal and average willingness to pay for public goods and quality changes of common access resources, and the associated risk parameters.

The second step in implementing integrated water management is to conduct a cost-recovery assessment of water services. This involves identifying the current water services costs by sector and the users and/or institutions that bear them. For example, operation and maintenance costs are often subsidized by the government and frequently, the social opportunity costs and external costs of extracting surface and groundwater are not reflected in market prices at all. Current cost-recovery levels must also be determined, incorporating all financial, environmental and resource costs and the institutional set-up for cost recovery such as the price and tariff structure, the existence of direct and indirect subsidies and cross-subsidies. If cost recovery is incomplete, the potential mechanisms available for this include taxes on water abstraction, charges for the use of the irrigation system, the selling of permits for water abstraction, and so on. Clearly, affordability for water users is also an important objective, and potential measures to address equity will also need to be identified. These may include subsidies to low-income households (mainly for agricultural water use) and capital subsidies on investments on infrastructure.

The third and final step is to conduct an economic assessment of potential measures for balancing water supply and demand. Least-cost measures may include the use of economic instruments such as abstraction and pollution taxes, and tradable permits; alternative measures to increase awareness regarding water scarcity; the use of direct controls on pollution charges to alleviate water quality issues; and the use of agri-environmental programmes to provide financial and technical assistance such as the adoption of water-saving technologies. These least-cost measures need to be assessed in terms of financial costs (capital, operation and maintenance, and administrative costs) and indirect costs (changes in environmental quality and the costs of preventative and mitigation measures). Finally, the impacts of these measures on key economic sectors and uses need to be evaluated. This includes the net impacts on public expenditures and revenues and the wider economic and social impacts such as on patterns of employment.

In the case that the achievement of good water status has significant adverse effects on the wider environment and human activities, then this constitutes 'disproportionality', in which case there may be time derogations or else the application of less stringent objectives may be applied.

The following section provides an overview of the market and government failures leading to the unsustainable use of water resources, in terms of overexploitation and excessive pollution. This provides a backdrop for section 6.4 which presents a typology of economic instruments and measures that are available for efficient surface and groundwater water resources management from both a water quantity and a water quality perspective. The advantages and limitations of these are identified and examples of where these have been implemented are described.

6.3   MARKET FAILURES IN WATER RESOURCES MANAGEMENT AND OPTIMAL USE

6.3.1   Market and Government Failures

Water services are public goods, that is, provision to one individual does not prevent others from using it. This is a form of market failure and can result in underinvestment and misallocation of resources. Other water services are characterized by economies of scale, which can lead to monopolistic power and socially inefficient allocation.

For groundwater, the prevailing externalities are of a different sort. Exploitation of a stock of groundwater is typically a common property problem since there is limited access to the resource. The finite stock implies that each unit of groundwater extracted is no longer available for others to use, therefore there is little incentive to save water for future use, which in turn leads to overpumping. Provencher and Burt (1993) call this the stock externality. In addition, there is a pumping cost externality: as the water table declines with increasing extraction, the pumping cost to the firm increases, as do the pumping costs of the other firms exploiting the resource. Since a firm does not take the other firms' costs into account, a second externality is generated. Finally, there is the risk externality, which is caused by the inherent value of groundwater as a substitute source of water in times of surface water shortages.

With regard to surface and groundwater quality, excessive pollution is caused by the existence of environmental externalities. Examples include effluent from waste treatment plants, factories and urban and agricultural run-off. In these cases, the social costs of producing the good are ignored, leading to artificially low production costs and hence overproduction of the good that generates the externality.

Importantly, economic decisions need to be made compatible with social objectives, that is, efficiency and equity considerations. Equity refers to the distribution of wealth among sectors and individuals. Government failures can also lead to misallocation of resources, as for example subsidies for agricultural production leading to the overexploitation of water resources for irrigation purposes.

6.3.2   Optimal Allocation of Scarce Water Resources

As a result of the above-mentioned issues, water supply and demand imbalances occur and water is not allocated efficiently amongst the resource users. Allocative efficiency requires the marginal value of water to be the same for the last unit of water consumed by each user and that it is equal to the cost of supplying water. Otherwise, society would benefit by allocating water to another sector where the returns would be higher. The efficiency criterion maximizes the total value of production across all affected sectors of the economy. Spatial and temporal considerations also need to be taken into account when valuing water which vary according to the quality and its use, thus making water a more challenging resource to manage efficiently.

The optimal price of water is illustrated in Figure 6.1. If there is a single source of water with several users at different locations then the marginal private cost (MPC) of water at the source is the cost of operating the facility plus the user cost. The marginal cost of water at a more distant location is the MPC (as before) plus the marginal cost of transporting the water from the source to the user, also known as the marginal conveyance cost (MCC). There are also environmental costs associated with removing water from a lake or a reservoir as this may have detrimental impacts on fish populations and other wildlife. The marginal environmental costs are denoted by MEC. Finally there may also be future costs associated with the extraction of water due to uncertainty in precipitation, denoted here by MFC. Examples of these costs include reduction in future productivity due to accumulation processes such as soil salinity or waterlogging.

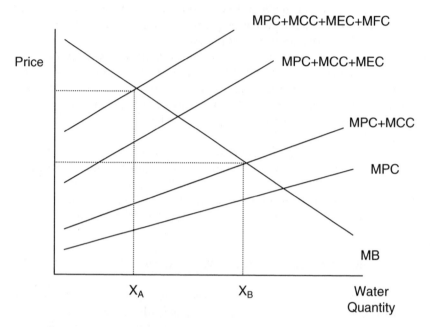

Note: MB is the marginal benefit curve and reflects the economic benefits that water buyers obtain from purchasing water. The intersection of demand (MB) with the sum of all costs reflect the socially optimum outcome where the amount of water extracted/used is given by quantity X_A. However, in most cases future and externality costs are not normally taken into account, leading to an equilibrium at point B, where the amount of water extracted/used is X_B, which is inefficiently high.

Source: Zilberman and Schoengold (2005).

Figure 6.1   The optimal price of water

6.3.2.1   Non-market valuation techniques

In part as a result of these market and government failures, degradation and loss of the environmental functions of water resources has been prolific in the last century. However, due to the observed loss of many ecological and hydrological services formerly provided free by aquatic systems, and the consequent environmental and economic costs of this loss, aquatic system protection and conservation has become an internationally important political issue.

In any aquatic system a number of processes may be occurring to a greater or lesser extent. These may be of a physical, chemical, biological or ecological nature. As a consequence of the occurrence of such processes, aquifers will perform a number of ecosystem preservation functions. For example the process of water storage in an aquifer may result in a wetland, which is performing the function of flood attenuation, while the processes of denitrification and plant nutrient uptake may contribute to the ability to perform the function of water quality maintenance through the removal of nutrients from surface water and shallow groundwater. Plant uptake of nutrients may also result in the performance of other functions such as the provision of support to the food web and habitat, demonstrating that an individual process may contribute to a variety of wetland functions.

The benefits of these water resources functions to society (and social welfare) however are not confined to their physical functions as referred to in the previous paragraph. For example they may be supporting wetlands used for recreation such as sailing, shooting and fishing; be held dear as intrinsic parts of landscapes or as wild places; and be valued, as habitats, for their biodiversity. Moreover water storage in aquifers may provide direct economic benefits but the value of aquatic systems, like that of nature in general, also has cultural and social dimensions. Such values, constituted through social processes, represent ethical, aesthetic and cultural concerns as much as scientific knowledge. In particular, nature's popular significance resides largely in meanings and values other than those bestowed by scientific understanding. But the physical functions performed by an aquatic system take place with or without the presence of society, usually as part of a self-sustaining ecosystem (intrinsic features), whereas other aquatic system values require the presence of society (extrinsic features), and these will vary over time and space while the functions may not.

Although the sources of aquatic system values are diverse and heterogeneous, much of national policy all over the world relating to aquatic systems (if existent at all) has arisen solely from scientific reports, which in some cases are flawed or only locally applicable. It is now widely accepted that decisions about environmental and groundwater resource management-related policies and projects should not be made on scientific and/or economic (including financial, management, restoration costs and benefits) grounds alone; social and cultural aspects also need to be heeded. For the integration of these values policy-makers have to explore water values held by 'ordinary' citizens in the context of developing a non-monetary approach to valuation, and suggest how these values should be integrated in water resources management policies.

In economics, the basis of value is determined by individual preferences (see figure 6.2). Preferences reflect the utilities that are expected to be derived from the consumption of resources, given the needs, wants and wishes of consumers. In order correctly to evaluate a given resource, one needs to consider the total economic value (TEV) of the resource, that is, the whole class of values that have a basis in human preferences. TEV is composed of direct

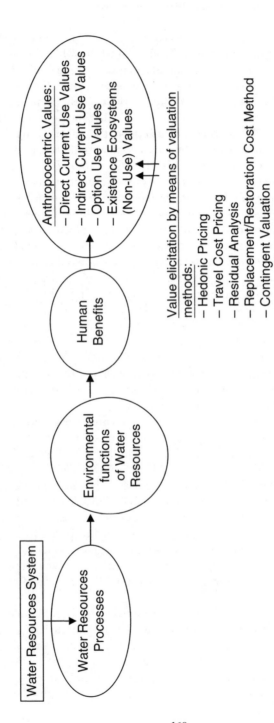

Figure 6.2 *A simple framework relating water resources to environmental functions, human benefits and anthropocentric values*

and indirect use values, as well as non-use values. Current use value derives from the utility gained by an individual from the consumption of a good or service, or from the consumption of others (for example parents may obtain utility from their children's consumption). Current use value is composed of direct use value (commercial and recreational) and indirect use value (such as amenity value or general ecosystem support). Option value derives from retaining an option to a good or service for which future demand is uncertain. If we are not certain about either our future preferences or about future availability, we may be willing to pay a premium (the option value) to keep the option of future use open. The option value is an additional value to any utility that may arise if and when the good is actually consumed.

Existence value derives from human preferences for the existence of resources as such, unrelated to any use to which such resources may be put. Individual preferences may exist for maintaining resources in their present forms even where no actual or future 'use' is expected to be made of the resource.

Given that many of these components of value are not reflected in market prices of water, economists will attempt to estimate the true resource value through user willingness to pay (WTP) for a given quantity and quality of supply. Valuation techniques are therefore necessary to assign appropriate prices that will enable water to be allocated in the most efficient manner. A variety of these techniques have been developed over the years to address this issue and are generally classified as revealed preference techniques and stated preference techniques. Revealed preference techniques use data on goods or services that are marketed and do have observable prices, in order to value some environmental attribute which is embodied in the marketed goods and services, but is not traded itself in any particular market. In stated preference techniques, individuals are provided with a constructed scenario in which they are asked how much they are willing to pay for changes in environmental quantity.

Within the category of revealed preference techniques for water resources, one approach is the residual value method which values all inputs for the good produced at market price, except for the water resource itself. The residual value of the good is attributed to the water input. For example one can value water as an input in the production of different crops. A problem with this methodology is that only part of the use value of water can be captured.

Another approach is the hedonic pricing method whereby implicit prices of characteristics which differentiate closely related goods are estimated. Suppose that an environmental resource that you wish to value is not itself traded in any market, possibly because the resource is a public good. As a result, no market price exists which can reveal preferences or willingness to pay for the resource. Suppose also that the resource can be defined in terms of services it yields or an 'attribute' it embodies. This attribute may be embodied in other goods or assets which are marketed, and which do have observable prices. For example farm prices in an area with good groundwater availability will be higher than areas with little or no groundwater availability. By comparing farm prices in different areas and accounting for other differences, the remaining difference in farm price can be attributed to groundwater availability. An example of hedonic pricing applied to evaluate water quality in Cyprus is given by Koundouri and Pashardes (2003). Using data on 193 parcels of land on variables such as price, usage (agriculture vs tourism), proximity to the sea and other variables, they estimate the marginal willingness to pay to avoid a marginal increase in the salinization of fresh groundwater supplies beneath owners' land.

A limitation of the hedonic pricing technique is that it is only capable of measuring that subset of use values for which people are willing to pay, and do so indirectly through the related market. It also relies on the assumption that consumers are fully informed about the qualities of the attributes being valued; otherwise hedonic price estimates are of little relevance. There are other problems in that the hedonic price equation and the second-step demand equation impose rather strong assumptions about separability of consumers' utility functions. The functional forms of regression models that are usually chosen impose weak separability. However standard consumer demand theory and evidence from applied studies doubt the validity of weak separability, particularly when large changes occur, as is often the case when dealing with environmental projects.

Travel cost models (also known as recreation demand models) are an alternative revealed preference technique which focuses on choice of trips or visits for recreational purposes and looks at the level of satisfaction, time and money spent in relation to the activity. Patterns of travel to a particular sight can be used to analyse how individuals value the site and, for example, the water quality of a river stretch. See Bockstael et al. (1987) for an example.

Within the category of stated preference techniques, one can use contingent valuation methods, choice modelling approaches, and meta-analysis. Many water quality evaluation problems occur in a framework for which no value measures can be derived from observing individual choices through a market. This is mainly due to the public good aspect of groundwater quality. Other examples where actual consumer choices are unobservable are cases where the policy change is potential rather than actual. In such cases, respondents are offered conditions simulating a hypothetical market in which they are asked to express willingness to pay for existing or potential environmental conditions not registered on any market. The most common form of questioning on hypothetical futures is called the contingent valuation method (CVM). This involves asking individuals directly what they would be willing to pay contingent on some hypothetical change in the future state of the world (Mitchell and Carson, 1989). Alternatively this can be expressed as the minimum monetary compensation they would accept to go without an increase in that good or tolerate a decrease (willingness to accept compensation WTAC). Thus an individual's WTP or WTAC will depend on the description of the contingent market, the information they have about the environmental good (which depends partly on what they are told about it as part of the CVM survey), their own preferences and their budget constraints, and the availability of substitutes and complements. In brief, a CVM exercise consists of a description of the environmental change in question and the contingent market, establishing a bid vehicle (for example an increase in monthly water bills), and a reason for payment (for example to reduce water shortage incidents from three times a month to once a month). The WTP bids can be elicited in a variety of methods including an open-ended format, a bidding game, a payment card or a single or double-bounded dichotomous choice mechanism. Once the mean and median WTP has been estimated, the average bid can be aggregated to a population total value.

There are many problems associated with CVM that may bias the value estimates (for example interviewing bias, non-response bias, strategic bias, embedding effects, yea-saying bias, hypothetical bias, information bias), and best practice guidelines for conducting CVM studies have been developed (NOAA, 1993). These recommend for example the use of dichotomous choice formats over other alternatives, that in-person interviews should be conducted as opposed to for example mail surveys, and that WTP, not WTAC, measures should be elicited.

Partly as a response to these problems, valuation practitioners are increasingly interested in alternative stated preference formats such as choice modelling (CM). CM is a family of survey-based methodologies (including choice experiments, contingent ranking, contingent rating and paired comparisons) for modelling preferences for goods, which can be described in terms of their attributes and of the levels they take. Respondents are asked to rank, rate or choose their most preferred alternative. By including cost as one of the attributes of the good, willingness to pay can be indirectly recovered from people's rankings, ratings or choices. An excellent critical review of CM alternatives and investigation of their potential to solve some of the major biases associated with standard CVM is provided by Hanley et al. (2001). In the class of CM alternatives, probably the one receiving the most attention is the choice experiment method (CEM). This is a survey-based technique which can estimate the total economic value of an environmental stock/flow or service and the value of its attributes, as well as the value of more complex changes in several attributes. Each respondent is presented with a series of alternatives of the environmental stock/flow or service with varying levels of its attributes and asked to choose their most preferred alternative in each set of alternatives. CEM eliminates or minimizes several of the CVM problems (for example strategic bias, yea-saying bias, embedding effects). An example of a choice experiment method applied to wetlands evaluation is that of Carlsson et al. (2003), who estimated the values of both use and non-use values of the Staffanstorp wetland in Sweden. The selection of attributes and levels that they selected included biodiversity (low, medium, high), fish (yes, no), surrounding vegetation (forest, meadow), walking facilities (yes, no), and a cost attribute (varying from SEK 200 to SEK 850). The choice sets were then constructed using experimental design methods and the survey sent out via mail to 1200 randomly selected individuals living in Staffanstorp. Using econometric models, they found that biodiversity levels and walking facilities were the two greatest contributors to welfare, whereas some other attributes led to a decline in welfare.

Recent years have seen a growing interest, from both academics and policy-makers, in the potential for producing generally applicable models for the valuation of non-market environmental goods and services, which do not rely upon expensive and time-consuming original survey work, but rather extrapolate results from previous studies of similar assets. Such methods are called meta-analysis for the use and non-use values generated by environmental resources. Meta-analysis is the statistical analysis of the summary of findings of empirical studies, that is, the statistical analysis of a large collection of results from individual studies for the purpose of integrating the findings. Meta-analysis offers a transparent structure with which to understand underlying patterns of assumptions, relations and causalities, so permitting the derivation of useful generalizations without violating more useful contingent or interactive conclusions.

The increase in meta-analytical research seems to have been principally triggered by:

1. Increases in the available number of environmental valuation studies.
2. The seemingly large differences in valuation outcomes as a result of the use of different research designs.
3. The relatively high costs of carrying out environmental valuation studies and the increasing demand for transferable valuation results.

Brouwer et al. (2004) present such a meta-analysis for the use and non-use values generated by wetlands across Europe and North America.

As can be seen, each of the valuation methodologies have advantages and disadvantages associated with them, and depending on the component of total economic value one is trying to estimate, some methods are more suitable than others. Once realistic estimates of surface and groundwater values are available, it is then necessary for governments to determine which policy measures are most suitable to achieve the desired outcomes.

6.4   ECONOMIC INSTRUMENTS FOR EFFICIENT SURFACE AND GROUNDWATER MANAGEMENT

A number of economic instruments are available that can provide the appropriate incentives for efficient surface and groundwater resources extraction and management. Though economic instruments to manage surface water and groundwater are similar, they are not identical due to certain special characteristics associated with groundwater. These include the relatively high cost and complexity of assessing groundwater, the highly decentralized nature of resource use and the ensuing high monitoring costs, and the long time-lags and near irreversibility of most aquifer contamination. The selection and use of economic instruments will also depend on current hydrology, economic, social and political considerations.

6.4.1   Standards and Quotas

A legal water standard or quota can be introduced that places restrictions on the amount of water that can be extracted for use. It will be effective if water users face substantial monetary penalties for lowering the water level below this standard or not adhering to the quota. Water quality standards may also be established. Standards and quotas do not strictly qualify as economic instruments as they do not improve economic efficiency and do not introduce incentives to innovate. The financial impact is not always equitably distributed among affected parties, since there are differences in the vulnerability of areas to changes induced by these instruments. Differentiated standards and quotas however will pose a large burden on the administrative capacity. Serious resistance is usually raised against the introduction of these policy instruments.

6.4.2   Water Abstraction Taxes

Theoretically a tax can be used to restrain water users from lowering the surface or groundwater level below a certain standard.

Area pricing is probably the most common form of water pricing whereby users are charged for water used per irrigated area, and may depend on crop choice, the extent of crop irrigated, and the irrigation method and season. In contrast, output pricing and input pricing are probably the least common forms of water pricing. Output pricing methods involve charging a fee for each unit of output produced per user whereas input pricing involves charging users for water consumption through a tax on inputs, for example a charge for each kilogram of fertilizer purchased.

The efficiency of water abstraction taxes is relative and depends on technical and institutional factors. Volumetric pricing is the optimal water tariff where price is equal to marginal cost of supplying the last unit. The choice of water pricing method however will also depend on factors such as institutions, administration and monitoring capabilities, the establishment and control of metering devices, the ability to collect fees, as well as enforcement issues. There are difficulties associated with marginal cost (MC) pricing because MC is multidimensional, that is, it includes several inputs such as water quantity and quality, and the fact that MC varies over the time period measured (that is, short-run vs long-run MC).

When sophisticated monitoring technology is available, then tiered pricing, and two-part tariffs (fixed and volumetric) are feasibly introduced. Tiered pricing for irrigation water for example is common in Israel (Yaron, 1997). This was initially introduced in 1974 but then abandoned in 1977 due to farmers' political pressure. Agricultural tier pricing was reintroduced in 1989 however and continues to be in effect today. For water from Mekerot, the national water company, farmers pay a progressively increasing price for the first 50, second 30, and final 20 per cent of their water quota. Farmers using more water than their quota provides pay much more for the excess. To avoid these punitive charges, farmers generally partake in inter-farm transfers of water. By allocating some water through quotas, it is believed that socially undesirable outcomes with respect to the distributional issues are prevented.

The effectiveness of a tax depends on the correct estimation of the marginal tax level and on how risk-averse farmers are with respect to damage from reduced water availability (both in quality and quantity terms). A differentiated tax level has to be created, because of local differences in both the monetary value of reserves and the vulnerability of the environment to changes in the groundwater level. An advantage of a tax is that it improves both economic and technical efficiency. Administrative costs are high, since a differentiated tax is not easy to control and monitor. The financial impact on affected parties depends on the restitution of revenues, which affects tax acceptability. Finally, there are practical implementation problems. It is hard to define a good basis for a tax. A volumetric tax on extraction is complicated, since it involves high monitoring costs. A tax on a change in the groundwater level is also complicated, because external and stochastic factors affect the level of groundwater, which is not uniform across any given aquifer. Charging water boards for lowering surface water levels will not influence an individual farmer's behaviour, but it will affect the strategy of groups of farmers represented in the governing body of water boards.

Specific taxes for groundwater abstraction have been adopted in the Netherlands and in France (OECD, 2002). In the Netherlands this was introduced in January 1995 at a standard rate of 0.15 €/m³, and at a rate of 0.025 €/m³ for infiltrated groundwater.

6.4.3 Pollution Taxes

Pollution taxes represent an efficient method of addressing water quality problems if these are adopted at the optimum level. Pigouvian taxes are statically and dynamically efficient as they induce users to innovate. Pollution taxes to address groundwater pollution have been implemented in the Netherlands, Sweden and Denmark, where they are targeted at non-point source pollution from agriculture, and are imposed on nitrogen fertilizers.

6.4.4 Subsidies

Subsidies can be directly implemented for water-saving measures to induce users to behave in a more environmentally friendly way. Alternatively, indirect subsidy schemes also exist which include tax concessions and allowances, and guaranteed minimum prices. Subsidies however are not economically efficient, they create distortions and do not provide incentives for the adoption of modern technologies. Acceptability however is not an issue, since participation in subsidy schemes is voluntary and has positive financial implications.

6.4.5 Tradable Permits

Another instrument prescribed by economists in the face of demand–supply imbalances is the introduction of water markets (Howitt, 1997) in which water rights, or permits, can be traded. The rationale behind water allocation through tradable rights is that in a perfectly competitive market, permits will flow to their highest-value use. Different types of tradable permit systems can be established which address different aspects of the water resource problem (Kraemer and Banholzer, 1999). These are:

● Tradable water abstraction rights for quantitative water resource management. These can be permanent and unlimited (property rights to the water resource) or temporary and limited (transferable rights to use water without right of abuse).

- Tradable discharge permits for the protection and management of (surface) water quality. Such pollution permits can be allocated to point or to non-point sources and trades can also be arranged among different kinds of sources. (For examples from the USA and Australia, see Kraemer et al., (2003.)
- Tradable permits to use or consume water-borne resources such as fish or the potential energy of water at height for example.

Generally, the government will determine the optimal level of water resource use over a specified time period (for example annually or seasonally) and will allocated a limited number of permits that reflect the optimal level to the different water users. Permit holders that gain lower benefits from using their permits (due to for example higher costs) have an incentive to sell them to users who value them more. The sale results in mutual benefit as each user is better off.

The financial impact on affected parties and related acceptability of tradable permits depends on the initial allocation of rights. These can either be distributed for free (for example depending on historical use or other criteria), or auctioned off to the highest bidders. If they are auctioned, revenues are created that the government can earmark for other environmental purposes. The use of tradable rights for groundwater seems to be complicated in practice, since the impact of changes in the groundwater level on agricultural production and nature depends on location-specific circumstances. To avoid transferring rights among areas with heterogeneous characteristics, trading has to be restricted.

Tradable water permit systems have been implemented in a number of countries including Chile, Mexico, Peru, Brazil, Spain, several states in Australia, and the Northern Colorado Water Conservancy District in the USA (Marino and Kemper, 1999).

6.4.6 Voluntary Agreements

Another policy option for controlling surface and groundwater use is voluntary agreements between farmers and government organizations. Participation in such control programmes is encouraged by means of positive incentives (a restitution of taxes). Such programmes try to convince farmers (through education) of the advantages of fine-tuned groundwater control. Voluntary agreements on controlling groundwater use are efficient, since they rely on specialized knowledge of participants about local conditions. When costs and benefits are not equitably distributed among affected parties, both parties can bargain about compensation payments. The allocation of such payments depends on the assignment of rights. Acceptability is not an issue, since it is a voluntary regime. Because of these advantages, participation of farmers in planning and decision-making at the local level is becoming more common. The principle of allowing the individual members of agricultural organization and water boards to make decisions on issues that affect them rather than leaving those decisions to be made by the whole group, the so-called 'principle of subsidiary', is widely accepted.

6.4.7 Liability for Damage

Environmental liability systems intend to internalize and recover the costs of environmental damage through legal action and to make polluters pay for the damage their pollution causes. If the penalties are sufficiently high, and enforcement is effective, liability for damage can provide incentives for taking preventative measures. For liability to be effective, there need to be one or more identifiable actors (polluters); the damage needs to be concrete and quantifiable; and a causal link needs to be established between the damage and the identified polluter.

Table 6.1 summarizes the advantages and disadvantages of all economic instruments mentioned in this section.

6.5 A METHODOLOGY FOR THE IMPLEMENTATION OF THE ECONOMIC ASPECTS OF THE WFD

In this section we outline the methodology we propose for application to the WFD. This methodology is based on: (1) the identification of the appropriate unit for management; (2) the agreement of the objectives of water allocation; (3) the evaluation of the various attributes of water demand within that unit; (4) the identification of optimal water resource allocations relative to objectives; and (5) the assessment of the impacts of the proposed reallocation.

6.5.1 The Appropriate Unit for Management

The watershed is a natural unit of analysis for addressing the balance of supply and demand for water, and the issues of efficiency, equity and sustainability for a number of reasons. Firstly, the aggregate availability of water resources, including sustainable yields, is bounded by the hydrological cycle of the watershed. Secondly, the interaction of different water sources (for example groundwater and surface water) is confined by the watershed. Thirdly, the demands for water interact within the watershed

Table 6.1   Classification of economic instruments

Economic Instrument	Advantages	Disadvantages
1. Standards and Quotas		Not economically efficient
2. Water abstraction charges	Adjustment of price signals to reflect actual resource costs; encourage new technologies; flexibility; generation of revenues	Low charges will have minimal impact on user behaviour and will continue in resource overutilization
3. Pollution charges	Same as water abstraction charges; polluter-pays principle	Same as water abstraction charges
4. Subsidies	Readily acceptable	Not economically efficient
5. Tradable permits	Quantity based targets that are able to attain least-cost outcome. Allows flexibility.	May entail high transaction costs.
6. Voluntary agreements	Readily acceptable	
7. Liability legislation	Assess and recover damages ex-post but can also act as prevention incentives	Require an advanced legal system; high control costs; burden of proof

and the hydrological impacts of one water user upon another and upon the environment; that is, externalities are defined by the watershed. For these reasons, an understanding of the hydrological cycle in the watershed area in question is a prerequisite for the determination of efficient, equitable and sustainable water resource allocation.

6.5.2   The Objectives of Water Allocation

Given the natural water resource constraints there is a clear need to address the pattern and growth of water demands in order to address the imbalance. The methodology proposed provides the policy-maker and planner with an objective approach to balancing the competing demands for water subject to the natural constraints. The approach is based on the comparison of the economic value of water in different sectors, in terms of quantity and quality, in comparable units of measurement. The overall objective of public policy is to maximize societal welfare from a given natural resource base subject to those valuations. The key objectives of public policy in the allocation of resources are as follows:

- Efficiency. Economic efficiency is defined as an organization of production and consumption such that all unambiguous possibilities for increasing economic well-being have been exhausted (Young, 1996). For water, this is achieved where the marginal social benefits of water use are equated to the marginal social cost of supply, or for a given source, where the marginal social benefits of water use are equated across users.
- Equity. Social welfare is likely to depend upon the fairness of distribution of resources and impacts across society, as well as economic efficiency. Equal access to water resources, the distribution of property rights, and the distribution of the costs and benefits of policy interventions, are examples of equity considerations for water policy.
- Environment and sustainability. The sustainable use of water resources has become another important aspect in determining the desirable allocation of water from the perspective of society. Consideration of intergenerational equity and the critical nature of ecological services provided by water resources provide two rationales for considering sustainability. In addition, the *in situ* value and public good nature of water resources should enter into water allocation decisions.

6.5.3   The Evaluation of Water Demand

For physical, social and economic reasons, water is a classic non-marketed resource. Even as a direct consumption good, market prices for water are seldom available, or when observable are often subject to biases through subsidies, taxes and so on. Similarly, environmental and ecological water values are rarely explicitly marketed and priced. Thus the economic value of water resources is seldom observed directly. The balancing of demands to resolve the resource conflicts described above requires the identification and comparison of the benefits and costs of water resource development and allocation among alternative and competing uses. In addition, water management policies have widespread effects on the quantity and quality of water within a watershed, and the timing and location of supplies for both in- and off-stream uses. In general, these impacts have an economic dimension, either positive or negative, which must be taken into account in policy formulation. Again, the value of these impacts is seldom observed directly.

Fortunately, economists have refined a number of techniques to value water resources and address objectively the balance of demands and evaluate the impacts of water management policy. The first step towards the evaluation of economic benefits requires the identification of the demands for the resource. Water is needed for all economic and social activities, so the evaluator is faced with the problem of identifying a multi-sectoral demand curve. The dimensions of demand include municipal and industrial, agricultural, tourism and environmental (recreation, amenity and ecological).

The valuation of each of the identified demands calls for a different approach for two main reasons: (1) the specific economic and hydrological context, data availability and so on; and (2) because the use of the resource is sector-specific. The residential and tourist sectors exploit the use value of water and use it as a consumption good; the agricultural sector derives use value from water as an input in production. The value of water-related environmental goods can be a use value or a non-use value, for example existence value. The overall evaluation strategy is shown in Figure 6.3.

The valuation techniques allow the estimation of the following desirable parameters:

- Marginal value of water. The efficient balance of demands from a given source is found where the marginal value (benefit) of water is equated across users. In any given context efficiency is achieved where the marginal value of water is equated to the marginal social cost.
- Price elasticities of demand (PED). Measures the responsiveness of demand to price changes. Characterizes the demand function and tells the policy-maker the extent to which prices must change to cause demand to fall to a particular, for example efficient, sustainable, level.
- Income elasticity of demand (IED). Measures the extent to which the demand for water varies with income. Tells the policy-maker whether water is a necessity or a luxury good and provides one way in which to assess the fairness of pricing policies. In combination with PED it can be used to estimate welfare changes resulting from policies.
- Marginal or average willingness to pay for public goods (WTP). Estimates the strength of demand for water as an environmental good. This determines in part the efficient environmental allocation of water.
- Marginal willingness to pay for quality changes of common access resources. Estimates the value of quality attributes of the resource, which are particularly important if the resource is used as a productive input.
- Risk parameters. Measurement of preferences towards risk and uncertainty. Useful for establishing policies which reduce the impacts of risk

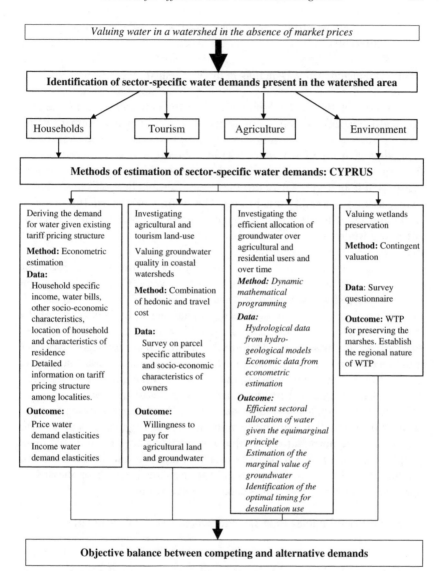

Figure 6.3   *The methodology for water demand valuation in a watershed area: examples from the Kouris watershed case study*

on consumer groups occasioned by reason of variability in water availability.

6.5.4   Balancing Water Demands in the Watershed

The outputs of the demand analysis allow the determination of the economically efficient allocations of water resources. The first element of an economically efficient allocation is the equi-marginal principle: this provides that each use of the water resource should achieve the same benefit from that water at the margin. In short, if water is more heavily valued at the margin in one sector than another, then it should be reallocated toward that sector until equality is achieved. The second element of the economically efficient allocation is that aggregate water resources are allocated efficiently where the marginal social benefit of their use is equated to the marginal social cost of supply.

One option for achieving an economically efficient water allocation is the use of the instrument of water pricing, where water is uniformly and universally charged at the marginal social cost of supply, which has the following implications. Firstly, competing demands will each make use of the supply until its marginal benefit is equated with marginal social costs of supply (the equi-marginal principle). Note that this implies that every use must receive an equal marginal benefit from water resources. The second implication is that aggregate demand for water will expand until the marginal benefit is equated with the marginal social cost of supply (aggregate efficiency). Note that this implies that demand is endogenous and managed within this model. The third implication is that the key to the success of the policy is the determination of the appropriate marginal social cost of supply and the marginal benefits to environmental uses. Note that this implies that the methodology used for implementing the policy is as important as the method that is used for determining it.

6.5.5   Deriving Policies from the Methodologies – Policy Impact Analysis

There is a second phase to the water allocation methodology that flows from the consideration of the implementation of the conclusions from the first. Firstly, the discussion here has largely been phrased in terms of the use of water pricing as the appropriate allocation mechanism, but this need not necessarily be the best or more appropriate instrument for allocating water in every context. There are many different approaches to enable the efficient allocation of water resources – pricing, marketable permits, even auctions. Ultimately the particular context (watershed) must be considered for the feasibility of the various instruments, and the policy-maker must determine the most appropriate allocation mechanism within that context.

Secondly, it is crucial to note that an economically efficient allocation need not necessarily be an equitable or sustainable one. Additional analysis is required to assess the distributional impacts of the allocation recommended by the equi-marginal principle. The hydrological impacts of the allocation need to be assessed, in order to assess whether the various demands are compatible within the existing watershed. Finally, the continued provision of basic environmental services within the watershed needs to be considered. In sum, the watershed needs to be double-checked for unforeseen externalities and for missing markets for watershed services to ensure intra- and inter-temporal efficiency is achieved and that equity and sustainability considerations are properly considered.

The methodology can be thought of as two complementary stages, the first consisting of an objective approach to ascertaining economically efficient water allocations and the latter phase consisting of the policy impact analysis.

6.5.6 Summary of Methodology

Stage I: Objective approach to balancing water demands

Evaluate demands   Apply appropriate methodologies to assess characteristics of the demand for water arising from individual, sectoral and environmental uses. Derive the parameters of water demand required for policy purposes: marginal value, PED, IED, WTP and risk parameters for all the relevant dimensions of demand. The evaluation process should be undertaken in accordance with carefully constructed methodologies, and be independent of any prior rights to water resources. This enables an evaluation of water uses according to the benefits that accrue to all of society from them.

Determine efficient allocations   Evaluate the relative values accruing to society by virtue of differing water allocations. Determine those water allocations that achieve an economically optimal balance. An economically optimal allocation is one in which aggregate demands are balanced with supply according to the equation of marginal social value (benefit) to the marginal social cost of supply, and in which each source of demand is achieving equal value from its marginal allocation of water.

Ascertain impacts of implementing efficient allocation   The policy-maker may choose from a wide variety of instruments to effect the desirable allocation (tradable permits, pricing, auctions). Any proposed method of implementation should be considered for feasibility within the relevant watershed, and then evaluated for its broader impacts on the society. This evaluation process leads into Stage II of the methodology.

Stage II: Policy impact analysis

Welfare distribution   The impact of the allocation policy options should be evaluated to establish the resulting distribution of the costs and benefits to society. That is, the change in social deadweight loss resulting from resource allocation changes should be determined, together with the actual distribution of this change. This is important both from the perspective of equity and often for reasons of political economy.

Market failures and missing markets   Consideration of sectoral demands in isolation may be insufficient to ensure efficient outcomes. Where water users are conjoined by the underlying hydrology of the watershed there are a number of potential impacts and externalities that may arise from the chosen allocation. For example policies implemented in upstream areas of a watershed will impact upon downstream users where the water resources are conjoined. Ignoring these effects will lead to inefficient allocations of water. In effect all the following facets of water demand should be considered: (1) sectoral allocation, that is, water demands should be balanced between sectors; (2) spatial allocation, that is, spatial variability and the conjoined nature of surface and groundwater; and (3) temporal allocation, that is conjoined users may impose externalities upon each other relating to allocation over time and the timing of resource use. Other externalities arise from the demand for public goods, which frequently extends beyond the watershed. Global and regional environmental goods for which existence, bequest and option values are held provide an example of this. Furthermore, where water scarcity is extreme, demands for water outside the watershed may induce investments in inter-basin transfers.

Institutional and legislative analysis   As one of the main obstacles to water reallocations, a review of the legislative and institutional environment required to effect the desired allocation may finally be required.

The methodology described above addresses the problem of water resource allocation at the level of the watershed and provides policy-makers and resource managers with a concrete procedure for attaining economic efficiency targets whilst considering equity and environmental sustainability. The methodology proposes that competing demands, including the environment, are traded off against one another and balanced against extant hydrological constraints using the notion of economic efficiency, the marginal valuation of water and the equi-marginal principle. The valuation exercises are undertaken independently of prevailing property rights regimes for water resources and hence allow the characterization of efficient or optimal allocations of water, rather than those tainted by property rights uncertainties, open access and missing markets.

However economic efficiency itself must be traded off against the contributions to social welfare derived from equitable distributions of resources and policy impacts such as employment. Similarly the complex nature of hydrological linkages requires additional analysis to establish the value of water resources in non-marketed watershed services such as drought mitigation or risk reduction and coastal wetlands. In addition demands for *in situ* environmental services external to the watershed need to be considered along with other potentially subtle market failures. Where not addressed in Stage I, these considerations are captured by Stage II of the methodology. In sum, the integrated water resource management approach attempts to provide a coherent procedure for overcoming the water resource allocation problem addressed at the level of the watershed.

6.6 CONCLUSION

The importance of appropriate economic considerations in all aspects of water resources management is becoming increasingly recognized. This chapter has presented the necessary procedures for implementing an integrated approach from an economic perspective which consists of the characterization of the river basin, an assessment of current cost recovery, and the identification of economic instruments and measures that are able to evaluate the true economic cost of water (including financial, environmental and resource costs), and to provide policy-makers with the tools to allocate water in an efficient manner. The theory and applications of these valuation methods (hedonic pricing, travel cost methods, contingent valuations and choice modelling, among others) and the economic instruments (abstraction and pollution taxes, subsidies and use of tradable permits) are described and illustrated with case studies.

Finally, we present a methodology for implementing the economic considerations of the EU Water Framework Directive. This takes into consideration the efficiency aspects of water allocation as well as the equity, environmental and sustainability issues. Together, these can help to provide policy prescriptions that endeavour to provide an integrated water resources management framework.

REFERENCES

Bockstael, N., Haneman and Kling (1987), 'Estimating the value of water quality improvements in a recreational demand framework', *Water Resources Research*, **23** (5), 951–60.
Brouwer, R., I.H. Langford, I. Bateman and K. Turner (2004), 'Meta-analysis of wetland contingent valuation studies' in R.K. Turner, S. Georgiou and I.J. Bateman (eds), *Environmental Decision Making and Risk Management: Selected Essays by Ian H. Langford*, Cheltenham, UK and Northampton, MA, USA: Edward Elgar Publishing.
Carlsson, F., P. Frykblom and C. Liljenstolpe (2003), 'Valuing wetland attributes: an application of choice experiments', *Ecological Economics*, **47**, 95–103.
Hanley, N., Mourato and Wright (2001), 'Choice modelling approaches: a superior alternative for environmental valuation?' *Journal of Economic Surveys*, **15** (3), 435–62.
Howitt, R. (1997), 'Market based conflict resolution', in R. Sanchez, J. Woled and D. Tilly (eds), *CWRC. Rosenberg International Forum on Water Policy: Resolving Conflict in the Management of Water Resources*, Report, 93, Davies, pp. 49–58.
Koundouri, P. and P. Pashardes (2003), 'Hedonic price analysis and selectivity bias: water salinity and demand for land', *Environmental and Resource Economics*, **26** (1), 45–56.
Kraemer, A. and K.M. Banholzer (1999), 'Tradable Permits in Water Resource Management and Water Pollution Control', in *Implementing Domestic Tradable Permits for Environmental Protection*, Paris: OECD, Organisation for Economic Co-operation and Development.
Kraemer, A., E. Kampa and E. Interwies (2003), 'The role of tradable permits in water pollution control', Institute for International and European Environmental Policy, Belgium, www.ecologic.de.
Marino, M. and K.E. Kemper (eds) (1999), 'Institutional frameworks in successful water markets: Brazil, Spain, and Colorado', USA WB Technical Paper 427, World Bank.
Mitchell, R.C. and R.T. Carson (1989), *Using Surveys to Value Public Goods: The ContingentValuation Method*, Baltimore, MD: Johns Hopkins.
NOAA (1993), 'Report of the NOAA Panel on Contingent Valuation', *Federal Register*, **58** (10), 4601–14, prepared by K. Arrow, R. Solow, P.R. Portney, E.E. Leamer, R. Radner and H. Schuman.
OECD (2002), 'Environmentally Related Taxes Database', www.oecd.org.
Provencher and Burt (1993), 'The externalities associated with common property resource exploitation of groundwater', *Journal of Environmental Economics and Management*, **24**, 139–58.
UNEP – United Nations Environment Program (2003), 'Vital water graphics', www.unep.org.

Yaron (1997), 'The Israel water experience: an overview', in Parker and Tsur (eds), *Decentralization and Coordination of Water Resources Management*, Boston, MA: Kluwer Academic Publishers.

Zilberman, D. and K. Schoengold (2005), 'The use of pricing and markets in water allocation', *Canadian Water Resources Journal*, **30** (1), 1–10.

7. Competition versus cooperation in groundwater extraction: a stochastic framework with heterogeneous agents

Marita Laukkanen and Phoebe Koundouri

7.1 INTRODUCTION

The most popular behavioural model in the groundwater literature is one in which farmers execute myopic pumping decisions; that is, the state equation does not enter the farmer's decision problem. Moreover a large part of the literature focuses on comparing the steady-state groundwater level under myopic behaviour (uncontrolled non-strategic interaction) and optimal control. See for instance Gisser and Sanchez (1980), Feinerman and Knapp (1983), Llop and Howitt (1983), Allen and Gisser (1984), Nieswiadomy (1985). This focus derives from the need to explain the paradoxical Gisser-Sanchez (1980) result stating that although serious depletion of aquifers is a major threat to many freshwater ecosystems all over the world, the benefits from managing groundwater extraction that have been derived in empirical studies are numerically insignificant.

Koundouri (2000) shows that the Gisser-Sanchez result does not hold in an aquifer with small storage capacity. Moreover in these aquifers, myopic groundwater pumping is not a good approximation of behaviour, as externality effects are more noticeable. Dixon (1989) Negri (1989) and Provencher and Burt (1993) model uncontrolled strategic interaction (feedback solution) under the common property arrangement. In these models farmers' behaviour is 'memoryless' in the sense that each farmer's pumping behaviour depends only on the current state of nature, and farmers take the state-dependent extraction rules[1] of their rivals as given. The empirical results from this literature indicate that the steady-state groundwater reserves attained when farms use feedback strategies are bounded from below by the steady state arising when farms are myopic, and from above by the steady state arising from optimal exploitation.

Although there exist groundwater studies that take rainfall stochasticity into account (Burt, 1964, 1967, 1970; Provencher and Burt, 1994; Knapp and Olson, 1995; Fisher and Rubio, 1997; Zeitouni, 2004), none of them is solved in a game theoretic framework. What is more, none of these studies consider heterogeneous farmers. In this chapter we consider a model that accommodates both strategic interaction between extracting agents and stochastic aquifer recharge, where recharge's stochasticity derives from stochastic rainfall. Each farmer makes their extraction choice facing uncertainty due to stochastic rainfall. Moreover we consider heterogeneous farmers with respect to their choice of irrigation technology, which results in different farmer-specific impacts on the aquifer recharge rate. The more efficient the chosen irrigation technology, the smaller the return flow of water in the aquifer, but it is also true that the more efficient the farmer the less water he or she will extract from the aquifer for irrigation purposes.

The objective of this study is to compare the socially optimal extraction strategy with the feedback extraction solution and the myopic solution, when farmers are heterogeneous and interact under uncertainty deriving from stochastic rainfall. We illustrate the implications of the different strategies on extraction rates, groundwater table levels and attained welfare, via simulations based on data from the Kiti aquifer in Cyprus, which is an aquifer of small storage capacity. The results support Koundouris's (2000) finding that the Gisser-Sanchez result does not apply to small aquifers: our results indicate significant differences between the solutions arising from competition versus optimal extraction.

The chapter is structured as follows: in this section we develop the model of groundwater extraction with heterogeneous agents under stochastic recharge and solve the non-cooperative and social planner problems. In section 7.2 we apply both of these solutions, via simulation, on data from the Kiti aquifer in Cyprus and discuss the results. Section 7.3 concludes the chapter.

7.1.1 Groundwater Extraction under Non-cooperation

We first examine non-cooperative extraction of groundwater, where each farmer makes their extraction decision without considering its effect on the other farmers' expected pay-offs. There are no negotiations or understandings between the farmers. Each farmer maximizes their expected pay-off, taking as given the other farmers' rates of extraction, which they can only infer from their knowledge of the other farmers' objective functions. Consider an aquifer where only the N farms with land overlying the aquifer have access to the resource. The farmers differ in terms of their choice of irrigation technology. By assumption, the farmers can be divided into two groups according to their efficiency and hence their effect on aquifer recharge rate: efficient farmers and inefficient farmers. Within each group, farms are identical in the sense that the profit function $\pi(q_{j,t})$ representing the benefits from groundwater extraction and the recharge rate α_k are identical for all the N_k, $k = e, i$, farmers in the group. The term $q_{j,t}$ denotes groundwater extraction by farmer j in period t, and the subscript $k = e, i$ refers to efficient and inefficient farmers. The per unit cost of groundwater pumping is determined by the level of the water table in period t, h_t. The costs of groundwater extraction, $c(h_t)$, then are identical for all the N farms. Farmer j/s ($j = 1, ..., N$) net revenue from water consumption is:

$$\pi_k(q_{j,t}) - c(h_t) q_{j,t} \tag{7.1}$$

By the assumption of farmers within each group being identical, the N_k farms in each group will pump the same amount of groundwater in period t, denoted by q_t^e and q_t^i, respectively for efficient and inefficient farmers. Total groundwater extraction in period t is then given by $N_e q_t^e + N_i q_t^i$. The state of the groundwater stock evolves according to:

$$h_{t+1} = g(h_t, \tilde{R}_t, q_t^e, q_t^i) = h_t + \frac{1}{AS}[\tilde{R}_t + (a^e - 1)N^e q_t^e + (a^i - 1)N^i q_t^i] \tag{7.2}$$

where $\tilde{R}_t$ denotes periodic rainfall, A the area of the aquifer, S the storativity coefficient, and a^k, $k = e, i$ the recharge rate. The annual rainfall is a random variable. By assumption, the farmers' planning horizon is infinite. The discount factor used to trade off current and future net benefits is δ, where $0 < \delta < 1$.

There are two hypotheses we might entertain about the farms' decision problem when the aquifer is common property. If the agents are myopic, they do not consider the effect of their extraction on the groundwater stock. Each farm sets its extraction rate so as to balance the marginal net benefit of groundwater extraction and the unit cost of extraction:

$$\pi_k'(q_{j,t}) - c(h_t) = 0, \qquad k = e, i \tag{7.3}$$

When the number of extracting agents is relatively small, a more realistic description of pumping behaviour would be that each agent considers the effect of its actions on the groundwater stock, but takes the other agents' extraction plans as given. An individual agent's perception of the stock equation is:

$$h_{t+1} = g(h_t, \tilde{R}_t, q_t^e, q_t^i) = h_t + \frac{1}{AS}[\tilde{R}_t + (a^e - 1)[(N^e - 1)q_t^{e^*} + q_{j,t}^e]$$
$$+ (a^e - 1)N^i q_t^{i^*}] \tag{7.4a}$$

when agent j is of the efficient type, and

$$h_{t+1} = g(h_t, \tilde{R}_t, q_t^e, q_t^i) = h_t + \frac{1}{AS}[\tilde{R}_t + (a^e - 1)N^e q_t^{e^*}$$
$$+ (a^i - 1)[(N^i - 1)q_t^{i^*} + q_{j,t}^i] \qquad (7.4b)$$

when agent j is inefficient.

The individual agent's problem then is to:

$$\max_{q_j} E\left[\sum_{t=0}^{\infty} \delta^t \{\pi_k(q_{j,t}) - c(h_t)q_{j,t}\} \right] \qquad (7.5)$$

subject to the state equation (7.4a)/(7.4b). The dynamic programming equation for the agent's problem is:

$$V_k(h) = \max_{q_j}\{\pi_k(q_j) - c(h)q_j + \delta E[V_k(g[h, \tilde{R}, q^{e^*}, q^{i^*}, q_j])]\} \qquad (7.6)$$

The first-order necessary condition to the problem on the right side of (7.6) is:

$$\pi_k'(q_j) - c(h) + \delta E\left[\frac{a^k - 1}{AS} V_k'(g[h, \tilde{R}, q^{e^*}, q^{i^*}, q_j]) \right] \qquad (7.7)$$

Benveniste and Scheinkman's formula (1979) implies that:

$$V_k'(h) = -c'(h)q_j + \delta E[V_k'(g[h, \tilde{R}, q^{e^*}, q^{i^*}, q_j])] \qquad (7.8)$$

since $\partial g/\partial h = 1$. Equations (7.7) and (7.8) jointly determine the individually optimal rate of extraction q^{k^*}, for $k = e, i$, given the water table h_t and the distribution of the level of the water table under the individually optimal feedback extraction policy. The term $V_k'(g(\cdot))$ represents the private shadow value of *in situ* groundwater, available in the next period. It depicts the agent's private user cost of pumping groundwater: each unit of groundwater extracted in the current period reduces the groundwater stock available for future consumption. An individual agent sets the marginal benefit of an additional unit of water extracted this year, equal to the private user cost in terms of a reduced reserve of water available in the following year.

7.1.2   Social Planner's Solution

We next turn to the problem of central (optimal) control. Consider the case where there exists a single manager with the authority to control each firm's rate of extraction. The social planner's problem is to maximize the aggregate net benefit of groundwater extraction:

$$\max_{q_t^e,\, q_t^i} E \sum_{t=0}^{\infty} \delta^t [N^e \{\pi_e(q_t^e) - c(h_t)\, q_t^e\} + N^i \{\pi_i(q_t^i) - c(h_t)q_t^i\}] \quad (7.9)$$

subject to the state equation:

$$h_{t+1} = g(h_t, \tilde{R}_t, q_t^e, q_t^i) = h_t + \frac{1}{AS}[\tilde{R}_t + (a^e - 1)N^e q_t^e + (a^i - 1)N^i q_t^i] \,(7.10)$$

There are N^e efficient agents and N^i inefficient agents among a total of N agents. Assuming that the social planner weighs each farmer's net benefits equally, the dynamic programming equation for the social planner's problem can be written as:

$$N^e V_e(h) + N^i V_i(h) = \max_{q^e,\, q^i} \{N^e[\pi_e(q^e) - c(h)q^e] + N^i[\pi_i(q^i) - c(h)q^i]$$

$$+ \delta E[N^e V_e(g[h, \tilde{R}, q^e, q^i] + N^i V_i(g[h, \tilde{R}, q^e, q^i])]\}$$

$$(7.11)$$

The first-order conditions are:

$$N^k\{\pi_k'(q^k) - c(h)\} + \delta E \frac{N^k(a^k - 1)}{AS}[N^e V_e'(g[h, \tilde{R},) q^e, q^i])$$

$$+ N^i V_i'(g[h, \tilde{R}, q^e, q^i])] = 0 \quad (7.12)$$

for $k = e,\, i$. Dividing by N^k yields:

$$\pi_k'(q) - c(h) + \delta E \frac{(a^k - 1)}{AS}[N^e V_e'(g[h, \tilde{R}, q^e, q^i]) + N^i V_i'(g[h, \tilde{R}, q^e, q^i])] = 0$$

$$(7.13)$$

for $k = e,\, i$.

Equation (7.13) together with the associated Benveniste and Scheinkman formula determines the socially optimal rates of extraction q^{k*} for $k = e,\, i$ given the water table h_t and the distribution of the level of the water table under the socially optimal extraction policy. As in (7.8), $V_k'(g(\cdot))$ represents the private shadow value of water left in the ground. In the social planner's solution, each farm's extraction rate is set to balance the marginal benefit of pumping in the current period to the opportunity cost it imposes on all agents in terms of a smaller reserve of water in the next period. A comparison of (7.7) and (7.13) shows that the individually optimal rate of groundwater pumping exceeds the socially optimal rate.

7.2 APPLICATION OF THE MODEL

The application of the model uses data from the Kiti agricultural region, an aquifer with small storage capacity located in the coastal southern part of the semi-arid island of Cyprus. The notion of common property characterizes ownership of groundwater reserves, as the doctrine of absolute landownership governs property law in the island. In particular, although the doctrine conditions ownership of groundwater on ownership of land overlying the aquifer (thereby limiting access), in all other respects owners of land own groundwater as a common property resource subject to the rule of capture.

7.2.1 The Data

Table 7.1 summarizes the hydrologic parameters for the region, supplied by the Water Development Department of Cyprus.

The more efficient the irrigation technology the smaller the return flow of water in the aquifer. Empirical results on the efficiency of irrigation methods can be summarized as follows. Irrigation efficiency for surface methods (basin, border, furrow irrigation) reaches 60 per cent, for sprinkler

Table 7.1   Hydrologic parameters

Parameter	Description	Parameter value
a^e	Return flow coefficient of efficient farmers	0.1000 pure number
a^i	Return flow coefficient of inefficient farmers	0.4000 pure number
A	Area of the aquifer	12 000 000 m^2
S	Storativity coefficient	0.1250 pure number
$\tilde{R}$	Rainfall	$\tilde{R} \sim \Gamma$ (20.5, 24.4)
h_o	Initial elevation of water table	3.45 m
SL	Maximum height of water table	47.5 m

irrigation (set systems, travelling guns, continuous move laterals) it reaches 85 per cent, and for localized irrigation (drip, micro-sprayer) it can reach 95 per cent. Most of the water not used by the plant is lost due to deep percolation, while a much lower percentage is lost by evaporation or run-off For the area under consideration 12 per cent of the farmers use surface irrigation systems, 8 per cent use sprinkler irrigation systems and 80 per cent use localized irrigation. For simulation purposes, farmers that use the two most efficient technologies are grouped into one category and are called 'efficient', while the remaining less efficient farmers are grouped in a second category and are called 'inefficient'. The return flow coefficient for efficient farmers (a^e) is taken to be equal to the average of the return flow of the farmers that use sprinkler and localized irrigation system $[1-(85\%+95\%)/2 = 0.1]$, assuming that evaporation is approximately equal to zero. The return flow coefficient for inefficient farmers (a^i) is equal to the return flow of the farmers that use surface methods $[1 - 60\% = 0.4]$, again assuming that evaporation is approximately equal to zero.

The distribution of stochastic rainfall was estimated using a time series of rainfall in the Kiti region for the years 1927–2003. The mean of the series is equal to 493.21mm and the standard deviation is 109.67mm. We used the test described by D'Agostino et al. (1990) with the empirical correction developed by Royston (1991) in order to identify the distribution from which our sample comes. This test indicates that at 98 per cent confidence level we cannot reject the hypothesis that rainfall follows a gamma distribution. Table 7.2 summarizes the socio-economic parameters for the region.

The discussion in the previous paragraph indicates that 85 per cent of the farmers in the area are efficient, while 15 per cent of them are inefficient. The total number of farmers is 60. With regards to the groundwater demand curve we use the one estimated by Koundouri and Christou (2000).

Table 7.2   Economic parameters

Parameter	Description	Parameter value
N	Total number of farmers	60
N^e	Number of efficient farmers (85% of N)	51
N^i	Number of inefficient farmers (15% of N)	9
k_1	Cost of pumping per m³ of water per metre of lift	0.3500 euros/m³
k_2	The intercept of the pumping cost equation	0.3672 euros/m³
g	Absolute value of the slope of agricultural water demand	9 500 000 m³/euros
k	The intercept of agricultural water demand	3 500 000 m³
$\pi(q_j)$	Benefit function for each farmer	$2.714q_j - 0.000014q_j^2$

Given the absence of observations over a wide range of prices, the derived demand for groundwater by farmers was estimated by linear programming. From this demand curve we derive the individual farmer's demand curve and calculate the benefit function for each farmer. The marginal cost function used in the solution of the system is

$$c[h(t)] = k_2 - k_1 \cdot h(t), \, k_1 > 0 \qquad\qquad 7.14$$

The difference $(SL - h)$ measures pumping lift, the distance from the water table to the irrigation surface. This pumping cost function (a specific form of a general cost function) is very popular in the literature; for example Gisser and Mercado (1973), Kim et al. (1989). Its derivatives have the desirable properties of a positive partial derivative with respect to (q) and a negative cross-partial derivative between (q) and the water table.

7.2.2   Simulation Results

Simulations were carried out in Matlab 6.0 using the CompEcon Toolbox for Matlab (see Miranda and Fackler, 2002). CompEcon is a set of Matlab routines developed by Mario Miranda and Paul Fackler for solving a variety of dynamic problems in economics. Of particular interest to the problem at hand, the CompEcon routines for solving continuous time-dynamic programming problems lend themselves to analysing both the social planner's problem and the feedback solution to the N agent groundwater extraction game. The dynamic groundwater extraction model gives rise to functional equations whose unknowns are entire functions defined on a subset of Euclidean space. In many applications, such functional equations lack known closed-form solutions and can thus only be solved approximately using computational methods. Among the numerical functional equation methods, the collocation method provides a flexible, accurate and numerically efficient alternative (see for example Judd, 1998, 1992, 1994). The CompEcon Toolbox provides a series of Matlab routines that perform the essential computations required in applying the collocation method.

Table 7.3 reports the numerical results for the steady state. The findings confirm Koundouris's (2000) result that in an aquifer of small storage capacity, competitive extraction results in serious depletion of the aquifer and significant welfare losses. In parallel to previous studies, the results indicate that a social planner would conserve the resource more than the status quo. Under optimal extraction, the mean elevation of the water table will approach 41 m, as opposed to the current level of 3.45 m. The feedback solution lies between the myopic solution and socially optimal extraction. However as the number of farmers sharing the resource is fairly large, the

Table 7.3   Empirical results

Policy	Extraction efficient farmers, m^3	Extraction inefficient farmers, m^3	Mean water table, m	Expected welfare, €
Myopic	155 300	155 300	2.7	113 100 000
Feedback	115 100	117 500	3.3	113 100 000
Social optimum	98 300	260 400	41	1 071 000 000

feedback solution is close to the myopic one, and there is practically no difference in expected welfare arising from the two competitive policies. The predictions of the empirical model are grim in terms of the losses arising from competitive extraction. Under socially optimal extraction the expected welfare would be close to tenfold compared to the competitive outcome, while the groundwater resource would be reserved. Compared to competitive extraction, the socially optimal solution allocates substantially more water to the inefficient relative to the efficient agents.

7.3   DISCUSSION AND EXTENSIONS

We have extended the literature on groundwater extraction to consider the case of stochastic recharge to the aquifer and heterogenous agents. Our results, based on empirical data for the Kiti aquifer in Cyprus, indicate that competitive extraction results in significant welfare losses: social welfare under competitive extraction is 90 per cent lower than what could be attained under optimal management of the resource. Moreover the groundwater resource is seriously depleted. Our results challenge the Gisser-Sanchez (1980) result that benefits from optimal (central) management are numerically insignificant. Substantial gains could be achieved through fully accounting for the effect of current extraction on future benefits from the groundwater resource.

Given that our results indicate significant differences between the solutions arising from competition versus optimal extraction, an interesting extension would be to investigate economic instruments that can be prescribed as remedies for the inefficiencies arising in the feedback solution. The remedy usually prescribed by the economics literature for the inefficiencies arising in common property groundwater extraction is central (optimal) control by a regulator, who uses taxes or quotas to obtain the efficient allocation of the resource over time. Another instrument considered to implement the full cooperative outcome is a tradable permit scheme. In the context of groundwater depletion Provencher (1993) and Provencher and Burt (1994) examined the applicability of the tradable permit scheme in which private shares to the groundwater stock are established. In their framework, farms are granted an endowment of tradeable permits to the *in situ* groundwater stock, which they control over time. Each farm's bundle of permits represents its private stock of groundwater. This private stock declines due to groundwater pumping and increases to reflect the farm's share of periodic recharge. It also changes in response to the farm's activity in the market for groundwater stock permits, increasing when permits are purchased and decreasing when permits are sold. As a practical matter, the market price for permits serves to allocate groundwater over time.

NOTE

1. An extraction rule expresses the groundwater pumping decision as a function of the observed groundwater stock.

REFERENCES

Allen, R.C. and M. Gisser (1984), 'Competition versus optimal control in ground-water pumping when demand is nonlinear', *Water Resources Research*, **20**, 752–6.
Burt, O.R. (1964), 'Optimal resource use over time with an application to ground-water', *Management Science*, **11**, 80–93.
Burt, O.R. (1967), 'Groundwater management under quadratic irrigation function', *Water Resource Research*, 3673–82.
Burt, O.R. (1970), 'Groundwater storage control under institutional restrictions', *Water Resources Research*, **6**, 1540–48.
D'Agostino, R.B., A. Balanger and R.B. D'Agostino, Jr. (1990), 'A suggestion for using powerful and informative tests of normality', *American Statistician*, **44** (4), 316–21.
Dixon, L.S. (1989), 'Models of groundwater extraction with an examination of agricultural water use in Kern County, California', unpublished PhD dissertation, University of California.
Feinerman, E. and K.C. Knapp (1983), 'Benefits from groundwater management: magnitude, sensitivity, and distribution', *American Journal of Agricultural Economics*, **65**, 703–10.
Fisher, A.C. and S.J. Rubio (1997), 'Adjusting to climate change: implications of increased variability and asymmetric adjustment costs for investment in water reserves', *Journal of Environmental Economics and Management*, **34**, 207–27.
Gisser, M. and A. Mercado (1973), 'Economic aspects of ground water resources and replacement flows in semiarid agricultural areas', *American Journal of Agricultural Economics*, **55**, 461–6.
Gisser, M. and D.A. Sanchez (1980), 'Competition versus optimal control in groundwater pumping', *Water Resources Research*, **31**, 638–42.

Judd, K. (1992), 'Projection Methods for Solving Aggregate Growth Models', *Journal of Economic Theory*, **58**, 410–52.

Judd, K. (1994), 'Approximation, perturbation and projection methods in economic analysis', in H. Amman, D.A. Kendrick and J. Rust (eds), *Handbook of Computational Economics, Vol. 1*, New York: North Holland, 509–86.

Judd, K. (1998), *Numerical Methods in Economics*, Cambridge, MA: MIT Press.

Kim, C.S., M.R. Moore and J.J. Hanchar (1989), 'A dynamic model of adaptation to resource depletion: theory and an application to groundwater mining', *Journal of Environmental Economics and Management*, **17**, 66–82.

Knapp, K.C. and L.J. Olson (1995), 'The economics of conjunctive groundwater management with stochastic surface supplies', *Journal of Environmental Economics and Management*, **28**, 340–56.

Koundouri, P. (2000), *Three Approaches to measuring natural resource scarcity: Theory and Application to Groundwater*, PhD Thesis, Faculty of Economics and Politics, University of Cambridge.

Koundouri, P. and C. Christou (2000), 'Endogenous dynamic adaptation to resource scarcity with backstop availability', mimeo, University of Cambridge.

Llop, A. and R. Howitt (1983), 'On the social cost of groundwater management: the role of hydrologic and economic parameters on policy actions', unpublished manuscript. University of California, Davis.

Miranda, M. and P. Fackler (2002), *Applied Computational Economics and Finance*, Cambridge, MA: MIT Press.

Negri, D.H. (1989), 'The common property aquifer as a differential game', *Water Resources Research*, **25**, 1–15.

Nieswiadomy, M. (1985), 'The demand for irrigation water in the High Plains of Texas, 1957–1980', *American Journal of Agricultural Economics*, **67** (3), 619–26.

Provencher, B. (1993), 'A private property rights regime to replenish a groundwater aquifer', *Land Economics*, **69** (4), 325–40.

Provencher, B. (1998), 'Issues in the conjunctive use of surface water and groundwater', in Daniel W. Bromley (ed.), *The Handbook of Environmental Economics*, Oxford, UK and Cambridge, USA: Blackwell.

Provencher, B. and O. Burt (1993), 'The externalities associated with the common property exploitation of groundwater', *Journal of Environmental Economics and Management*, **24**, 139–58.

Provencher, B. and O. Burt (1994), 'A private property rights regime for the commons: the case for groundwater', *American Journal of Agricultural Economics*, **24**, 875–88.

Royston, P. (1991), 'Tests for departure from normality', *Stata Technical Bulletin*, **2**, 16–17. Reprinted in *Stata Technical Bulletin Reprints*, **1**, 101–4.

Zeitouni, N. (2004), 'Optimal extraction from a renewable groundwater aquifer with stochastic recharge', *Water Resource Research*, **40**: W06517.

PART V

A co-evolutionary approach to adaptive, integrated water management under changing utilization conditions: the Aquadapt project

8. Socio-cultural influences on water utilization: a comparative analysis

Antonio Aledo Tur, Guadalupe Ortiz Noguera, Paul Jeffrey, Mary Gearey, Jean Daniel Rinaudo, Sébastien Loubier,Tatjana Veljanovski and Natasa Ravbar*

8.1 INTRODUCTION

Strategies for sustainable water use are now widely recognized to be promoted by an understanding of the perceptions, attitudes, behaviours and opinions of the final users. This dimension to sustainable development is explicitly stated as an element of Agenda 21 statements that prioritize social participation as a key factor in the construction of environmentally and socially fairer water governance arrangements. The culture of water is created from the interactions between communities and their water environments. This is a constant process of adaptation involving the redefinition of attitudes and behaviours. These processes of the production of environmental cultures are influenced not only by the economic, political and social power structures that define their frames of action (Donahue and Johnston, 1998) but also by global cultural trends that generate new meanings for the environment (Plumwood, 2002). The socio-cultural influences on water utilization are therefore a set of dynamic meanings that generate attitudes and behaviours (Strang, 2003). The scientific effort to understand these socio-cultural determinants produces knowledge that allows us to design new formulas for the sustainable use of water with a higher level of confidence.

However when developing an understanding of the socio-cultural influences on attitudes to water and its use, we are not simply adding another tool for better and more efficient management. We are also realizing a wider ambition. This ambition is premised on the belief that neither scientists nor technicians have the absolute legitimacy to design new ways of managing water and that final users must be incorporated in the process of diagnosis, decision-making and response (Ostrom, 1990). The data presented in the following pages are intended to provide insights into the ways in which citizens wish to construct the future use of water in their regions.

The innovation introduced by this research lies in presenting a comparative analysis of data from four catchments in France, Spain, the United Kingdom and Slovenia. To date, studies regarding domestic water use have been developed exclusively at a national level. The Eurobarometer reports do supply comparative data about the attitudes of the Europeans towards the environment, but without focusing specifically on water issues. Therefore the data provided by the survey reported below provide an opportunity to investigate which local factors may influence the design of strategies for sustainable use of water, and also to start to explore the existence of a common water culture among Europeans.

The broad aim of the study reported here is to expose variations in the determinants of water use at individual, family, community and catchment levels across four European countries (France, Spain, the UK and Slovenia). We are particularly interested in why and under what conditions individuals might alter or modify their water usage patterns (quantities used, quality required or accepted, and timings of use) in response to changing economic conditions and demand management tools such as price and education initiatives. We investigated the attitudes of consumers towards water (for example, as a communal resource, as a right, as a commodity) and the use of it for domestic, leisure, industrial and agricultural purposes, focusing on variations in water quality and water availability (in terms of both volumes and the timing of access).

This general aim has been developed into more specific objectives:

- Objective 1: To understand the political, socio-cultural, economic and technological determinants of collective and individual water consumption.
- Objective 2: To investigate the attitudes of consumers towards water as a communal resource, as a social right and as a commodity.
- Objective 3: To understand the linkages and the differences between four case studies to determine the scope of local, regional and international integrated water management challenges.

This chapter has been structured into five sections. First, we will describe the main goals of the research and then describe the main characteristics of the four catchments involved in the research. Next, we present the results of the national surveys together with a comparative analysis. In the fourth section we will reflect on the emergence of a coherent European water culture. Conclusions are developed in the last part of this chapter.

8.2 DESCRIPTION OF THE CASE STUDY REGIONS AND STUDY METHOD

Four case study regions were selected in order to investigate the functions of socio-cultural variables in water use and management: the Hérault watershed, France; the Kras plateau, Slovenia; the Marina Baixa region, Spain; and the Nene catchment, UK. (Figure 8.1). The four case study regions show sharp climatic and geographic differences that determine the quantity and quality of the water that is available for the populations in these regions. The Marina Baixa represents an extreme case characterized by its semi-arid climate, where water is a scarce and valuable resource. The central issue in the Slovenian case study is the difficulty of extracting water from the karst aquifers. In all four regions agriculture is an important sector of the local economy. Industry is also a significant activity in the UK, French and Slovenian cases. The service sector in all four countries is growing rapidly, mainly due to the expansion of the tourism industry (in the Spanish and Slovenian cases) which can trigger water use conflicts among water consuming sectors.

The River Nene Catchment

The River Nene is located in the east of England, originating in Northamptonshire and running through Cambridgeshire and Lincolnshire into East Anglia. This region has the lowest average level of rainfall in England and Wales. The catchment also includes areas which are below sea level, which leads to the implementation of management strategies to prevent flooding events in times of heavy rainfall and sea surges. There are two cities located in the catchment, Northampton and Peterborough, along with many smaller towns and villages. The region is affected by high levels of in-migration attracted to the area around Peterborough and Cambridge.

The River Nene has not been subject to water quality problems in the recent past. Neither is water quantity a significant problem. However a major threat to the water quality of the river is eutrophication; in particular the Nene has suffered from excess nitrates and phosphates. The surrounding landscape has a mainly agricultural economy, but in recent years the river has become a big attraction for the regional leisure industry. The Nene is therefore a vital resource for the local economy and ecology.

The Marina Baixa

The Marina Baixa is a semi-arid region located on the northern coast of the Alicante province in south-east Spain. It is 680 km^2 in area, and it

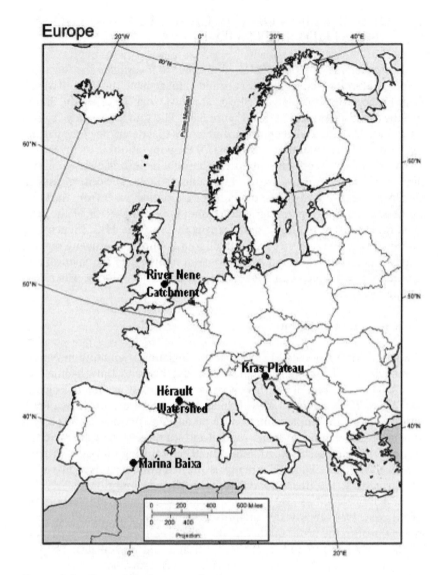

Figure 8.1   Location of case study sites

has a permanent population of 125 088. The region's relief is divided into
a coastal plain area and a mountainous interior. The Marina Baixa has a
Mediterranean climate, with mild winters (a little colder inland) and warm
summers. Rainfall is higher inland, at times registering three times the
amount of rain that falls on the coast. The pluvial regime is characterized

by its long, dry summer and its irregularity, as a few hours of rain can equal half of the annual rainfall.

During the first half of the twentieth century the demographic dynamic of this area was characterized by stagnation. Emigration was very high and agriculture and fishing were the main economic activities. Increased tourism and associated development in Benidorm at the end of the 1950s totally changed the economic and demographic structure of the Marina Baixa. Nowadays tourism services and urban development, along with the activities associated with these two sectors, support the Marina Baixa's economy. The area suffers from a hydrological deficit. A decrease in agricultural activity and improved (more efficient) water use practices have driven a reduction in agricultural water consumption. However this consumption decrease in the agricultural sector is counteracted by the rapid development of residential tourism and the high population growth in the region.

The Hérault Watershed

The Hérault is a river located in the south of France, flowing into the Mediterranean Sea near the town of Agde. The river is 160 km long and the river basin covers an area of 2500 km². Significant differences in annual rainfall can be observed between the low altitude in coastal areas (500–600 mm) that are semi-arid and the elevated mountainous zone (more than 2000 mm). The river basin population is about 152 000, divided amongst 166 towns and villages. Most of the population of the watershed is concentrated on the coast. It represents 12 per cent of the river basin area and 38 per cent of its permanent population, with a density of 165 persons/km². Agde and Vias are the most densely populated cities, having permanent populations of more than 24 000.

Agricultural activity is dominated by wine production, which represents the mainstay of the economy. The improvement of the road network has led to the development of industrial and service-related activities. The local economy is also influenced by the demand generated by the arrival of immigrants, particularly in the construction sector. The Hérault and its alluvial aquifer are the two major water resources of this region. Waters from the Hérault river are mostly used for crop irrigation and hydropower production. Overabstraction occasionally generates tensions with non-consumptive uses of the river such as fishing, swimming and canoeing. The alluvial aquifer of the Hérault river is also the main source of drinking water for the municipalities of the area, making the overall water supply highly vulnerable to accidental pollution.

The Karstic Environment of South-West Slovenia

The Slovenian case study region is located in the south-west of the country and has six different geomorphologic areas. The south-west of Slovenia has a sub-Mediterranean climate that becomes increasingly continental in nature towards the interior. Karst regions are poor in surface waters. Therefore, more than half of the water resources are obtained from karst aquifers which makes it difficult to obtain water for domestic use. In spite of sufficient rainfall, water stress is present in the area mainly because of the poor quality of drinking water supply systems and because of the vulnerability of karstic water resources to pollution.

Population growth is largely due to immigration from remote areas, is concentrated in the valleys and coast, and is a key stress driver in the catchment. Agriculture is the main activity inland. Other crucial stress drivers are urbanization in the valleys and industrialization on the coast, as well as the development of tourism resorts on the coast. Although the inflow of tourists occurs mainly in the summer months, uncoordinated planning of tourism development may be a threat to the stability of the water balance in the region. In spite of sufficient rainfall, water stress is present in the area mainly because of the poor quality of drinking water supply systems.

Survey Methodology

Survey sample profiling considered socio-demographic variables such as age, gender, geographical area and (with the exception of the Spanish case) type of living accommodation. This guaranteed a statistically representative sample of the whole population of each area and gave the survey a margin of error of ± 5 per cent and a confidence level of 95 per cent. Completed and validated questionnaires from each case study gave 421 responses from Slovenia, 400 from France, 411 from Spain and 380 from the British case study.

The survey was conducted through an administered questionnaire conducted in respondents' own homes. Questionnaire development involved collaboration between the four regional teams and the final set of questions included a core set of queries common to all four case studies (divided into eight sections: environmental concerns; individual perception and knowledge of water resource management; individual knowledge of the drinking water cycle; water uses and water quantity; water uses and perception of water quality; water prices and related behaviours; and water-saving behaviours), and a set of case study-specific questions. Survey translation and piloting was conducted in each case study location.

8.3   SURVEY FINDINGS

We now go on to report the results from the surveys as derived from two analytical procedures: (1) national differences in attitudes to water stress, based on a comparison of basic frequencies; (2) a consumer profile analysis to understand the attitudes and behaviours towards the use and consumption of water of the respondents, constructing three different typologies: (a) based on level of concern about water issues; (b) based on how informed respondents feel they are with respect to water issues; (c) based on water-saving behaviours.

National Differences in Attitudes to Water Stress

Analysis of the survey results confirm an already well-documented feature of European attitudes to the environment. Data from surveys carried out across Europe suggest that the environment is not a primary concern of Europeans. For example the Eurobarometer data between September 2003 and August 2004 show that when responding to the prompt: 'the two most important issues facing (our country) at the moment are' our respondents ranked 'protecting the environment' in twelfth place. The first three places were taken by unemployment, economic situation and crime (EC, 2003).

Data from the survey reported here allows us to put some detail on this rather general trend. Amongst our four sets of respondents, Spanish respondents seem to have the highest level of concern about environmental issues in general, and more specially, with regard to water problems. Conversely, respondents from the UK displayed the lowest level of concern about water issues. When asked about the environmental issue that concerned them the most at a global level, it is the Spanish sample that seems to be more concerned with water, rating it third in importance, while the French and Slovenians placed water issues as the sixth most concerning issue.

Whilst a majority of respondents in all four case studies agreed that the main function of water is to support natural life, we have detected some differences among the samples. In the French case, the difference between those who answer that the function of water is to satisfy human needs (43.8 per cent) and those who say it is to support natural life (56.2 per cent) is much smaller than the difference that we found with the Slovenian respondents, of whom only 24.5 per cent selected the first option, in opposition to 75.6 per cent that selected the second one.

An unwillingness to be directly involved in discussions and debates on the management of water resources is also a common characteristic of the four national response sets. This finding may be related to the lack of

Table 8.1   Willingness to support off-peak pricing

		Country				Total
		Spain	Slovenia	France	UK	
Acceptance of	Yes	61.5%	67.0%	71.4%	62.3%	65.6%
off-peak tariff	No	38.5%	33.0%	28.6%	37.7%	34.4%
	Total	100.0%	100.0%	100.0%	100.0%	100.0%

consideration of water as an important concern (as reported above), as well as with distrust of the effectiveness of their participation in public debates about water. The Spanish and Slovenian respondents are the most predisposed to participate, while the French and British samples are the least willing to get involved in public debates on water issues.

In terms of knowledge of the water cycle and its management, the Slovenian sample most clearly demonstrates an understanding of the water cycle, while the UK sample seems to be poorly informed about these issues. This difference might be explained by the predominance of a more rural lifestyle in Slovenia that fosters a direct relationship with the resource.

Although respondents in all four samples do not consider themselves to be high consumers of water, we detected evidence of water-saving behaviour in all the cases. For example the proportion of respondents that ensure that the washing machine and/or the dishwasher has a full load before switching them on is above 80 per cent in the Spanish, Slovenian and French cases. Closing the taps to avoid unnecessary wastage of water was also a commonly articulated behavioural trait among the respondents with between 84 per cent and 91 per cent indicating that they always follow such guidelines. This generally positive attitude towards behaviour modification is confirmed by responses to questions on attitude towards or willingness to accept more personal effort and time-consuming measures with the aim of decreasing household water consumption.

For example, when asked if they would accept a pricing system which differentiates between peak and off-peak use, the majority of respondents in the four countries answer affirmatively (Table 8.1).[1] Spain is the country where we find the most negative responses, and we might infer that behavioural changes are more difficult to introduce here than in the other countries. French respondents are the most predisposed to this kind of change to tariff structures.

When asked the question, 'If your normal water bill was projected to increase by a quarter, do you think you would take measures to reduce your consumption?' (Table 8.2) only one national response group (Spanish

Table 8.2   Willingness to reduce water consumption

		Country				Total
		Spain	Slovenia	France	UK	
Willingess to take	Yes	54.0%	28.9%	49.3%	39.0%	43.0%
measures to reduce	No	46.0%	71.1%	50.7%	61.0%	57.0%
water consumption	Total	100.0%	100.0%	100.0%	100.0%	100.0%

Table 8.3   Willingness to pay to protect water in the environment

		Country				Total
		Spain	Slovenia	France	UK	
'I would be willing to pay an additional	Strongly agree	25.3%	12.8%	16.0%	4.9%	14.9%
charge in my household	Agree	39.1%	53.7%	33.2%	40.7%	41.8%
water bill to directly	Neither	16.4%	5.9%	22.8%	18.0%	15.7%
support the protection	Disagree	13.3%	23.2%	16.5%	31.1%	20.9%
of water in the environment.'	Strongly disagree	5.9%	4.4%	11.5%	5.3%	6.7%
	Total	100.0%	100.0%	100.0%	100.0%	100.0%

respondents) had a majority which answered in the affirmative. The remaining groups, especially Slovenia, had majorities resistant to taking such measures.

Respondents were also asked if they agreed with the statement, 'I would be willing to pay an additional charge in my household water bill to directly support the protection of water in the environment' (Table 8.3). Here, the response from Slovenian citizens is interesting as, even though responses to other questions show that this is the sample group that considers tap water to be more expensive than the rest, it is also the one that agrees more clearly with an increase in water bills to protect the water environment. The French sample is more reluctant to support increases in the price of water, which may be due either to their perception of it as an expensive resource or to the lack of any significant water scarcity problems in this case study region.

When asked to what extent they agreed with the statement, 'In my region, water is very abundant; there is no need to save it' (Table 8.4), a majority of the Spanish sample responded 'Strongly disagree'. The immediacy of water scarcity problems in Spain and the related social debate about this resource may explain the distribution of responses here.

Table 8.4   Opinions regarding water availability

		Country				Total
		Spain	Slovenia	France	UK	
'In my region, water is very abundant; there is no need to save it'	Strongly agree	2.7%	0.6%	5.3%	1.6%	2.6%
	Agree	5.7%	11.3%	17.8%	20.2%	13.6%
	Neither	4.7%	1.0%	13.3%	11.0%	7.4%
	Disagree	34.5%	49.8%	36.2%	48.0%	42.1%
	Strongly disagree	52.4%	37.3%	27.4%	19.2%	34.3%
	Total	100.0%	100.0%	100.0%	100.0%	100.0%

Profiling Consumers with Respect to their Attitudes towards Water Use

The construction of characteristic consumer profiles was made difficult by the absence of well-defined socio-demographic clusters. In other words, a combination of socio-demographic variables (age, sex, type of living accommodation, ownership of the property, educational level, occupation and number of people per home) has not enabled the identification of groups of respondents with significant differences with regard to their water-saving behaviour, the extent to which they feel themselves informed about water issues, or their level of concern about water issues. Only age and educational level were partially correlated with these aspects of water use. This is, in itself, an interesting finding. We now go on to report the results of a profiling analysis which categorize types of respondent in terms of (1) their level of concern about water issues; (2) the extent to which they feel themselves informed about water issues; and (3) their water-saving behaviour.

Level of concern about water issues

A factorial analysis of the data was undertaken and revealed that the population group with the highest level of concern about water issues are young adults with a high educational level. Many of them are members of families of four people that live in their own apartments. This group is also likely to believe that the main function of water is to support natural life and they are more willing than average to get involved in discussions and debates on water issues. They also believe that the highest volumes of water are consumed by the tourism and leisure sectors. They generally show a critical attitude towards the quality of tap water: they do not trust tap water, its quality, and probably because of this, they usually consume bottled water. They consider potable water to be expensive and its price to have gone up over recent years.

Those who are least concerned about water issues are more likely to be older adults with a lower standard of education. These respondents tend to consider the main function of water to be to satisfy human needs, and not to support natural life. They do not seem willing to get involved in debates or discussions on water problems, and they point out that agriculture is the sector that consumes the highest amount of water. In general, this group is quite satisfied with the quality of their tap water, as they trust it and they believe it has an appropriate quality and price (they also think its price is quite stable), and they consume it as a habit rather than purchase bottled water.

Informed about water issues

Analysis of this issue involved a two-step cluster analysis which included a consideration of nationality. From this we conclude that the respondents that declare themselves to be well informed about water issues are most likely to be older Slovenian males, of an average age of 53 years. They would typically live in a detached house which is their own property. They are more willing to get involved in discussions and debates about these issues than to consider themselves ill-informed, and they believe that tourism, and secondly, industry, are the economic sectors that consume the highest volumes of water. They are more likely to think that water is expensive and are less willing to consume their highest volumes of water at off-peak hours, although they would pay additional charges in their normal water bills if these charges were directed to protect water in the environment.

Those respondents who indicated that they are uninformed about water issues are most likely to be British women who live in apartments and in rented households. They seem to be less disposed to become involved in debates about these issues, and they believe that the agricultural sector, followed by tourism, are the economic sectors with the highest water consumption. They perceive water as a cheaper resource than do well-informed respondents, although they seem to be more willing to consume their highest volumes of water at off-peak times to save money on their water bills, and they are more reluctant to pay new charges to protect water in the environment.

Water-saving behaviour

A two-step cluster analysis was also completed to support analysis of this issue. Analysis focused on the socio-demographic characteristics of the respondents and their more or less active water-saving behaviour. The Spanish sample with an age range between 61 and 80 years old are the most active in water-saving behaviour. The least active in this kind of behaviour are the British respondents and those between 21 and 30 years old. The most active respondents in terms of water-saving behaviour are more willing to get involved in discussions and debates on water management issues. They believe that tourism and leisure are the economic sectors that consume the highest volumes of water, and they are more likely to drink filtered or bottled water. They usually have a water meter installed, and they believe that water is expensive, and indicate their willingness to consume their highest volumes of water at off-peak times to reduce their water bills.

The least active in water-saving behaviours state that they would not get involved in debates on water issues, and they believe that industry and agriculture are the economic sectors that consume the highest volumes of water. They prefer to drink water directly from their taps. Water meters are less likely to be installed at their households, and they think water is not expensive. They are also disinclined to consume water at off-peak hours.

We conclude this profile analysis by making some general observations on the relationships between respondent characteristics and the dimensions to water management discussed above. Firstly we would note that younger respondents display the highest level of concern about water issues but also demonstrate the least water-saving behaviour, whilst older respondents are the most active group in terms of water saving, although they are the least concerned about water issues. Country by country, Spanish respondents are more likely to be concerned about water issues, whilst conversely, we find that British respondents have a lower level of concern and water-saving behaviour. In general, those most concerned and more informed are also the most active in water-saving behaviours, more willing to get involved in public debates and discussions on water issues and more critical about the price of water. The least concerned, informed and active in water-saving behaviours are less worried about the price of water. The least concerned and the least active in water-saving behaviours also seem to trust the quality of their tap water, and the least informed and the least concerned are less willing to participate in public debates on water issues.

Once the profiles were constructed they were compared with the aim of identifying correlations between levels of concern, levels of information and water-saving behaviour. The results obtained illustrate an important level of coherence among these constructed profiles. We observed that it is more probable to find respondents from the group of 'the most informed' about water issues in the group of the most concerned respondents about water issues (Table 8.5).

Also, respondents who are most active in water-saving behaviours are more likely to be found in the group with the highest concern about water issues (Table 8.6).

Table 8.5   Relationship between levels of concern and knowledge about water issues

			The least/the most concerned about water issues		Total
			The least	The most	
Informed about water	No	% Informed	66.7%	33.3%	100.0%
		% The least/The most	64.0%	47.6%	57.4%
	Yes	% Informed	50.6%	49.4%	100.0%
		% The least/The most	36.0%	52.4%	42.6%
Total		% Informed	59.8%	40.2%	100.0%
		% The least/The most	100.0%	100.0%	100.0%

Finally, the most active respondents in water-saving behaviours can be divided into two groups of the same size: one of these groups considers itself as informed about water issues and the other does not. Only 29.4 per cent from the group which is least active in water-saving behaviours also declare that they are informed about water issues, while 70.6 per cent say they are not informed. Therefore, among the informed respondents we can find more respondents active in water-saving behaviours (77.3 per cent) than in the group of the uninformed (59.3 per cent) (Table 8.7).

Are there 'Typical' Europe-wide Attitudes to Water Use?

The relative homogeneity of the results of this survey across the four case study areas indicates a generally positive attitude towards water and its management. Specifically, the findings seem to reflect: (1) the existence of shared environmentalist values in the samples; and (2) a special concern about water. We now intend to expand on these findings, drawing on additional data from the survey to support our thesis. Our interest here is the possible existence of a shared perspective on water and its use: a water culture? By culture we mean the mechanism of adaptation to the social and environmental context. Adaptation to the social context is achieved by the transfer, from generation to generation, of a whole symbolic complex that allows interaction with the social context, and endows it with meaning. In this sense, a water culture would comprise the symbolic and practical elements of interactions between society and water, providing it with a meaning that encourages specifically admissible attitudes and behaviours for each society. A European water culture would involve many of the cultural meanings of water, a set of perceptions, attitudes and behaviours towards water which are

Table 8.6 Relationship between conservation behaviour and level of concern about water issues

			The least/the most concerned about water issues		Total
			The least	The most	
The most/The least active in water-saving behaviours	The most active in water-saving behaviours	% The most/The least active in water-saving behaviours	37.0%	63.0%	100.0%
		% The least/The most concerned	61.4%	82.9%	73.4%
	The least active in water-saving behaviours	% The most/The least active in water-saving behaviours	64.2%	35.8%	100.0%
		% The least/The most concerned	38.6%	17.1%	26.6%
Total		% The most/The least active in water-saving behaviours	44.2%	55.8%	100.0%
		% The least/The most concerned	100.0%	100.0%	100.0%

Table 8.7 Relationship between levels of concern and conservation behaviour

			The most/The least active in water-saving behaviours		Total
			The most active in water-saving behaviours	The least active in water-saving behaviours	
Informed about water	No	% Informed about water	59.3%	40.7%	100.0%
		% The most/The least active in water-saving behaviours	50.7%	70.6%	57.3%
	Yes	% Informed about water	77.3%	22.7%	100.0%
		% The most/The least active in water-saving behaviours	49.3%	29.4%	42.7%
Total		% Informed about water	67.0%	33.0%	100.0%
		% The most/The least active in water-saving behaviours	100.0%	100.0%	100.0%

Table 8.8   Issues of concern to respondents

		Country			Total
		Spain	Slovenia	France	
At national level,	Law and order	35.3%	43.7%	32.0%	37.0%
I'm concerned	Education	19.8%	9.0%	27.0%	18.5%
about . . .	Economy	5.4%	18.5%	10.8%	11.6%
	Employment	13.1%	22.7%	20.2%	18.6%
	Health and SS	17.3%	5.4%	6.0%	9.6%
	Environment	7.9%	0.5%	3.8%	4.0%
	International policy	1.2%	0.2%	0.4%	0.6%
Total		100.0%	100.0%	100.0%	100.0%

shared by most of the European population. Although the Aquadapt survey has been confined to four specific basins that limit this hypothesis, the high level of coherence shown by the responses from these four samples from four distant and little-related river basins seem to indicate at least a kernel of coherence and commonality.

As stated earlier, the environment is not a priority concern for our respondents. In all four countries, 'law and order' is ranked as the highest concern. The environment is ranked sixth by the French, Slovenian and English respondents, while for the Spaniards it is ranked fifth. The priority given to the issue of law and order could well be a reflection of global perceptions of the risks associated with the events triggered by the attacks of 11 September 2001 and the Iraq war. It follows logically that there is concern about economic issues in a framework of a global process of rapid economic change that is due to a high level of competitiveness among regions and states. We would characterize these issues as 'strong' issues or 'hard cultural concerns' for European culture. On the other hand, concern about the environment, housing issues or international policy are placed into the category of 'weak issues' or 'weak cultural concerns' (O'Riordan, 1976).

The coherence of results across the four case studies seems to indicate a shared European culture, at least with regard to: (1) environmental issues (Tables 8.8 and 8.9); (2) agreement on the need to reduce water consumption (Tables 8.1, 8.2 and 8.3); and (3) water-saving behaviour undertaken by the respondents from the four countries (Table 8.10).

So does this common culture of water extend to the profiles described earlier in this text? As we have already pointed out, only age and educational level are relevant socio-demographic features. However we can say that younger respondents are more likely to display higher levels of environmental concern whilst older respondents exhibit lower levels of concern, even

Table 8.9   Opinions on the function of water

		Country				Total
		Spain	Slovenia	France	UK	
The function of water is to . . .	Satisf. human needs	36.7%	24.4%	43.8%	42.6%	36.9%
	Sustain natural life	63.3%	75.6%	56.2%	57.4%	63.1%
Total		100.0%	100.0%	100.0%	100.0%	100.0%

Table 8.10   Water conservation behaviour

			The most/the least active in water-saving behaviours		Total
			The most	The least	
Country	Spain	% Country	78.5%	21.5%	100.0%
		% The most/The least	33.3%	22.6%	30.2%
	Slovenia	% Country	70.7%	29.3%	100.0%
		% The most/The least	37.9%	38.7%	38.1%
	UK	% Country	64.7%	35.3%	100.0%
		% The most/The least	28.8%	38.7%	31.6%
Total		% Country	71.2%	28.8%	100.0%
		% The most/The least	100.0%	100.0%	100.0%

though they are more active in water-saving behaviour (Figure 8.2). A priori, it might be expected that the level of concern about water issues would show an increasing trend as educational level rises. However the range of the data in the graph in Figure 8.3 indicates that there is little difference in the level of concern between the 'primary education' group and the group with university education.

With regard to the coherence between attitudes and behaviours, in the results obtained we observed that attitudes towards water are reflected in coherent behaviours. For instance among the group of those most active in water-saving behaviours from the four catchments, we found that 63 per cent of them are also found in the cluster of the most concerned, and the other 37 per cent are among the least concerned. Moreover among the most concerned we find 82.9 per cent of the respondents that are also in the group of

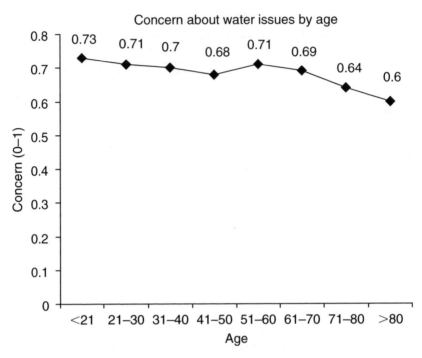

Figure 8.2   Relationship between age and level of concern about water issues

the most active in water-saving behaviours, while 17.1 per cent is among the group of the least active in water-saving behaviours (Table 8.6).

Although this is a clear difference, it is from our point of view insufficient to demonstrate the point. It might have been expected that, in a group more or less concerned (25 per cent are the most concerned and 25 per cent are the least concerned) about water issues, the behavioural coherence would be higher. That is, we found an even higher percentage of concerned respondents in the group of the most active in water-saving behaviours, and a higher percentage of less concerned people among the least active in water-saving behaviours. In this sense, we can see that among the group of the least concerned from the four case studies we continue to detect that 61.4 per cent also belong to the cluster of the most active in water-saving behaviours, which entails the existence of some kind of latent incoherence in the atti-tude– behaviour relationship, as well as the broad introduction of environ-mental values into European society. This fact confirms the former statement about the high homogeneity among perceptions, attitudes and behaviours towards water.

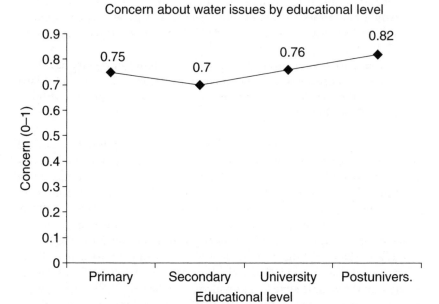

Figure 8.3   *Relationship between level of education and level of concern about water issues*

8.4   EMERGENCE OF A COHERENT EUROPEAN WATER CULTURE

Our research leads us to conclude that people display water-saving behaviours in a more consistent way than would have been expected if we observe the attitudes related to this kind of behaviour. Moreover it can be asserted that the water-saving behaviour has been internalized by the surveyed population. A possible explanation may be related to the multiple meanings and uses of water. In terms of the whole population and their attitude towards water, it would appear that water is not only a natural resource, but also a valuable and scarce economic resource. This fact is reinforced by their daily behaviour. It could also explain the generalization of post-materialistic values among the respondents.

In other words, we believe that the population understands that water has a dual role:

1. Water is perceived as a basic resource. From the responses, we can detect that the willingness to change consumption habits after an

    increase in the price of water is rather low (57 per cent of the sample would not reduce their consumption) (Table 8.2); and that in general, water is perceived as a cheap good (45.9 per cent say it is not expensive) (Table 8.11).

2.   Water also has an environmental aspect, of a significant symbolic nature, as we have been able to see when analysing this factor. For example 63 per cent of the sample believe that the main function of water is to support natural life (Table 8.9).

Taken in total, we would propose that these results not only demonstrate that there is a shared European culture of water, but also that environmental values, attitudes and behaviours have been internalized – although at a superficial level – by most of the population. This assertion does not contradict the distinction between strong cultural concerns and weak cultural concerns. The sociological theory about cultural change in developed societies proposed by the British sociologist Ronald Inglehart (1989) forecast in the 1980s that there would be an increase in the post-materialistic-environmentalist values in Western Europe, as a consequence of the material safety that the welfare state had provided since the mid-1950s. However the European social dynamic during the 1980s and until today has not placed environmental values into hard cultural concerns, but into weak cultural concerns (Blühdorn, 2000).

The European water culture clearly has contact with local water cultures. These local cultures are the result of the interaction of local populations with water, of their socio-cultural history and of the local environmental characteristics of water with regard to its quantity and quality. Along with this reality of local cultures, in constant dialectics and interaction with the global culture, is the beginnings of an explanation for those differences we find when comparing the results of the four case studies, and the internal coherence that the results illustrate when they are analysed at a regional scale.

For example, the 'basic resource' perspective would anticipate the results obtained from the point of view of the local culture, as we find that the respondents from the Spanish sample are the main components of the group with the most concern over water issues and that are the most active in water-saving behaviours (Tables 8.12 and 8.13). In Maslownian terms, scarcity creates the necessity, and necessity generates the values. In a region where the water deficit is a structural feature, water is a valuable resource, and this is reflected in the attitude and behaviour of the Spanish consumers.

Along with the Marina Baixa catchment, the Slovenian case study is also characterized by significant water problems due to the difficulties imposed by the karst landscape. In this sense, scarcity or difficult access to water would be directly related to the perception of this basic resource, its care and saving.

Table 8.11   Opinions regarding the price of water

		Country				Total
		Spain	Slovenia	France	UK	
I think price of water is . . .	Cheap					
	% I think price of water is . . .	24.1%	22.4%	21.1%	32.5%	100.0%
	% Country	15.7%	13.7%	13.3%	21.3%	15.9%
	Neither					
	% I think price of water is . . .	25.8%	18.0%	19.7%	36.5%	100.0%
	% Country	42.0%	27.7%	31.2%	60.1%	40.0%
	Expensive					
	% I think price of water is . . .	23.5%	34.5%	31.8%	10.2%	100.0%
	% Country	42.3%	58.5%	55.5%	18.6%	44.1%
Total						
	% I think price of water is . . .	24.5%	26.0%	25.2%	24.3%	100.0%
	% Country	100.0%	100.0%	100.0%	100.0%	100.0%

Table 8.12 Concern over water issues by country

			Country				Total
			Spain	Slovenia	France	UK	
The least/the most concerned about water issues	The least	% The least/the most concerned about water issues	14.6%	14.6%	35.8%	34.9%	100.0%
		% Country	24.4%	32.1%	60.5%	83.2%	48.4%
	The most	% The least/the most concerned about water issues	42.5%	29.0%	21.9%	6.6%	100.0%
		% Country	75.6%	67.9%	39.5%	16.8%	51.6%
Total		% The least/the most concerned about water issues	29.0%	22.1%	28.6%	20.3%	100.0%
		% Country	100.0%	100.0%	100.0%	100.0%	100.0%

Table 8.13 Water conservation behaviour by country

		Country			Total
		Spain	Slovenia	UK	
The most/the least active in water-saving behaviours	The most active	% The most/the least active in water-saving behaviours	33.3%	37.9%	28.8%	100.0%
		% Country	78.5%	70.7%	64.7%	71.2%
	The least active	% The most/the least active in water-saving behaviours	22.6%	38.7%	38.7%	100.0%
		% Country	21.5%	29.3%	35.3%	28.8%
Total		% The most/the least active in water-saving behaviours	30.2%	38.1%	31.6%	100.0%
		% Country	100.0%	100.0%	100.0%	100.0%

However it is not only scarcity or the difficulty of abstracting water which add value to this resource. As responses to the questions about measures to reduce the consumption of water in the future demonstrate, there must be other elements that increase the value of this resource. These values promote a pro-sustainable attitude amongst the users. For example when questioned as to whether they would be willing to accept an increase in their water bills if the additional charge was used for the protection of water in the environment, British respondents most readily agree with this kind of measure. In this sense, when asked about the option of shifting water consumption to off-peak times, the French respondents offer the highest number of affirmative answers while, contrastingly, the Slovenians are most likely to resist this measure. Therefore campaigns aimed at improving water use at a household level should take into account these local differences. Campaigns should be adapted to local water cultures and be extremely sensitive towards the kind of relationship, symbolic perception and physical interrelation that citizens maintain with water.

8.5   CONCLUSIONS

The results that this research provide are in many aspects hopeful signs for the sustainable future use of water. Although the environment and water are not considered as a major problem for European citizens, survey results demonstrate that respondents have a high concern about water issues. The high willingness to accept different kinds of measures to decrease water consumption must be taken into account when making decisions to activate such demand-side strategies. On the other hand, the lack of knowledge about the processing of tap water and the lack of interest in participating in public debates are the main challenges to be addressed in order to design sustainable strategies of water use.

Sustainability is a collective project and the sustainable use of water is a task that every citizen is committed to. However the attitudes and behaviours of water users are influenced by the power structures that define their frames of action. In other words, attitudes towards water and daily behaviours are determined by the way that sustainability values are broadcast by the mass media and taught at school, by the contradictions in water supply strategies found in public policies, or by the lack of water-saving devices in urban environments. These determinants are a product of pre-existing power structures that have an influence on global and local water cultures. Therefore the goal of sustainable water use is also a political issue, a dialectic between power structures and human agency.

NOTES

* Specifically, we would acknowledge the contributions of Raquel Huete, (University of Alicante, Spain) and José Andrés Domínguez (University of Huelva). The authors would like to thank Denise Eisenhuth for her help in the task of translating the Spanish draft of this chapter into English, and also her intellectual advice in the analysis of the results of this research.
1. All tables presented in this chapter show statistically significant data.

REFERENCES

Blühdorn, I. (2000), *Post-Ecologist Politics: Social Theory and the Abdication of the Ecologist Paradigm*, New York: Routledge.

Donahue, J. and B.R. Johnston (1998), *Water, Culture and Power: Local Struggles in a Global Context*, Washington, DC: Island Press.

European Comission (2003), *Eurobarometer 60.1: Public Opinion in the European Union*, Brussels: EC.

Inglehart, R. (1989), *Culture Shift in Advanced Industrial Society*, New Jersey: Princeton University Press.

O'Riordan, T. (1976), *Environmentalism*, London: Pion.

Ostrom, E. (1990), *Governing the Commons: The Evolution of Institutions for Collective Action*, Cambridge: Cambridge University Press.

Plumwood, V. (2002), *Environmental Culture: The Ecological Crisis of Reason*, New York: Routledge.

Strang, V. (2003), *The Meaning of Water*, Oxford: Berg.

9. Some evidence of landscape change, water usage, management system and governance co-dynamics in south-eastern Spain

Andreu Bonet, Juan Bellot, Denise Eisenhuth, Juan Peña, Juan Rafael Sánchez and Julio César Tejada

9.1 INTRODUCTION

The identification and characterization of co-dynamic processes between landscape, resource usage, management system and governance is crucial to determine the causes of structural change in socio-natural systems. A clearer understanding of the co-dynamic processes that can occur in socio-natural systems could help to illuminate further the rapid and unforeseen changes that are inherent to the environmental, socio-economic and governance contexts within which water supply and demand patterns develop. The processional logic here infers that if co-dynamic processes cause structural change in socio-natural systems, then structural change could offer the key through which to identify the characteristics of both the type of resilience and the adaptive capacity that maintains the long-term sustainability of a socio-natural system.

The literature pertaining to the concepts of resilience and adaptive capacity recognizes that resilience refers to the potential of a natural or social system to reorganize or restructure (Walker et al., 2002; see also Gunderson and Holling, 2002). Adaptive potential is understood to be the capacity of an ecological system to transform itself, and in a social system to promote innovation; such change facilitating a reconfiguration of the system without a significant decline in its crucial functions.

The study reported here takes as its frame of reference the Marina Baixa catchment area in Spain (Figure 9.1). The catchment covers 671 km^2 and is located on the border between a semi-arid rainshadow climate and a dry climate. It comprises a complex and varied topography characterized by

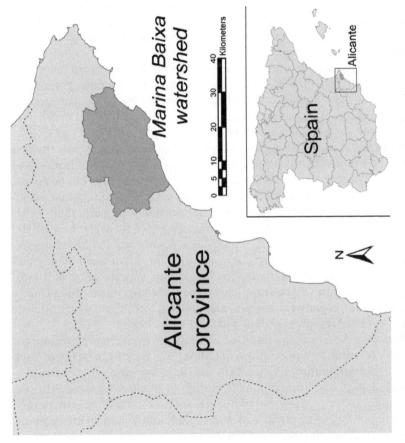

Figure 9.1   Study area map: location of Marina Baixa County watershed in the Alicante province

dense land occupation where irrigated crops (medlars, citrus and other fruits) and dry crops (carobs, olives and almonds) predominate together with developed and industrial areas as well as a well-defined area of Mediterranean woodland. It is one of the nine counties that together constitute the province of Alicante and is located in a region that has undergone great socio-economic changes due to the fact that today it hosts over 60 per cent of the Valencian community's tourist activity. In its turn, the Marina Baixa county comprises 18 municipalities which for the period under study (1956–2000) exhibit a mosaic of different change trends due to their proximity to the coast (tourism) and the availability of irrigation water (intensive irrigation crops).

As we will see later, water management in the Marina Baixa has a long history. Currently, the State bears prime responsibility for water governance issues and the Confederaciones Hidrográficas (river basin management authorities) are state bodies. Water is considered a public good with a concession for use as established in the 1985 Ley de Aguas (Water Law).

Concessions for water use can be administrative or shared, as is the case with the Comunidades de Regantes (irrigation water user associations) or can be private concessions that were granted prior to the 1985 Ley de Aguas. The Comunidades de Regantes were formalized as semi-autonomous institutions in 1985. A fairly complicated arrangement of property rights exists amongst these institutions despite the amendment of the Water Law in 1999 to deal with this situation. Ayuntamientos (local councils) are also semi-autonomous institutions and are responsible for urban water supply and sanitation. These semi-autonomous institutions allocate water at a local level and therefore can be considered to be embedded institutions. That is, local cultural, cognitive, structural and political institutions which allocate environmental resources (Zukin and DiMaggia, 1990).

However there is a long tradition of water governance in the region: the history of water user associations in Callosa d'en Sarriá can be traced back to the fifteenth century which means that there have been at least five centuries of local and autonomous allocation of a scarce resource. Also the autonomy of water in this part of Spain dates back to the thirteenth century. A distinguishing characteristic of water supply and demand patterns in this region is that in some municipalities there has been no traditional separation of land and water rights as there has been in others.

Because of its geographical location, the Marina Baixa has a history of water deficiency. Local water-using communities have devised complex supply and demand management arrangements to accommodate this deficiency. The Consorcio de Aguas de la Marina Baixa (a consortium of coastal municipalities) is one of these complex management arrangements that emerged in 1977. Another administrative body with responsibility for responding to the ever-increasing demand for water supply is the Junta Central del Usuarios del Alto y Medio Vinalopó, l'Alicanti y la Marina Baixa, the central unit that will administer the proposed Júcar-Vinalopó water transfer.

The water resource governance process in the Marina Baixa is influenced by determinations made by disembedded institutions, that is, global water institutions, non-governmental organizations (NGOs), the European Union parliamentary departments, the relevant state ministries, the relevant departments of the autonomous community and provincial governments. The Junta Central and the Consorcio, because of their roles in the governance process, are also considered to be disembedded institutions. Together with the embedded institutions described above, there exist other types of embedded water user associations and local NGOs that complete the governance process. Accordingly, management responsibilities overlap in a relatively complicated hierarchical arrangement (Figure 9.2).

Institutions that we consider to be embedded function on at least three different levels: at community, municipal and local NGOs level. However the Comunidades de Regantes that extract and allocate water predominantly for irrigation and the Ayuntamientos that source and allocate potable water appear to be the significant local actors in the allocation process. Despite the apparent hierarchy of embedded and disembedded institutions, both institutional context and water resource legislation is such that these embedded institutions operate with a fair degree of autonomy, which would seem to imply that it is at this level that the capacity to adapt to changes in water supply and demand pattern changes could be detected. These institutions maintain constant and direct interaction with the resource. It can be therefore assumed that if there is evidence of resilience and adaptive capacity at an institutional level, it is most likely to be in these embedded institutions.

However high volumes of this water are extracted and transferred in fairly complex intra-basin and inter-basin transfer arrangements to maintain the sustainability of the water management system. Holling et al. (2002) describe sustainability as the capacity of a system to 'create, test, and maintain adaptive capacity'. Water transfers can be described as engineering responses or resilience to maintain the stability – or the sustainability – of the hydrological system. The result of continued and increasing engineered resilience to maintain stability of the hydrological system challenges both the adaptive capacity of other ecological systems, as well as social adaptive capacity (McGlade, 2002; see also Gunderson and Holling, 2002). Consequently in many of the Comunidades de Regantes there is a general lack of knowledge regarding the area of extensions of land under irrigation, the annual volumes of water used to irrigate or the sources of water. Hence

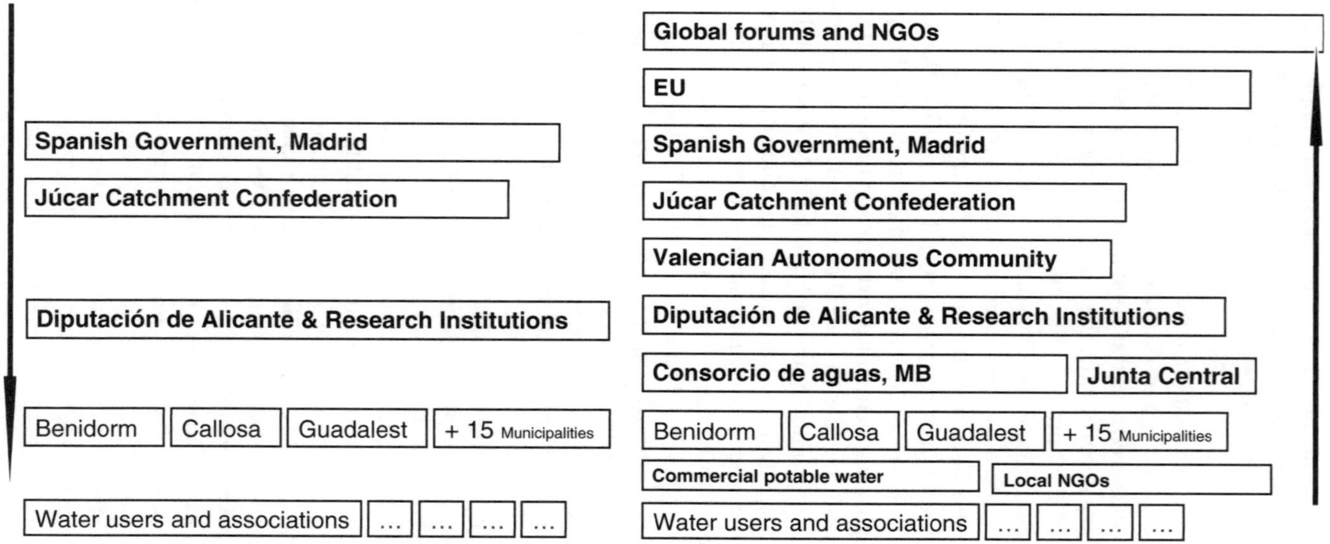

Global forums and NGOs

EU

Spanish Government, Madrid

Júcar Catchment Confederation

Valencian Autonomous Community

Diputación de Alicante & Research Institutions

Consorcio de aguas, MB

Junta Central

Benidorm | Callosa | Guadalest | + 15 Municipalities

Commercial potable water

Local NGOs

Water users and associations | ... | ... | ...

Spanish Government, Madrid

Júcar Catchment Confederation

Diputación de Alicante & Research Institutions

Benidorm | Callosa | Guadalest | + 15 Municipalities

Water users and associations | ... | ... | ...

Note: Down arrow represents law and policy; Up arrow represents information and claims flux.

Figure 9.2 Embedded and disembedded (bold) institutions concerned with water management during periods 1956–60 (left) and 1960–2000 (right) in Marina Baixa

there are variations between the extensions of land that can legally be irrigated and actual irrigated areas. These variations come about as the result of either cyclical water scarcity or new clearances of land. In the Marina Baixa some of the Comunidades de Regantes do not know the exact amount of water that is used on an annual basis and even fewer know exactly how much water is extracted and/or transferred from different water sources. This situation would seem to suggest that there is a distinct lack of the type of social adaptive capacity that leads to innovation in water supply and demand patterns. Despite the introduction of drip irrigation, the general lack of knowledge in the embedded institutions regarding areas of land under irrigation, the volumes of water applied to irrigation and water sources indicates that the water-using culture of the Marina Baixa, particularly in terms of irrigation, is one that promotes the philosophy of supply augmentation.

In terms of the effect of disembedded institutions it is difficult to neglect the emergence of the Consorcio in 1977, a municipal consortium whose sole task is to seek and administer water supply for the coastal municipalities where tourism development has been concentrated, or the formation of the Junta Central that is to administer the proposed Júcar-Vinalopó water transfer, of which the Marina Baixa is to receive 11.5hm^3. The emergence of these two institutions – whose character is to source and administer water supply – has established path-dependence for the governance context of the Marina Baixa. That is, the current water governance context is one that is difficult to change because of the existence of these two institutions and their respective roles. This is primarily because these institutions only exist to promote water transfers (Eisenhuth, 2005).

The nature of the problem in this particular study is that the inter-basin and intra-basin water transfers (engineering resilience) that maintain the global stability of the hydrological system could have ultimately locked out the type of desired co-dynamic processes and structural change that can lead to the creation and testing of alternative water sourcing and usage practices. In this study the characteristics of the type of resilience we are interested in locating provides a socio-natural system with the potential to adapt or reorganize in a desirable way following disturbance-driven change (Gunderson and Holling, 2002) that is caused by significant and regular water transfers. Therefore the ultimate challenge of this study is to locate the reciprocal co-dynamic processes that promote the type of structural change that increases the ecological as well as the social resilience and adaptive capacity of the water-using communities in the Marina Baixa. The aim then is to analyse structural change in both the natural and the social systems, and the nature of the reciprocal co-dynamic processes that promote ecological and social adaptive capacity.

In the remainder of this chapter we attempt to analyse the nature of the co-dynamic processes that have led to structural change in the landscape, water-usage patterns and management systems in three municipalities of the Marina Baixa, each with radically different land-use change patterns. By comparing and contrasting structural change in the landscape and water management system, as well as supply and demand patterns, it is possible to identify reciprocal relationships between the co-dynamics of water supply and demand patterns, institutional change, landscape change and physical change to the water management system during the time-frame for this study.

9.2   LANDSCAPE CHANGE

Understanding the ecological effects of landscape dynamics has attracted the attention of ecologists for many years now (Turner et al., 2001). The rate of alteration of landscape is increasing dramatically worldwide due to the increase in and intensification of human land use (Richards, 1990; Dale et al., 2000), particularly with regard to the effects of modifications to the structure of the landscape upon environmental quality and biodiversity (see for example Krummel et al., 1987; Holling, 1992; Levin,1992; Alés et al., 1992; Bonet, 1997; Romero-Calcerrada and Perry, 2004). This phenomenon has also been analysed in the context of semi-arid Mediterranean country-side, concentrating especially on the results of the abandonment of farm-land and afforestation carried out on different scales (Bonet et al., 2001; Chirino et al., 2001, Bonet, 2004; Bonet et al., 2004; Chirino, 2003).

Specific cause – effect relationships have been determined concerning the effects of these changes in the landscape upon the conservation of water resources (Omerick, 1977), and more specifically those caused by modifica-tions in the landscape's structure and metrics (Hunsaker et al., 1992). Water limitations in Mediterranean conditions have interacted with landscape changes, altering the relationships between the different compartments in hydrological cycles and limiting the availability and use of water as a human resource due to a reduction in the recharge of aquifers (Bellot et al., 2001).

Studies undertaken in semi-arid Mediterranean landscapes, where the availability of water limits the development of plant cover, have found that landscape changes as a result of land management alters water balances. Increases in vegetation density caused by afforestation of pine woodlands or the increase of shrubland cover as a consequence of farmland abandon-ment, produce less surface run-off and greater infiltration than if the plant cover is maintained as dry pasture (Cerdá, 1995; Bellot et al., 1999; Chirino 2003; Chirino et al., 2003). Similarly, studies in wetter forested Mediterranean areas (Piñol et al., 1988; Bellot et al., 1999; Piñol et al., 1999) indicate that a greater degree of plant cover reduces run-off, increasing real evapotranspiration.

For decades, agriculture and tourism have been the main productive sectors in such limiting environments. This is indeed the case for the Marina Baixa county (Alicante, Spain), where these drivers have caused a noticeable attrition in the landscape and water balances. The area is often presented as an example of where landscape, water usage and the water management system and governance have changed co-dynamically over time. However the environmental impact of such change has been largely ignored and has not been the subject of considered review.

Traditional land use activities are at least partly responsible for main-taining the high levels of ecological quality found in Mediterranean land-scapes (Blondel and Aronson, 1999). Although the ecological concepts of balance and stability are contested (for example see Perry, 2002) we refer here to a state of dynamic equilibrium in which socio-cultural activities, biological diversity and ecosystem function are maintained.

Changes in land cover, water use and management of the land have occurred throughout history in Mediterranean regions and other parts of the world (Dale et al., 2002). The total land area dedicated to human usage has grown dramatically, and increasing production of goods and services has intensified both use and control of the land. Water availability through-out the landscape varies seasonally and from year to year in response to changing weather conditions and water use demands. Land use and climate changes have a potential effect on hydrological cycles, flow damages, groundwater recharge and water demand (Turner et al., 2001), thus affecting the availability of water resources. The consequences or impacts of such changes on risk or resource availability and reliability depend not only on biophysical changes in landscapes, water recharge and water quality, but also on the characteristics of the water management system.

In order to determine co-dynamic processes for the Marina Baixa region of South-eastern Spain, we identified the links between landscape struc-ture, water usage and institutional and management systems during a recent change period between 1956 and 2000. The analysis of the physical changes is focused on (1) transitions patterns that are evaluated in terms of ecological sustainability; and (2) the identification of the key elements on water balances.

9.3   LAND USE AND LAND COVER CHANGE

In order to identify the factors which shape landscape dynamics in the Marina Baixa, three different patterns of land cover and land use change, demonstrating varying development strategies are analyzed. These patterns relate to three sub-regions: Benidorm (51 873 inhabitants, 3860 hectares), Callosa d'en Sarriá (7057 inhabitants, 3430 hectares) and Guadalest (180 inhabitants, 1610 hectares). The first of these is one of Europe's main coastal resorts, welcoming over 3 million tourists per year. Hotel and other vacation accommodation provides almost 20 million pernoctations per year. Maximum occupation occurs during the summer months with more than 300 000 people per day (Ivars and Juan, 1998). Guadalest, located inland, has followed a development strategy completely different to that of Benidorm. It welcomes more than 2 million visitors per year who come to see the castle and its surroundings, yet typically do not stay in the area overnight. The village therefore has hardly grown since 1956 and indeed the local population has fallen during this period. Callosa on the other hand is located between the above two municipalities and its strategy has been to develop the specialized irrigated cultivation of citrus fruit and medlars, a large part of the latter destined for export to EU markets.

Taking 1956, 1978 and 2000 land use and land cover maps obtained from aerial photography as our point of departure; the space–time dynamic of land use has been studied, considering five general categories of hydrological interest (urban, dry crops, irrigated crops, shrublands and pine woodlands). Its structure at a patch level is calculated using the landscape's metrics. Data to characterize the landscape's components has been extracted using Arc*Fragstats, employing landscape and class (land use and land cover types) indices usually used to describe landscape structure (MacGarigal and Marks, 1995). Indices used for describing landscape structure are: number of patches (PN) equals the number of patches in the landscape; patch density (PD) equals the number of patches in the landscape, divided by total landscape area (m^2), multiplied by 10 000 and 100 (to convert to 100 hectares); average patch size (APS) equals the mean area (m^2) of all the patches, divided by 10 000 (to convert to hectares); average nearest neighbour (ANN) defined as mean distance (m) to the nearest neighbouring patch of the same type, based on shortest edge-to-edge distance; form index (aggregation) (AI) equals the number of like adjacencies involving the corresponding class, divided by the maximum possible number of like adjacencies involving the corresponding class, which is achieved when the class is maximally clumped into a single, compact patch, multiplied by the proportion of the landscape comprised of the corresponding class, summed over all classes and multiplied by 100 (to convert to a percentage); Shannon Diversity Index (SD) equals minus the sum, across all patch types, of the proportional abundance of each patch type multiplied by that proportion.

Class type indices used here are: total class number of patches (NPc) of a particular patch type is a simple measure of the extent of subdivision or fragmentation of the patch type; class patch density (PDc) equals the number of patches of the corresponding patch type divided by total landscape area; class average patch size (APSc) calculated for each land cover type.

Patterns of landscape change have been very different across the three municipalities even though the initial situations in all three cases were very similar. Forest land use, which includes natural cover (for example pine-woods, dense and clear shrublands and abandoned farmland), has decreased during the study period in both Callosa and Benidorm, in favour of agriculture and urban development (caused by tourism) respectively. In Guadalest however the tendency has been towards an increase in all types of natural vegetation (20 per cent), except for pine woodlands which have decreased due to forest wildfires. As a result, the predominant plant cover is shrublands both with and without the presence of pine trees.

Since 1978 agriculture has been in steady decline in Guadalest (13 per cent) and Benidorm (30 per cent), while in contrast since the same year irrigated farming, especially under plastic, has grown by 300 per cent. Dry crop farming has fallen considerably in Callosa, somewhat less in Guadalest, and in Benidorm it has disappeared (Figures 9.3 and 9.4).

Associated urban use (settlements and infrastructure) reflects the degree of anthropization of the territory, the specific type of use evolving differently in different municipalities. There has been almost no change in Guadalest and Callosa since 1956 while Benidorm's initial urban area has increased fiftyfold (Figures 9.3 and 9.4). Although this land use category occupies less land area than forest and agricultural use, it is a new use with important consequences for the conservation of resources such as water. Its impact occurs predominately during the latter period (2000) with the appearance of industrial, commercial and above all recreational and leisure areas. Road networks have also grown on a large scale, although they are concentrated around the town. Access to the developed areas and improvements to arterial roads have multiplied 1978's values by factors of 6 and 2.

Infrastructure with which to move water has also appeared in the territory since 1956. In 1978 the dam to regulate the river Guadalest's flow came into service. Although the dam did not result in significant changes to the amount of water flowing through the area, it substituted an active natural system for a controlled, passive system. Due to the intermittent presence of water, dry river bed vegetation appeared, increasing land connectivity between the territories adjacent to the river bed. The number of irrigation dams and swimming pools in the region has also increased during the last period in both Callosa and Benidorm, thus raising the risk of evaporation of waters that had previously been underground.

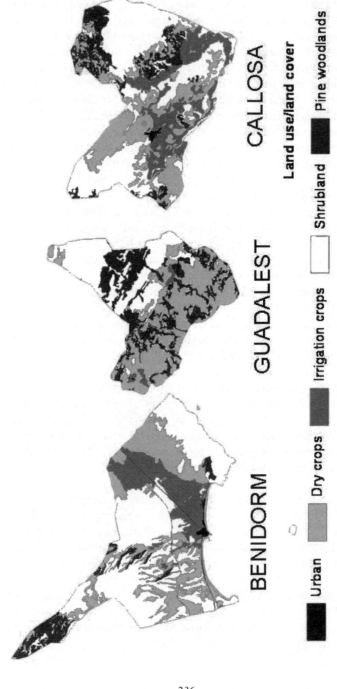

Figure 9.3   Land use/land cover maps of Benidorm, Guadalest and Callosa (MB) from 1956 aerial photographs

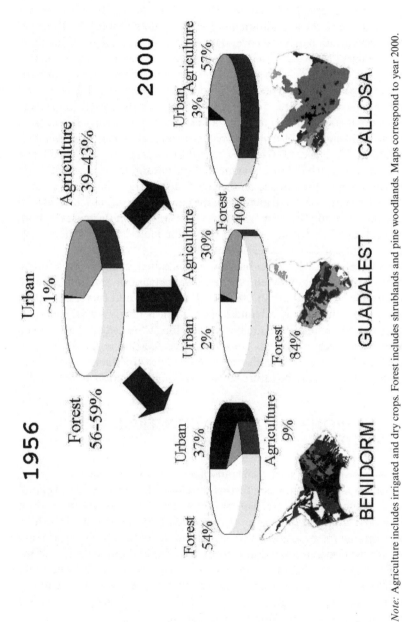

1956

Urban
~1%

Agriculture
39–43%

Forest
56–59%

2000

Urban
3%

Agriculture
57%

CALLOSA

Urban
2%

Agriculture
30%

Forest
40%

Forest
84%

GUADALEST

Urban
37%

Agriculture
9%

Forest
54%

BENIDORM

Note: Agriculture includes irrigated and dry crops. Forest includes shrublands and pine woodlands. Maps correspond to year 2000.

Figure 9.4   Changes in land use/land cover in Benidorm, Guadalest and Callosa (MB)

237

9.4 LANDSCAPE STRUCTURE CHANGE

With regard to changes in the structure of the landscape, a greater unifor-
mity has been observed in Guadalest where the fragmentation of forests has
diminished due to the abandonment of crop farming (Table 9.1). However
there is also variation in forest cover owing to the abandonment of farmland
and forest fires (Table 9.2). Conversely, an opposite trend has been noted in
Callosa and Benidorm where the area of forest has decreased whilst the
number of patches of all types of cover increases (Figure 9.4, Tables 9.1 and
9.2). The reason for this trend in the case of Callosa is the growth in irrigated
crops that penetrate natural territory and substitute dry crops, leading to a
decrease in the number of irrigation patches and their density together with
an increase in their average size and concentration (Table 9.2). In Benidorm,
the expansion of urban fabric fragmented the natural territory, creating an
extensive patch of human use on the coast, displacing other types of land
use away from the coast. An increase in the connectivity of agricultural land
use patches can only be seen clearly in Callosa, while it decreases in both
Guadalest and Benidorm, causing a rise in the landscape's global average
nearest neighbour value (Tables 9.1 and 9.2).

The adjacency of land cover has also been studied, using information on
the length of borders between patches. The increase of total edge length
between pine cover and urban use (from 0 to 72 km) and to a lesser extent
between urban use and shrubland in Benidorm is highly significant. This
value is directly related to a greater risk of forest fires which have indeed
increased over recent decades. The progressive decrease in the dry crops –
shrublands border-length is also of interest since this factor might have
a negative influence on the future recolonization of abandoned farmland.

9.5 ENVIRONMENTAL QUALITY TRANSITION MODELS

Our analysis of the links between landscape, water use, management system
and governance co-dynamics is further developed by first considering landscape transition patterns. Transition patterns can be analysed using three
dimensions: temporal dimension (speed, size and time period), scale level
dimension (micro, meso and macro scale) and the nature of change (break-
down, innovation and restructuring). We have focused our attention on the
last of these approaches, fixing the temporal dimension between the 1950s
and 2000, and the scale is fixed at municipality, county and catchment resolution. A conceptual framework for describing and analysing landscape
transitions is provided by Martens and Rotmans (2002).

Table 9.1 General landscape metrics

PN	1956	1978	2000
BENIDORM	135	147	168
CALLOSA	172	197	80
GUADALEST	90	112	89

PD	1956	1978	2000
BENIDORM	3.5	3.8	4.7
CALLOSA	5.0	5.7	2.3
GUADALEST	5.6	6.9	5.5

APS	1956	1978	2000
BENIDORM	28.6	26.3	23.0
CALLOSA	19.9	17.4	42.8
GUADALEST	17.8	14.3	18.0

ANN	1956	1978	2000
BENIDORM	196.4	107.1	101.1
CALLOSA	96.0	107.9	210.3
GUADALEST	91.4	82.9	70.8

FI	1956	1978	2000
BENIDORM	10.4	11.9	12.1
CALLOSA	11.7	11.4	6.2
GUADALEST	9.1	9.3	6.7

SD	1956	1978	2000
BENIDORM	1.23	1.52	1.35
CALLOSA	1.29	1.45	1.14
GUADALEST	1.14	1.27	1.28

Note: PN – total number of patches; PD – patch density (no./100ha); APS – average patch size (ha); ANN – average nearest neighbour (m); FI – form index (aggregation); SD – Shannon Diversity Index.

Table 9.2   Class landscape metrics

URBAN	APSc			PDc			PNc		
	1956	1978	2000	1956	1978	2000	1956	1978	2000
BENIDORM	17.5	33.5	77.4	0.05	0.41	0.47	2	16	18
CALLOSA	7	5.5	13.5	0.05	0.38	0.23	2	13	8
GUADALEST	24.6	3.9	5.3	1.68	0.19	0.19	27	3	3

DRY CROPS	APSc			PDc			PNc		
	1956	1978	2000	1956	1978	2000	1956	1978	2000
BENIDORM	19.8	7.0	0.0	1.25	0.60	0.07	48	23	3
CALLOSA	10.7	13.7	11.5	2.57	1.34	0.35	82	46	12
GUADALEST	5.7	13.0	9.2	0.25	2.36	2.91	4	38	47

IRRIGATION	APSc			PDc			PNc		
	1956	1978	2000	1956	1978	2000	1956	1978	2000
BENIDORM	40.47	42.30	6.55	0.36	0.60	1.40	14	23	54
CALLOSA	23.52	30.36	112.35	0.67	0.93	0.46	23	32	16
GUADALEST	30.40	4.02	15.15	0.99	0.99	0.18	16	16	3

SHRUBLAND	APSc			PDc			PNc		
	1956	1978	2000	1956	1978	2000	1956	1978	2000
BENIDORM	36.0	29.8	28.6	1.42	0.96	0.96	55	37	37
CALLOSA	23.5	20.4	81.0	0.78	1.34	0.41	27	46	14
GUADALEST	30.4	20.4	55.2	0.99	1.24	0.68	16	20	11

PINE WOODS	APSc			PDc			PNc		
	1956	1978	2000	1956	1978	2000	1956	1978	2000
BENIDORM	17.4	22.7	20.6	0.36	1.19	1.27	14	46	49
CALLOSA	13.7	15.3	13.7	0.87	1.55	0.52	30	53	18
GUADALEST	10.6	18.3	20.7	2.55	2.11	1.49	41	34	24

Note: APSc – class average patch size (ha); PDc – class patch density (no./100ha); PNc – class total number of patches.

Table 9.3   Transition classes between 1956 and 2000

1956	2000				
	Urban	Dry crops	Irrigation	Shrublands	Pine woods
Urban	N	A	A	A	A
Dry crops	D	N	D	A	A
Irrigation	D	A	N	A	A
Shrublands	D	D	D	N	A
Pine woods	D	D	D	D	N

Note: A, aggradative; D, degradative; N, no transition.

To characterize co-dynamic processes between different land uses and their corresponding hydrological balances we apply a measure of ecological sustainability, defined as the tendency of a system or process to be maintained or to be preserved over time. This is a measure of persistence of state rather than a measure of process or structural change. Therefore land use could be sustainable locally over the long term due to external subsidies, but this practice would result in an inevitable loss from the system providing the subsidies and thus would not be seen as sustainable when viewed at a larger scale. We considered a set of surrogate indicators of the ecological sustainability of the water management system: ecological complexity and stability; ecosystem services (Costanza et al., 1997) provided as steady environmental returns from natural capital.

A simple, non-spatial model analogous to the Markov chain transition method was generated for each combination of map pairs; 1956–78, 1978–2000 and 1956–2000 (Dale et al., 2002). The transition's qualification criteria for ecological sustainability have taken into account the increase or reduction in indicators such as biomass, successional status, irreversibility of change, land fragmentation, variations in water consumption, evaporation and evapotranspiration. This has enabled us to group together the transitions based on the processes that have occurred in the territory (succession, degradation, etc.) into aggradative (A) degradative (D) and no-transition (N) classes. In order to do this, a reduced number of land use categories have had to be considered giving $5 \times 5 = 25$ types of transition (see Table 9.3). Therefore any transformation of pine forests or forest formations will be degradative while that occurring on urban land will be aggradative. Also in this context the change from dry crop farming to irrigation is considered as degradative due to the increase in water consumption and evaporation, while the change from irrigation to dry crop farming is considered as aggradative.

The results of applying these evaluation criteria to the transition matrix in the selected cases, show that during the total study period of 1956–2000 Guadalest exhibits the greatest proportion of no-transition classes and is also that which has the least degree of degradative changes. Callosa and Benidorm share the same percentage of degradative changes. Finally, Benidorm has the largest number of transitions and is characterized by its low proportion of no-transition patches and high level of degradation. However it also has the highest percentage of aggradative transfers, due to the abandonment of crop farming and reforestation (Figure 9.5).

Aggradative and no-transition changes are proportionally more relevant in inland municipalities than in coastal municipalities when considering the Marina Baixa county as a whole (Figure 9.6). Municipalities situated in more coastal positions exhibit high proportions of degradative transitions due to a higher degree of irreversibility of the transformations of the landscape (that is changes from agriculture to urban use). Unsustainable transformations of the landscape are related to the increase of the urban and irrigation uses, thus indicating also an increase in water demand.

9.6   WATER USAGE AND MANAGEMENT SYSTEM

Changes in the pattern of water consumption in the region are primarily driven by urban and recreational growth, with high demand for water from both outside the area (transfers) and water from reservoirs. Even though this link is significant, little of the water used in the engineered storage and supply system returns to the aquifer (Figures 9.7 and 9.8).

In environmental terms, Benidorm has lost most of its natural character since 50 per cent of its territory is now occupied by urban development and associated infrastructure. A global view of the situation in 1956 reflects a more rational use of the territory and greater sustainability in water consumption in that year. However whilst Benidorm, Callosa and Guadalest had similar land use compositions in 1956 (<1 per cent urban, 39–43 per cent agriculture and 56–59 per cent forest), the region has been transformed in recent decades, irreversibly degrading the environment and overexploiting hydraulic resources. Lower intensity of agricultural activity in Callosa and of tourism in Benidorm during the early years of the study period resulted in a water balance that was almost in equilibrium (a deficit of 0.9 hm^3). However the increased complexity of water exploitation has been accompanied by greater rationalization (Figures 9.7 and 9.8).

To better understand the hydrological flows and water use at plot scale for forest, agriculture and urban land cover classes, we have constructed a model as illustrated in Figure 9.9. The model indicates the percentage of

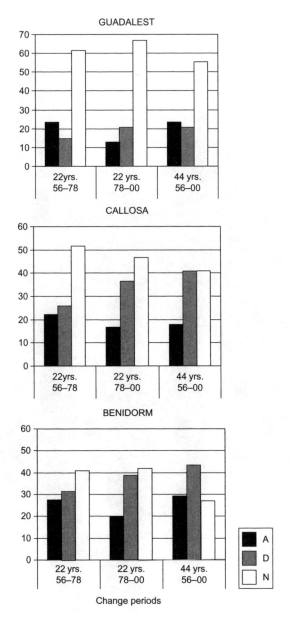

Note: A, aggradative; D, degradative; and N, no-transition, over two 22-year periods (1956–78; 1978–2000) as well as for the whole 44 years (1956–2000). For definition, see Table 9.3.

Figure 9.5   Types of transition

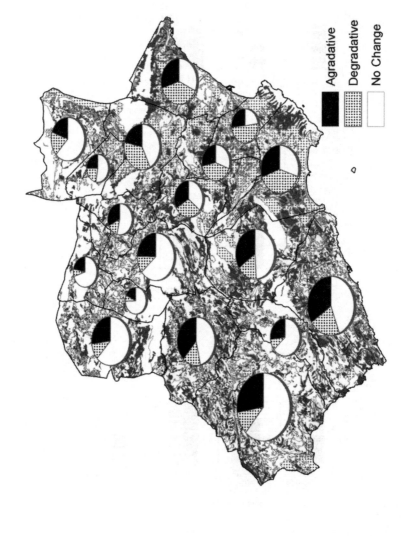

Figure 9.6   Environmental sustainability transition analysis map for the period between 1956 and 2000. Pie charts show transition proportions for each municipality in the Marina Baixa county

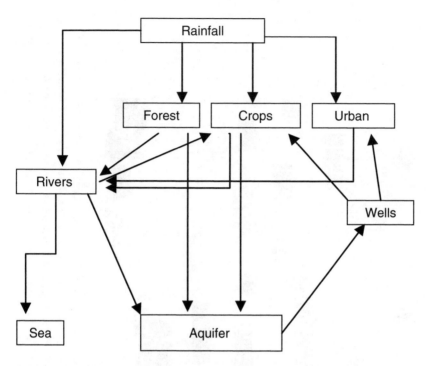

Figure 9.7   Water use system during the 1950s in the Marina Baixa

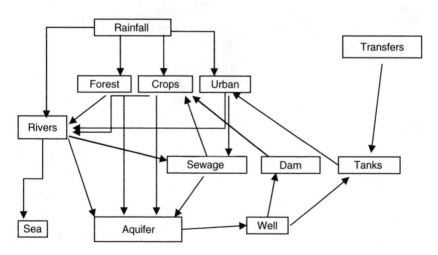

Figure 9.8   Water use system during the year 2000 in the Marina Baixa

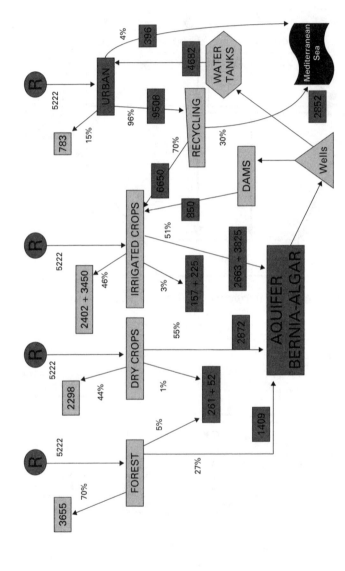

Figure 9.9   Hydrologic model schematic applied in Marina Baixa. Average values of water flows by plot type based on the Ventos hydrological model (Bellot et al., 2001) and field work in Marina Baixa. Per cent values are portions of rainfall (R) volumes; values above the sector boxes are evapotranspiration losses (m³ ha⁻¹ yr⁻¹) and value below are infiltration volumes (m³ ha⁻¹ yr⁻¹) to soil or aquifer recharge, input to dams, runoff and recycling fluxes.

water received by type of water use as well as volumetric flows in m^3 year^{-1}. The most significant feature of the data associated with the model is the evapotranspiration losses due to irrigation.

As we have indicated previously, a large part of the water used for irrigation in the region is recovered wastewater. The recovery system in the Marina Baixa is complex, involving several treatment plants and distribution networks. The quantity of wastewater treated is approximately 15.12 hm^3 year^{-1} between the different recycling plants in the county, and 70 per cent of this volume is reused (10.32 hm^3 year^{-1}). However with 6230.1 hectares of irrigated land in the county, recovered water can only cover the supply for 80 per cent of this area using drip irrigation.

A gross water balance at county scale indicates that natural inputs reach 355.49 hm^3 year^{-1} in the Marina Baixa (Table 9.4). The annual outputs produced by uncontrolled run-off to the sea and by evapotranspiration are elevated to 14.71 and 257.58 hm^3 year^{-1}, respectively. So the balance is positive, and on an annual basis we can assume that water inputs to the county are sufficient to meet demand and provide an excess of 83.2 hm^3 year^{-1}. However the temporality of demands places the balance in disequilibrium, making other contributions necessary that are obtained from the aquifers or from transfers external to the system.

Owing to the fact that both the agricultural and urban sectors exhibit large seasonal differences with maximums in summer, precipitation is insufficient to cover their requirements of 104.69 hm^3 year^{-1}. Consequently, extractions and transfers are required to satisfy the seasonal peak demands, leaving precipitation the work of recharging the aquifers and the dams. Although 10 Hm^3/year^{-1} are notionally required to cover the annual deficit in the county, this value is, in reality, greater owing to the temporal disequilibrium of peak demands.

9.7 CONCLUSIONS

The evolution of rapid and intensive land use change in coastal and valley municipalities of Marina Baixa (that is, Benidorm and Callosa) can be linked to changes in water supply and demand patterns that can be traced to the 1970s. As a consequence of these degradative landscape changes, there is evidence of reciprocal co-dynamic processes in the physical characteristics of the water management system. Structural change to the physical systems, along with the change in the water supply and demand patterns, can then be linked to the evolution of a water-using culture in the 1970s that is dependent on continual and increasing intra-basin and inter-basin water transfers. Also, structural change in the institutional context, that is, the

Table 9.4 *Annual inputs (rainfall, irrigation, urban supply) and outputs (actual evapotranspiration; Eta) for usage categories in plots of 1 ha and for overall county*

Uses	Year 2000 Surface area	Irrigation	Urb.Suply	Inputs Ha	Inputs Tot County	Eta %	Eta Ha	Outputs Eta County
Industrial, commercial and leisure	932.59		7300	5222.3	11678171.8	0.15	783.3	730539.7
Low density residential: surface	2252.82		2217.3		4995177.8			
Low density residential: houses	420.6			5222.3	2196499.4	0.15	783.3	329474.9
Low density residential: garden	901.57	5200		10422.3	9396433.0	0.90	9380.1	8456789.7
Low density residential: pavement	382.3	221.86		5444.2	2081302.4	0.15	816.6	312195.4
Low density residential: pools	90.56		6383	11605.3	1050976.0	1.00	11605.3	1050976.0
Low density residential: vegetation	457.54			5222.3	2389411.1	0.70	3655.6	1672587.8
Low density residential: inhabitant	101377			290 L/p/d				
Medium density residential: surface	391.49		11755.5		4602160.7			
Medium density residential: garden	7.47	5200		10422.3	77854.6	0.90	9380.1	70069.1
Medium density residential: pavement	80.84	1176.8		6399.1	517305.7	0.15	959.9	77595.9
Medium density residential: pools	0.39		6383	11605.3	4526.1	1.00	11605.3	4526.1
Medium density residential: houses	279.4			5222.3	1459110.6	0.15	783.3	218866.6
Medium density residential: vegetation	23.33			5222.3	121836.3	0.70	3655.6	85285.4
Medium density residential: inhabitant	93308			150 L/p/d				
High density residential: surface	311.34		19311.8		6012535.8			
High density residential: garden	64.13	5200		10422.3	668382.1	0.90	9380.1	601543.9
High density residential: pavement	127.62	1953.6		7175.9	915785.8	0.15	1076.4	137367.9
High density residential: pools	7.22		6383	11605.3	83790.3	1.00	11605.3	83790.3
High density residential: houses	62.33			5222.3	325506.0	0.15	783.3	48825.9
High density residential: bare soil	50.03			5222.3	261271.7	0.50	2611.2	130635.8
High density residential: inhabitant	122021			157 L/p/d				
Dryland crops	7960.45	3000		8222.3	65453208.0	0.44	3617.8	28799411.5
Irrigated crops by flood	4018.14	7500		12722.3	51119982.5	0.46	5852.3	23515192.0
Irrigated crops by drop	1962.41	4950.2		10172.5	19962596.1	0.46	4679.3	9182794.2
Crops under plastic cover (drop)	249.66	4950.2		10172.5	2539663.9	0.46	4679.3	1168245.4

Note: Data $m^3 \, ha^{-1} \, year^{-1}$, and m^3 or hm^3 in total county. Considered values for reference evapotranspiration (Eto) are 11605 and total rainfall 5222.3 mm.

emergence of the Consorcio and the Junta Central, has established path-dependency in terms of institutional context and water-using culture in these municipalities. Both the Consorcio and the Junta Central exist to source and administer water transfers. It is therefore difficult to foresee a change to either the water-using culture, institutional context or water supply and demand patterns in the foreseeable future. This could lead to further decline in ecological sustainability in coastal and valley municipal-ities, together with diminished resilience and social adaptive capacity in the embedded institutions.

Conversely inland (that is, Guadalest), the relative stability of the land-scape, the associated water supply and demand patterns, as well as the water management system during the bulk of the study period can be attributed to the fact that there has been no requirement for supply augmentation or the intervention of disembedded institutions in the allocation process. However it is difficult to predict if the embedded institutions in these municipalities embody the capacity to adapt to extensive land use change or the associated water supply and demand patterns, simply because the long-term stability of both the natural as well as the social system, has not led to the requirement for the embedded institutions to adapt to change.

NOTE

This work has been financed by the European AQUADAPT (EVK1-CT-2001-00104) project.

REFERENCES

Alés, R.F., A. Martin, F. Ortega and E.E. Alés (1992), 'Recent changes in landscape structure and function in a Mediterranean region of southwest Spain', *Landscape Ecology*, **7**, 3–18.
Bellot, J., A. Bonet, J.R. Sanchez and E. Chirino (2001), 'Likely effects of land use changes on the runoff and aquifer recharge in a semi-arid landscape using a hydrological model', *Landscape and Urban Planning*, **778**, 1–13.
Bellot, J., J.R. Sanchez, E. Chirino, N. Hernandez, F. Abdelli, and J.M. Martinez (1999), 'Effect of different vegetation type cover effects on the soil water balance in semi-arid areas of south eastern Spain', *Physics and Chemistry of the Earth* (B), **24**, 353–7.
Blondel, J. and J. Aronson (1999), *Biology and Wildlife of the Mediterranean Region*, Oxford: Oxford University Press.
Bonet, A. (1997), 'Efectos del abandono de los cultivos sobre la vegetación en la cuenca del Alt Llobregat (Barcelona). Relación con factores ambientales y de usos del suelo', *Ecología*, **11**, 91–104.
Bonet, A. (2004), 'Secondary succession on semi-arid Mediterranean old-fields in

south-eastern Spain: insights for conservation and restoration of degraded lands', *Journal of Arid Environments*, **56**, 213–33.

Bonet, A., J. Bellot and J. Peña (2004), 'Landscape dynamics in a semiarid Mediterranean catchment (SE Spain)', in S. Mazzoleni (ed.) *Recent Dynamics of Mediterranean Vegetation Landscape*, Reading: Gordon & Breach, pp. 41–50.

Bonet, A., J. Peña, J. Bellot, M. Cremades and J.R. Sánchez (2001), 'Changing vegetation and landscape patterns in semi-arid Spain', in Y. Villacampa, C.A. Brebbia and J.L. Usó (eds), *Ecosystems and Sustainable Development III*, Southampton: WIT Press, pp. 377–86.

Cerdà, A. (1995), 'Factores y variaciones espacio-temporales de la infiltración en los ecosistemas mediterráneos', Monografías científicas, Geoforma ediciones.

Chirino, E. (2003), 'Influencia de las precipitaciones y de la cubierta vegetal en el balance hídrico superficial y en la recarga de acuíferos en clima semiárido', Universidad de Alicante, Facultad de Ciencias, Departamento de Ecología, Tesis doctoral, Alicante, Spain.

Chirino, E., J. Bellot, A. Bonet and J.M. Andreu (2003), 'Efecto de diferentes tipos de cubierta vegetal en el control de la erosión en clima semiárido. SE- España', en R. Bienes and M.J. Marqués (eds), *Control de la Erosión and Degradación del Suelo*, Madrid: Fórum Calidad, pp. 183–7.

Chirino, E., J.R., Sánchez, A. Bonet and J. Bellot (2001), 'Effect of afforestation and vegetation dynamics on soil erosion in semi-arid environment (SE Spain)', in Y. Villacampa, C.A. Brebbia and J.L. Usó (eds), *Ecosystems and Sustainable Development III*, Southampton: WIT Press, pp. 239–48.

Costanza, R., R. d'Arge, R. de Groot, S. Farber, M. Grasso, B. Hannon, K. Limburg, S. Naeem, R. O'Neill, J. Paruelo, R. Raskin, P. Sutton and M. van den Belt (1997), 'The value of the world's ecosystem services and natural capital', *Nature*, 387253-260.

Dale, V.H., S. Brown, R.A. Haeuber, N.T. Hobbs, N. Huntly, R.J. Naiman, W.E. Riebsame, M.G. Turner and T.J. Valone (2000), 'Ecological principles and guidelines for managing the use of land', *Ecological Applications*, **10** (3), 639–70.

Dale, M., P. Dale and T. Edgoose (2002), 'Using Markov models to incorporate serial dependence in studies of vegetation change', *Acta Oecologica*, **23**, 261–9.

Eisenhuth, D. (2005), 'Overview of the Water Governance Process in Alto and Medio Vinalopó', Alicante and Marina Baixa, WWF/ADENA, Madrid.

Gunderson, L.H. and C.S. Holling (2002), 'Resilience and Adaptive Cycles', in L.H. Gunderson and C.S. Holling (eds), *Panarchy Understanding Transformations in Human and Natural Systems*, Washington, DC: Island Press, pp. 25–62.

Holling, C.S. (1992), 'Cross-scale morphology, geometry, and dynamics of ecosystems', *Ecological Monographs*, **62**, 447–502.

Hunsaker, C.T., D.A. Levine, S.P. Timmons, B.L. Jackson and R.V. O'Neill (1992), 'Landscape characterization for assessing regional water quality', in D.H. McKenzie, D.E. Hyatt and V.J. McDonald (eds), *Ecological Indicators*, Vol. 2, New York Elsevier Applied Science, pp. 997–1006.

Ivars, J.A. and F. Juan (1998), 'La descentralización de la actividad turística en Benidorm', *Revista valenciana d'estudis autonòmics*, **25**, 245–58.

Krummel, J.R., R.H. Gardner, G. Sugihara, R.V. O'Neill and P.R. Coleman (1987), 'Landscape patterns in a disturbed environment', *Oikos*, **48**, 321–4.

Levin, S.A. (1992), 'The problem of pattern and scale in ecology', *Ecology*, **73** (6), 1943–67.

Martens, W.J.M. and J. Rotmans (2002), *Transitions in a Globalising World*, Lisse, The Netherlands: Swets & Zeitlinger Publishers.

McGlade, J. (2002), 'Landscape sensitivity, resilience and sustainable watershed management: a co-evolutionary perspective', discussion paper prepared for the AQUADAPT Workshop, Montpelier, 25–27 October.

McGarigal, K. and B.J. Marks (1995), 'FRAGSTATS: spatial pattern analysis program for quantifying landscape structure', Gen. Tech. Rep, USDA Forest Service, PNW-GTR-351, Portland, OR.

Omerick, J.M. (1977), 'Nonpoint Source-stream Nutrient Level Relationships: A Nationwide Study', EPA-600/3-77-105, US Environmental Protection Agency, Corvallis, Oregon, USA.

Perry, G.L.W. (2002), 'Landscapes, space and equilibrium: some recent shifts', *Progressive Physical Geography*, **26**, 339–59.

Piñol, J., A. Àvila and A. Escarré (1999), 'Water balance in catchments', in F. Rodà, J. Retana, C. Gracia and J. Bellot (eds), *Ecology of Mediterranean Evergreen Oak Forest*, Ecological Studies, pp. 273–82.

Piñol, J., M.J. Lledó, J. Bellot, A. Escarré and J. Terradas (1988), 'Evapotranspiration estimation and runoff response of two Mediterranean forested watersheds', in F. Di Castri, Ch. Floret, S. Rambal and J. Roy (eds), *Time Scales and Water Stress*, IUBS, pp. 197–201.

Richards, J.F. (1990), 'Land transformations', in B.L. Turner II (ed.), *The Earth as Transformed by Human Action, Global and Regional Changes in the Biosphere Over the Past 300 Years*, London: Cambridge University Press.

Romero-Calcerrada, R. and G.L.W. Perry (2004), 'The role of land abandonment in landscape dynamics in the SPA "Encinares del río Alberche and Cofio, Central Spain", 1984–1999', *Landscape and Urban Planning*, **66**, 217–32.

Turner, M.G., Gardner, R.H. and R.V. O'Neill (2001), *Landscape Ecology in Theory and Practice. Pattern and Process*, New York: Springer Verlag.

Walker, B., S. Carpenter, J. Anderies, N. Abel, G.S. Cumming, M. Janssen, L. Lebel, J. Norberg, G.D. Peterson and R. Pritchard (2002), 'Resilience management in social-ecological systems: a working hypothesis for a participatory approach', *Conservation Ecology*, **6** (1), 14; http://www.consecol.org/vol6/iss1/art14/.

Zukin, S. and P. DiMaggia (1990), *Structures of Capital, the Social Organisation of the Economy*, Cambridge: Cambridge University Press.

PART VI

Conclusion

10. Conclusions and policy recommendations for the EU Water Framework Directive

**Katia Karousakis, Phoebe Koundouri,
Dionysis Assimacopoulos, Paul Jeffrey
and Manfred A. Lange**

This book has presented a selection of results from the ARID Cluster of projects. The three projects have explored aspects of water scarcity and demand in arid and semi-arid regions, as well as participatory and adaptive approaches to defining and applying appropriate management strategies. Given the importance, multiple uses and competing demands for water, we have adopted an interdisciplinary perspective on water resources management. More specifically, the adopted perspectives have included an engineering approach, namely the use of a decision support system that can simulate water supply and demand under different scenarios and management options and strategies (Part II); a stakeholder-participatory approach for addressing conflicting demands and varying hydrological conditions for the sustainable use of water on Mediterranean islands (Part III); an environmental economic perspective on efficient integrated water resources management (Part IV); and finally, a co-evolutionary approach to adaptive, integrated management under changing utilization conditions (Part V).

Part II of the foregoing text emphasized the need for a systematic evaluation of water management interventions over extended time-scales, simulating long-run accumulative effects and anticipating potential future changes and uncertainties. Following an analysis of water management practices and problems in different regions, and the analysis of stakeholder perspectives for addressing water planning, the adopted methodology employs a GIS-based decision support system that enables simulation of alternative water availability and demand scenarios. In contrast to previous methodologies and other decision support systems, the WaterStrategyMan DSS allows a more thorough incorporation of social, environmental, economic and technological dimensions and interrelationships in the simulation analysis. The application of the DSS platform to a case study in Portugal illustrates how the DSS can be used in other parts of the EU as well and how it might inform the implementation of the EU Water Framework Directive (WFD).

The main conclusions of Part III are that the implementation of indicators facilitates an integrated approach, which is able to combine the natural and socio-economic aspects of water management while allowing stakeholder involvement. Following the 'Driving forces – Pressures – States – Impacts – Responses' (DPSIR) approach on the islands of Corsica, Crete, Cyprus, Majorca and Sicily, the policy recommendations include demand management improvements (water saving and storage measures), institutional policy and capacity-building (especially in the agricultural sector), as well as the introduction of a differentiated pricing system amongst water users and public awareness and educational programmes.

In Part IV, the challenge of integrated sustainable water management is addressed from the field of environmental and resource economics. The importance of the efficient (or optimal) pricing of this resource is emphasized, and a non-technical description of the valuation methods to account for the total economic value of water is provided. The appropriate choice of economic instruments to provide users with the correct incentives for consumption will vary from region to region, depending on for example the metering technology that is available and the likely size of transaction costs associated with the different methods. The transaction costs associated with tradable water permits for example is likely to vary from one country to another depending on administrative capacity, the number of participants in the market, the existence of brokers and other issues, making such trading more or less favourable from one country to another. An important and generic conclusion for all policy-makers involved in making decisions that have long-term implications (that is, greater than 30 years) is that they should consider the application of a declining discount rate, as opposed to the more traditional flat discount rate, to obtain net present values of potential projects.

Part V examines the relationships between natural resource availability and the development of human societies. The first of these chapters analysed the socio-cultural determinants of water utilization in more detail by conducting four survey-based case studies. Findings suggest commonalities in behavioural patterns with respect to consumer perceptions regarding the availability of water, and the quality of information and education regarding water scarcity. In contrast, the surveys indicate that different cultures are likely to be more conducive to certain policy instruments over others. In the final chapter, structural change in both natural as well as social systems is analysed, as is the nature of the reciprocal co-dynamic processes that promote both ecological and social adaptive capacity in the Marina Baixa region of Spain.

The purpose of this final chapter is to identify the common themes of the three projects (WSM, MEDIS and Aquadapt), to integrate and harmonize the results and approaches adopted by each, and to discuss conclusions and potential policy implications that can feed into the EU Water Framework Directive. The knowledge that has emerged from the three projects has been principally obtained from case study analyses. These have examined competing water use patterns, compared governance structures and how these have evolved in response to scarcity, and structural and non-structural instruments to address water deficiency. The experiences and lessons learned from these studies are summarized below. First however we briefly describe the general circumstances, or pressures and driving forces, that are common to the case studies examined in the ARID Cluster of projects.

Most of the case studies examined lie in the Mediterranean region and are thus subject to similar climatic conditions. Some countries are more vulnerable to changes in water availability than others. Cyprus for example is classified as a semi-arid environment, whereas Corsica is categorized as a dry sub-humid environment. The various countries, regions, and islands studied vary with respect to characteristics such as population density, the amount of tourism they handle on a seasonal or annual basis, agricultural dependence and the types of crops that are grown. However it is seasonal and geographical variations and differences in water availability throughout the year that make water planning and availability difficult, especially in the summer due to high demand for water from the tourism sector.

The importance of taking a holistic approach to the issue of sustainable water resources management is a common feature of all aspects of the projects. This is typified by the material contained in Part II of the book where the described DSS includes economic, hydrological and environmental components to evaluate the different water management options and strategies. Part III emphasizes the importance of examining the physical and environmental, the economic and regulatory, and the social, institutional and political aspects related to water management. Part IV presents the methods that have been developed to evaluate environmental and social goods and services that do not have market prices in economic terms, thus enabling a more accurate reflection of costs and benefits to aid in policy-making decisions. Finally, Part V examines how water uses are interrelated and affected by a number of different factors, namely by landscape changes, management systems and governance co-dynamics in South-eastern Spain. In addition, four case studies are undertaken in different parts of Europe to examine the socio-cultural determinants of water usage. Within this, various technological and economic approaches to water management are also addressed.

The holistic approach is important because water needs to serve a multitude of different purposes and contributes disproportionately to lives and

livelihoods across a landscape. From an economic and development perspective, water affects the wider economy and society, including land use
changes and settlement growth, and changes in agricultural and industrial
activity. From an environmental perspective, water provides recreational
benefits and, most importantly, life-support functions for wildlife and of
course, human health. Examining water scarcity from a holistic, multidisciplinary perspective and involving different stakeholders ensures that a full
consideration of relevant influences and options for action are considered.

The importance of demand-side management in addition to the more
traditional supply-side management of water scarcity is another common
underlying theme of the projects. It is becoming increasingly clear that, in the
face of continued urban growth, water quality degradation and new uncertainties brought on by climate change, supply-side mechanisms for water
scarcity are unlikely to yield long-term sustainable solutions. Demand-
side management options such as the efficient use of water through the
reduction of losses, conservation and water recycling and reuse will become
a more important component of sustainable water management. Demand-
side management will entail a change in individual attitudes, and hence
behaviour, towards water use such that this is more efficient and more cost-
effective. Policy recommendations for the improved efficiency of water use
that derive from the ARID Cluster case studies include the following:

- the adoption of new technologies for reducing consumption;
- the modification of crop patterns in agriculture to reduce water use;
- the use of indicators to identify significant inefficiencies; and
- the alignment of policies in other sectors (for example the elimination
  of subsidies to energy used for pumping groundwater for irrigation).

With regard to water conservation, reuse and recycling, the main policy
recommendations that have come out of the case studies are the application of the following:

- rainwater harvesting;
- the reduction of evapo-transpiration by covering open reservoirs
  where this is feasible; and
- waste water recycling and the utilization of reclaimed and brackish
  water.

For the latter, these will likely need to be encouraged via the use of educational programmes for farmers to accept treated sewage water, and the
imposition of lower tariffs than those to surface and groundwater to
provide economic incentives for its use.

Integral to demand management is the application and use of economic instruments. Policy-makers should begin to implement water pricing programmes that go beyond the objective of revenue generation to actually inducing a reduction in water wastage and promoting water-saving behaviour instead. These can be achieved via the introduction of appropriate water prices. In addition, pilot programmes can be set up to obtain experience with other economic instruments such as tradable water permit systems, as has been done in the US, Australia, Canada, Chile and other countries (Easter et al., 1998). Lessons can be learned from previous experiences and shortcomings.

Sustainable water management in the agricultural sector may deserve special attention given that in the major Mediterranean islands it uses up more than 50 per cent of available water resources, and further it is the least efficient sector in water use since irrigation efficiency is in some cases less than 55 per cent. The policy recommendations here are clear and straightforward. Sustainable water management in agriculture can be achieved by adopting improvements in irrigation practices, best soil and crop management practices, water pricing, the reuse of marginal waters (reclaimed or brackish) for irrigation, wider and more effective participation of farmers in water management, and capacity-building. For these policies to work effectively, governments or policy-makers will need to ensure that any existing distortionary subsidies for agricultural production are eliminated.

The need for effective monitoring and enforcement, as well as the consistent application of monetary and civil penalties when existing regulations have been breached is important for effective water management. Good administrative capacity, institutional coordination and economic stability within a country are also prerequisites for the successful application of efficient water management policies and measures.

From a social perspective, it is clear that intra- and inter-generational equity with respect to water use is also of vital importance. With regard to intra-generational equity, this applies both within a particular sector and between sectors. For example within the domestic sector, low-income and marginal households will still need to be able to afford a secure supply of water, despite the introduction of a more efficient water pricing system (which will often entail higher water prices). Similarly, between sectors, many of the case studies show a distinct conflict between the agricultural and farming sector *vis-à-vis* the tourism sector.

Public awareness, educational campaigns and outreach are important as well so as to change and correct public perceptions. The four case studies that were undertaken in France, the UK, Spain and Slovenia to establish why and under what circumstances individuals are willing to alter or modify their water usage patterns indicate that those who are most concerned about water quantity and quality issues are those who claim to be the most active in water-saving behaviour. Similarly, those who are most informed on water issues also tend to be those who are most active in water-saving behaviour. This form of coherent behaviour is common across all of the four case studies, suggesting that public awareness and educational programmes should have positive effects towards attaining sustainable water consumption and a raised awareness for sensible water use at the European level as well.

In contrast, the study reported in Chapter 9 finds that the demand management and policy prescriptions adopted in a country should be adapted to the local water cultures within each country. For example it is concluded that local cultures across countries have different preferences with regard to management policies and prescriptions: the British for example are more willing to accept higher water bills for the protection of the environment, whereas the French are against this and would prefer to change their water consumption patterns to off-peak hours. The policy implications this has for the implementation of the EU Water Framework Directive is that some policies may vary in their acceptability across countries, whether this is due to existing previous experience with similar measures or to other differences in the local culture. This may indicate that some policies may also be more successful in certain countries than in others, and that the decision-maker should take these considerations into account when selecting the appropriate policy responses to provide incentives for efficient water resources use.

It seems appropriate here to examine potential next steps and to conclude with some recommendations for future research. Two issues seem particularly important: (1) additional resources should be allocated to the collection and monitoring of accurate household, firm-level and farm-level water data; and (2) local and regional water pricing pilot schemes should be introduced in different areas to obtain experience with various economic instruments. These will enable empirical studies to be undertaken that evaluate the effectiveness of various economic instruments[1] under different scenarios which can feed directly into tangible policy recommendations of the Water Framework Directive at the European level.

NOTE

1. Similar European studies that have focused on the effectiveness of economic instruments for air emissions include those by Sterner and Hoeglund (2000), and Millock and Nauges (2003).

REFERENCES

Easter, W., A. Dinar and M. Rosegrant (1998), *Markets for Water: Potential and Performance*, The Netherlands: Kluwer Academic Publishers.

Koundouri, P., P. Pashardes, T. Swanson and A. Xepapadeas (2003), *Economics of Water Management in Developing Countries: Problems, Principles and Policies*, Cheltenham, UK and Northampton, MA, USA: Edward Elgar Publishing.

Koundouri, P. (2004), *Econometrics Informing Natural Resources Management: Selected Case Studies*, New Horizons in Environmental Economics Series, Cheltenham, UK and Northampton, MA, USA: Edward Elgar Publishing.

Millock, K. and C. Nauges (2003), '*Ex post* evidence on environmental taxes: an assessment of the French tax on air pollution', FEEM Working Paper 44.03.

Sterner, T. and L. Hoeglund (2000), 'Output based refunding of emissions payments: theory, distribution of costs, and international experience', RFF discussion paper 00-29, Resources For the Future, Washington DC.

Index

and pollution taxes 175
and water pricing 166
in WaterStrategyMan decision
support system 18, 24, 31–3, 35
in WaterStrategyMan Project case
study 44, 45, 48, 63, 67
see also domestic water quality;
groundwater quality; surface
water quality
water resources 44, 45, 46, 47–8, 56,
128, 142
see also aquifers; dams; reservoirs;
precipitation; rainwater
harvesting; rivers; transfers,
water
water reuse
costs 77, 84–6
and demand management 258
in MEDIS Project 123, 143, 154
in WaterStrategyMan Project case
study 63, 68, 72–3, 74–5, 76, 77,
78–9, 82, 87, 89, 94, 98
see also marginal water; salinization;
wastewater, treated; wastewater
treatment plants
water rights 31, 128, 175, 228
water-saving behaviour
and attitudes to water stress 208,
217–18, 224, 260
consumer profiles 211–13, 214–15
in demand management 258
and European water culture 216,
217–18, 219, 223, 224
water scarcity
attitudes 207–10
beliefs 209–10
consequences 162
definition 111–12
and global climate change 107
holistic approach 258
integrated assessments 110–15
Mediterranean islands 107–10
(*see also* MEDIS Project)
seasonal water shortages 107, 117,
119–21
and transfers, water 184, 229, 231,
235, 245, 247
and water concerns 220
in WaterStrategyMan decision
support system 29, 31, 33

in WaterStrategyMan Project case
study 45, 55, 56–7, 88
water supply
Mediterranean islands 118
sources 44, 45, 46, 47–8, 56, 128,
142–3
and water demand 44, 163–4, 228–9,
231, 247, 249
in WaterStrategyMan decision
support system 33, 34
see also domestic water supply;
irrigation water supply costs;
marginal social costs of supply;
network enhancements;
network loss reduction; network
losses; primary water supply
system; secondary water supply
network losses; secondary water
supply system; supply links;
supply nodes
water use
attitudes 210–13, 214–15, 216–19,
220, 222, 224, 258, 260
and landscape change 232, 233
in Marina Baixa region 242, 245–7,
249
in MEDIS Project 122, 127, 142
wastefulness 123–5, 126–7, 128, 129,
137, 164
see also Aquadapt Project
water use efficiency 122, 127, 147,
150–52, 258
water user associations 228, 229, 230,
231
see also farmers' associations
water values, in WaterStrategyMan
decision support system 32–3
watersheds 26, 177–8, 181–4
see also Hérault watershed
WaterStrategyMan decision support
system (WSM DSS)
architecture 16–20
economic factors 15, 17, 18, 24–5,
29, 32–3, 34, 35, 36, 39
evaluation 36–7, 38
framework 15–16
indicators, additional 15–16, 17,
34–7
modelling water management
options 33–4